PILGRIM LIFE IN THE MIDDLE AGES

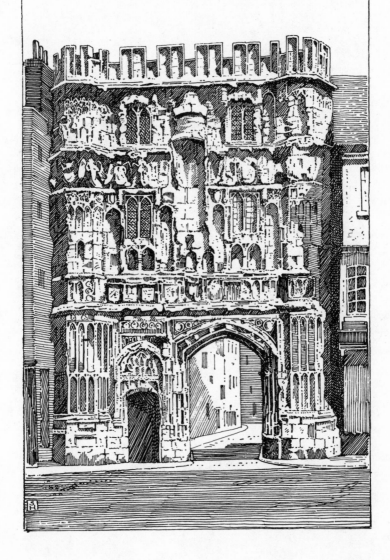

Christ Church Gate, Canterbury

PILGRIM LIFE IN THE MIDDLE AGES

By SIDNEY HEATH

WITH 43 ILLUSTRATIONS

KENNIKAT PRESS
Port Washington, N. Y./London

PILGRIM LIFE IN THE MIDDLE AGES

First published in 1911
Reissued in 1971 by Kennikat Press
Library of Congress Catalog Card No: 72-118524
ISBN 0-8046-1146-7

Manufactured by Taylor Publishing Company   Dallas, Texas

TO

ERNEST W. HASLEHUST, R.B.A.

AS A SMALL TOKEN

OF FRIENDSHIP AND ESTEEM

THIS BOOK IS DEDICATED

NOTES ON MAPS

THE only road taken by the pilgrims of old that remains practically in its entirety is that which runs along the shoulder of the downs from the daughter city of Winchester to the mother one of Canterbury. This is a very ancient trackway, a veritable "harrow," or hoary old road, that was in existence for centuries before the shrine of Becket became the most hallowed in Europe.

The road itself maintains a fairly uniform level throughout, a few feet below the crest of the downs, and although it passes within half a mile or so of many important places, it goes directly through few. The pilgrims could look down on the towns and avoid them if they wished.

There are three ways by which the modern tourist may follow the route taken by the mediæval pilgrim :—

1. By treading literally in his footsteps—*i.e.*, by walking.

2. By cycle.

3. By train or motor-car to convenient centres from whence the trackway can be explored in sections.

Notes on Maps

The railway has many advantages for the busy man. It runs parallel to the road for considerable distances, and the stations are conveniently placed, so that it is possible, by a series of daily or weekly excursions, to cover the whole of the route in the course of a summer.

By far the best way is to tramp along the trackway ; for even if the cycle enables one to make good time over the well-defined and level portions, the machine has to be pushed for considerable distances when the " Pilgrims' Road " crosses ploughed fields, or merges into a rough and brier-tangled woodland path.

On whichever method of travelling one's choice may fall—and a caravan would probably prove an ideal method—the modern pilgrim has one great advantage over his mediæval predecessor, in that he can procure, at a trifling cost, excellent maps that cover the entire route.

The well-known Ordnance maps have probably done as much to popularise modern pilgrimages as Wynkyn de Worde's " Informacion for Pylgrymes " did for the mediæval ones. Be this as it may, the old-time pilgrimage has left its mark on our modern cartography, and the magic words " Pilgrims' Way " appear still on many a modern map.

For all purposes, and for every class of traveller who would journey along or near what is probably the most ancient, as it is surely the most interesting, road in England, the Ordnance Survey maps are unequalled. They fold easily for carrying in the

Notes on Maps

pocket ; and armed with a set of these excellent maps, the traveller may leave the fair city of Winchester in full confidence that if he read them aright, they will direct him faithfully to the first city of the Anglo-Saxon race and the mother city of all the Englands of the Seven Seas.

The large sheet maps of the new series on the one-inch-to-the-mile scale are the best for general purposes. The numbers of the sheets required are 124, 125, 115, 116, and 117. These sheets cover the whole of the route to within a short distance of Canterbury. The prices of these sheets are 1s. 6d. paper, and 2s. mounted. Mr. T. Fisher Unwin, 1, Adelphi Terrace, London, W..C., is the sole wholesale agent for these maps, which can be obtained from any bookseller.

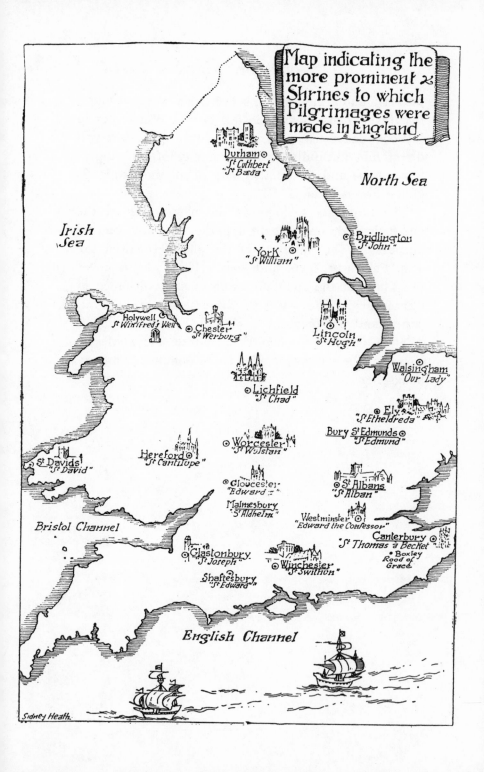

PREFACE

THIS book is designed to serve and entertain the general reader who is interested in the religious pilgrimages of olden days, of which so many memorials remain throughout the country.

Regarded from any standpoint—religious, archæological, or architectural—the subject is a vast one, and these pages are but portions of the whole story. The information set forth in this book has been gathered from many sources, owes much to the labours of others, and is the result of a considerable amount of searching, collation, and selection.

In dealing with such a multiplicity of dates, one can hardly hope to be immaculate in chronology, and the author would ask indulgence if some of his statements lean more to the legendary and traditional than to the purely scientific and historical sides of the subject. The sceptical antiquary may dissect the folklore, traditions, and religious customs of the past, and prove to his own satisfaction that they are nothing but myths. Yet to some of us our old English garden of legend and romance, with its beautiful flowers of chivalry and devotion, is infinitely sweeter to live with than are the dry and barren acres

Preface

given over to the cultivation of nothing but proven facts.

At any rate, let us keep enough romance to moisten the antiquary's dry treatises on those ancient days, when, with all their faults, religion was exhibited by the chivalrous invasion of infidel lands, and love was attested by daring deeds of arms done in honour of bright eyes.

The thanks of the author are due to, among others, Dr. Colley March, F.S.A., Mr. Herbert Batsford, Mr. Philip Norman, F.S.A., the proprietors of the *Builder*, Miss Ida M. Roper, and Mr. W. A. Dalziel, the Honorary Secretary of the Chaucer and Early English Text Society.

S. H.

Upwey, Dorset.

CONTENTS

ILLUSTRATIONS

Illustrations

PILGRIM LIFE IN THE MIDDLE AGES

CHAPTER I

INTRODUCTORY

THE word " pilgrimage " comes from the old French *pelegrinage*, Latin *peregrinatio*, and means a journey undertaken in a devotional spirit to some sacred place. The fundamental idea of the Christian pilgrimage was that the Deity exercised a benevolent influence operating through sacred *media* in some definite building or locality. Every nominal Christian of the Middle Ages yearned to make a pilgrimage to some hallowed shrine or sacred place, in much the same manner as at the present time in India, the home of pilgrimage, the pious wish of every Brahmin is to visit the holy city of Benares, and to be washed clean in the waters of the Ganges. To quote Macaulay : " In times when men were scarcely ever induced to travel by liberal curiosity, or by the pursuit of gain, it was better that the rude inhabitant of the North should visit Italy and the East as a pilgrim, than that he should never see anything but those squalid cabins and uncleared woods amidst which he was born. In times when life and female honour were exposed to daily risk from tyrants and marauders, it was better that the precinct of a shrine should be regarded with an irrational awe, than that there should be no refuge inaccessible to cruelty and licentiousness. . . . Had not such retreats been scattered here and there, among the huts of a miserable peasantry, and the castles of a ferocious aristocracy, European society would have consisted merely of beasts of burden and beasts of prey." Further, "Even the spiritual supremacy arrogated by the Pope was productive of far more good than evil."

Just as the Crusades contributed to the culture of the Middle Ages, so pilgrims did much to advance civilisation and, while they furthered the common use of letters, were not infrequently the bearers of peaceful messages between warlike nations, and before it became abused the pilgrim's badge was a sign of Christian fellowship and the revered token of international brotherhood.

During their sojourn in Palestine and the East the Crusaders, and after them the pilgrims, learned something of the conditions of Eastern life, and brought back with them, in addition to a vast number of holy relics, an appreciation for the peculiar products of that region—jewels, silks, perfumes, and spices. With a brisk commerce throughout the length and breadth of the Mediterranean, the wealth of Genoa, Pisa, Florence, and Venice was founded, and the inland sea was covered with sails trafficking from the ports of Italy to those of Syria and Egypt. The necessity of transporting merchandise from the East to supply the demand thus created in the West stimulated commerce, advanced the science of navigation, and encouraged manufactures. From the Greeks the Italians learned the art of weaving silk.

Introductory

Arabia was made to yield her secrets for tempering and inlaying military weapons ; and Constantinople furnished the Christians with splendid specimens of her native art. Nearly all our early Christian churches owed something to the trade from the Orient that followed the romantic wars of the Crusades, and to the wonder with which the churches of Byzantium were regarded by the pilgrims of Western Europe.

It is obvious, therefore, that, in spite of the particular vices the pilgrims acquired beneath a warmer sun than that which shone upon their native lands, the effect of pilgrimages was to strengthen the intercourse with Eastern nations which the Crusades had commenced, and to create a demand in the West for the products, arts, and industries of the East. In mediæval days the importance of a city depended far less on the number of its inhabitants, the volume of its trade, or the advantage of its climate than on the number and quality of its holy things. The richest city was that which possessed the greatest number of miracle-working relics to attract the pilgrim. In the Middle Ages pilgrimages, acting through the virtue of relics, had the same practical influence on the minds of men as have the themes of science or political economy at the present day, and it is doubtful if we shall ever appreciate to the full the profound effect produced by these pilgrimages, in the days when every idea was a belief, when legends were realities.

To us, the religious memorials of the past, the desecrated shrine and the dishonoured reliquary, are merely examples of ancient art, trinkets that supply a study for the jeweller, a subject for the lecturer, and, most frequently of all, a specimen in

Pilgrim Life in the Middle Ages

the museum. To our forefathers these things were living forms, voices which were heard, and teachers to be obeyed. Doctrines and historical traditions which echoed and were transmitted from nation to nation, from age to age, became the natural inheritance of the devout pilgrim, and so tended to feed and nourish the mysterious spirit of intense reverence with which saintly relics and hallowed shrines were regarded by the law, the laity, and the hierarchy of mediæval days.

As an anonymous writer has said : " In most countries hospitals were maintained at every stage for the accommodation of the pilgrim ; and chivalry in arms kept watch and ward wherever he was in danger of pagan insult or aggression. For him the Teutonic brotherhood guarded the German forests ; for him the knights of Santiago patrolled the Moorish frontier ; and for him the galleys of St. John maintained ceaseless and most gallant warfare with the merciless rovers of the Mediterranean. Kings and councils took care of his interests while engaged in these holy excursions, and hedged his household and estate from all assault. Creditors were forbidden to dun and enemies to assail, and the severest form of excommunication was denounced against his wife did she dare to contract another marriage during his absence."

At the present day, when locomotion has been so wonderfully facilitated that the means of communication to and from the most distant parts of the world offer the traveller an almost bewildering choice of routes, we can scarcely realise what our feelings would be should we find ourselves without the transporting aids of the railway, steamship, motor-car, and other mechanically-propelled vehicles.

Introductory

The mediæval lover or diplomat, instead of availing himself of the post, regular in departure and true in arrival, was compelled either to transmit his letters by a special messenger or to entrust them to any person who happened to be journeying towards the place of address, to the knight returning to his own estate after a foreign war, the priest soliciting a benefice, the monk changing his monastic abode, and, above all, to the pilgrim or palmer on his way to pay his devotions at some famous shrine or holy well.

Slow and tardy indeed were the modes of communication so irregularly obtained; for upon "the best estafetted [1] road in Europe, the road to Rome," three months elapsed before the pilgrim, quitting the shrine of Becket at Canterbury, could stand before the great basilica of St. Peter. The geographical knowledge of the earlier years of the Middle Ages apart from that personally acquired by travellers, consisted mainly of brief extracts from the pages of Pliny and Solinus. The terrestrial sphere, as portrayed in the first quarter of the fourteenth century, shows a circular projection, in the exact centre of which appears Jerusalem, while the Temple is depicted in the exact centre of the city. On the outermost margin is the ocean surrounding the whole domicile of mankind, and beyond the countries of Christendom nothing is shown but representations of camels and ostriches, elephants and tigers, designs that, by covering the regions unknown to the cartographer, hide his ignorance as they amuse the spectator. The lucid idea which an Ordnance map conveys at once to us was wholly wanting, and the forms and positions of the various portions of the

[1] Guarded by military couriers.

globe, the boundaries of the kingdoms, the localities of the great cities, and the courses of the rivers were all enveloped in vagueness and uncertainty.

For the transmission and diffusion of thought, ideas, and opinions we now depend almost entirely on the printing press ; but it is quite possible that as much was effected without its aid, for it is beginning to be admitted that the ideas imparted by means of printing obliterate each other by their numbers.

We can readily understand that when the printing press did not exist the smaller quantity of mental stimulants was more than compensated by their intensity. In the tale brought home by the knight who had won his spurs in foreign wars, and the impassioned narrative of the pilgrim recounting the glories of the shrines of Europe, there was a vivid vitality that must have carried conviction to the minds of whole masses of the population.

It is, of course, easy for us to sneer at the superstitious customs and the love of pilgrimage which played so prominent a part in the lives of our ancestors, but the sneering can be, and indeed has been, overdone. All impartial historians are agreed that there was a peculiar fitness in the mental qualities of the mediæval period, when considered as introductory to our own. Stationary, or even retrograde as the Middle Ages may appear to be with respect to some of the faculties of the intellect, others were exhibited in full and beneficial activity. To understand rightly any age or customs with a view to estimating fairly their character and influence, we must, by the force of sympathetic imagination, transport ourselves into that age, acquaint ourselves with its leading activities, and endeavour to feel and think

Introductory

as the people who lived under its social and religious influences must have felt and thought. It is neither wise nor just to measure the customs of a past age by the standards of our own.

As the great German writer Frederick Schlegel reminds us : " The Middle Ages are sometimes regarded as a chasm in the history of the human intellect, a void space, as it were, between the genius of antiquity and the civilisation of modern times. Art and science are, by an ingenious fiction, supposed to terminate their existence, only to start into life from chaotic nothingness after a sleep of ten centuries : this is inaccurate, nay, untrue, for the essence of ancient knowledge and culture never entirely perished, whilst much that is noblest and most excellent in the improvements of modern times *was born of mediæval genius.*"

At the same time, we cannot dissociate the present from the past if we would, for continuity is as inevitable in manners and customs, in psychical processes, as it is in physical facts. Thus the mediæval pilgrimage and the pointed Gothic arch are, like the saintly relic, the hallowed shrine, and the whole celestial hierarchy, our heritage and our destiny. With the advent of Christianity in England the Holy Land and Rome naturally became points of attraction to the devout adherents of this faith, and the ancient British Christians often made pilgrimages to these places, as we learn from St. Jerome, who speaks as though the practice was liable to lead to abuse, for, says he, " it is as easy to find the way to heaven in Britain as at Jerusalem." Christian pilgrimages to the Holy Land are mentioned as early as the third century, and by the fourth they were more or less common from all parts of the Roman Empire.

Pilgrim Life in the Middle Ages

At the same time, we have not many records of pilgrimages made to the Holy Land by the Saxon Christians ; but Adamnan, Abbot of Iona in Beda's lifetime, wrote an account of the holy places which was taken from a description of Palestine given him by Arcwulf, a French bishop, who, having made the " grand tour " of Jerusalem, Damascus, Constantinople, and Alexandria, was carried by a storm to the coast of Scotland, where the ship found shelter at Iona.

Adamnan's chronicle does not seem to have kindled much desire among his contemporaries to visit the Holy Land ; and, with a few notable exceptions, the Saxon pilgrimages from these islands ended at Rome, the scene of so many martyrdoms and the grave of so many saints, where one of the first to appear was Cedwella, formerly King of Wessex, who, after being well received and baptized by Pope Sergius, died within seven days afterwards, April 20, 689 A.D.

It is not difficult for us to understand the passion for pilgrimage which soon seized upon our early Christian ancestors when the warm glow of romance began to encircle about

> " Those holy fields,
> Over whose acres walked those blessed feet."

The restless spirit of their barbarian fathers seemed still to work in them, a spirit that is by no means an expended force at the present day, although directed into a different channel. The pilgrims, Crusaders, buccaneers, merchant adventurers, colonisers, and explorers of the Middle Ages have handed down to us the spirit of *wanderlust*, although the modern tourist travels by motor-car for pleasure

Introductory

and worldly profit, whereas his mediæval prototype journeyed afoot for the welfare of his soul. In early days, not only Cedwella, and enthusiastic youths like the two sons of St. Richard, the King of the Englishmen, but great warriors and statesmen renounced their dignities for the pilgrim's garb ; and Ina, the greatest of English kings before Alfred, was the most distinguished of the band. Pilgrimages to Rome became highly popular, and before long noble and simple, clerk and layman, men and women, caught the infection, wishing, as Beda says, " to live as pilgrims on earth that they might be welcomed by the saints when they were called away from their earthly sojourn."

The Church itself was not behind in encouraging the people to enrol themselves in one or other of the many bands of wanderers, with the result that a perpetual inducement was held out to pilgrimage and vagrancy to rise into a regular profession. In addition to many advantages to his body spiritual, the pilgrim enjoyed particular privileges of a temporal nature, with the result that proscribed criminals or hunted debtors helped to fill the ranks of devout pilgrims. If a priest, the pilgrim drew his full stipend, providing that his absence did not exceed a term of three years. If a layman, he was excused the payment of all taxes. The property of all pilgrims was secured from confiscation and injury while on pilgrimage, nor could they be arrested or cast in any civil court. Their sanctity was universally respected, for once the sacred cross was sewn upon his garment and he had received the blessing of Holy Church, the pilgrim was above all law except the ecclesiastical. He was protected by St. Peter and the Pope.

Pilgrim Life in the Middle Ages

Another, and one of the greatest factors that helped to swell the ranks of pilgrims and tended to the formation of bands of penitents, was the frequency with which famine and pestilence swept over the land. First famine, then the plague would lay whole districts desolate. The people, being taught that these calamities were manifestations of Divine wrath at sinful indulgence or religious backslidings, were easily led to believe that the only remedy was to resort to penance by a course of severe asceticism, when penance became a mania and fraternities were established for its better practice.

During the whole of the mediæval period it is doubtful if the plague was ever entirely absent from this country, while every now and then, usually about every ten years, it would rage with extraordinary violence.

The insanitary condition of the towns and the dirty habits of the people were, no doubt, largely responsible. In reading any contemporary accounts regarding the personal habits of the people of this country during the Middle Ages, it is significant to notice how any allusions to personal cleanliness are conspicuous by their absence ; and even when we do happen upon such reference it is confined to the washing of the face and hands. In the reign of Edward IV. soap was provided in the King's household only for the washing of clothes, although it is possible that it was used for other purposes as well. The filth of all classes of the population, excepting perhaps the ecclesiastical, was simply indescribable, and even princes were no strangers to vermin and other accompaniments of dirt.

As late as the reign of Henry VIII., and possibly for many years later, the scullions lay naked in the

Introductory

kitchens, and were so filthy that in 1526 a special ordinance was passed " for the better avoydyng of corruption and of all uncleanness out of the king's house," making provision " for such scolyons as shall not goe naked or in garments of such vileness as they now doe, and have been accustomed to doe, nor lie in the nights and dayes in the kitchens or ground by the fireside."

We are told that Cardinal W.olsey, when going to Westminster Hall, held in his hand " a very fair orange," the inside of which was filled with a vinegar-soaked sponge, " against the pestilent odours of his many suitors."

Erasmus makes many references to the plague, which he states was due to the filth of the streets and houses. Of the latter we read that " the floors are commonly of clay, strewed with rushes, under which lies unmolested an ancient collection of beer, grease, fragments, bones, spittle, excrements and urine of dogs and cats, and everything that is nasty." That even such a terrible scourge as the plague had its beneficial as well as its purely harmful and destructive forces is obvious to all students of history. The epidemics that depopulated the towns and denuded the agricultural districts of labourers played a considerable part in the welfare as in the desolation of nations. Our English hedgerows, which, until the advent of the motor-car, were the pride and glory of the countryside, are memorials, or at any rate are reminders, of the plague, for they mark the change in land tenure that followed the Black Death. It was the scarcity of men that dealt the final blow to villeinage and serfdom, and so released the English agricultural labourer from slavery. As a modern writer says : " Plague helped to kill the textile industries of the eastern counties and laid the foundations of the modern prosperity of Lancashire and Yorkshire. It was largely responsible for the decline of the power and wealth of the monasteries, and thus brought nearer the Reformation. It revolutionised Church life and greatly modified Church architecture. It even facilitated the growth of English literature. Up to the time of the Black Death French was the principal language of the schools and of the wealthy. So many teachers died in the epidemic that a new race of educationists arose who insisted on giving instruction in the English tongue, and the way was thereby paved for ' Piers Plowman ' and Chaucer." [1]

When we read of the loss of life due to warfare or to epidemics during the mediæval period, we must bear in mind that the total population of England was under two millions at the time of the Norman Conquest, and Professor Creasy tells us that the census showed no advance on this figure in the reign of John. It is necessary that we should keep this in mind, or we may fail to attach sufficient importance to the epidemics that carried off a few thousands of the inhabitants, and wonder why such destruction of life should have been regarded as a national catastrophe that sent the survivors weeping to the shrines of the saints.

It is probably no exaggeration to describe the modern tourist, who " does " Italy in ten days or Norway in five, as a direct descendant of the mediæval pilgrim, and but for the Reformation the making of pilgrimages might have suffered no breach of historical continuity.

The old-time pilgrimage was touring and sight-

[1] *Daily Mail*, February 15, 1911.

Introductory

seeing at its best, notwithstanding many disadvantages, and there were more wonders to be witnessed between Venice and Jerusalem than the most enterprising traveller would now encounter in a voyage round the entire world. Of the thousands of pilgrims who wended their way to the smaller domestic shrines we have no records, but an English traveller in the fourteenth century has related that he saw lying in the harbour of Corunna eighty shiploads of pilgrims, of which vessels thirty were from England. At the shrine of Becket at Canterbury the annual number of pilgrims exceeded for many years the remarkable figure of two hundred thousand, and the extraordinary devotion paid to this saint appears at one time to have almost, if not quite, effaced the adoration of the Deity. At God's altar, for example, the offerings in one year totalled the meagre sum of £3 2s. 6d., while the shrine of Becket received no less than £832 12s. 3d. The year following the disproportion was still greater, for not a single penny was offered at God's altar, although St. Thomas had for his share £954 6s. 3d., representing some thousands of pounds of our present currency.

Other equally famous shrines, apart from the most famous of them all, the Holy Sepulchre at Jerusalem, were those of the Holy Blood of Hayles ; St. Andrew, in Scotland ; St. David, in Wales ; St. Edmund, at St. Edmundsbury ; St. Patrick's Purgatory, in Ireland ; St. Ninian, in Galloway ; St. James of Compostella, in Spain ; and the Virgin's House, at Loretto, in Italy. In England the shrine of Becket, at Canterbury, and that of Our Lady of Walsingham, in Norfolk, rank easily first, both in popularity and in the numbers of pilgrims who visited them.

The English domestic shrines surpassed in point

of numbers, variety, and wealth those of any other country, there being no fewer than thirty-eight of these pilgrims' Meccas in the county of Norfolk alone.

There is little reason to doubt that the organisation of bands of pilgrims for transmarine voyages developed into a regular trade, and one that may be said to have been the first great commercial speculation of mediæval days. The foundation of the wealth of Venice is traceable to the great influx of foreign pilgrims, and the same may be said of Pisa, Rheims, Corunna, Genoa, and other favoured places. Many of our old cities and towns like Canterbury and Walsingham must have derived much pecuniary benefit from the pilgrims.

When pilgrimages became the fashion almost anything, from a scolding wife to a great offence, was excuse sufficient for the making of one. A knight of old about to undertake some dangerous mission of love or war invariably prepared himself for the ordeal by making a pilgrimage, and, returning in safety, he made another one as the most approved form of thanksgiving for having been preserved from disaster or death.

So Richard I., on his escape from the Austrian dungeon, wended his way barefooted from Sandwich to the shrine of Becket, and the first act of Columbus on recrossing the Atlantic was to make a pilgrimage. Gibbon hints that Peter the Hermit became a pilgrim to escape from matrimony, and a certain Guy de Crema is said to have gone all the way to Ararat in the hope of obtaining a piece of the Ark, with which to fashion a talisman for his wife to wear against a too rapid increase of family. Louis VII. had a perfect mania for pilgrimages, for, having got

Introductory

rid of a bad wife by some such promenade, he married again, and immediately set out on another from gratitude at getting a good one. These, however, were trifles, for he made a series of such pedestrian exercises through Europe, extending over a period of twenty-eight years, in order to induce the saints to provide him, as they eventually did, with a son and heir. For a pilgrimage-maker, this monarch's record would be hard to beat.

Pilgrimages could be performed by proxy, a consequence, perhaps, of the common doctrine of the mediæval Church that an individual could occasionally depute his religious duties to others without detriment to himself. Generally, however, it will be found that such pilgrimages were made only after the death of the person to whom they referred, although there are a few instances to the contrary.

Provision for these *post-obit* pilgrimages are frequently met with in the wills of the twelfth to the sixteenth century. In the earlier instances they were mostly directed to Rome or Jerusalem, but in later times, like other pilgrimages, they were more commonly made to domestic shrines.

A pious dame whose will is given in an old "History of Norfolk" provided for a pilgrim to visit, after her death, no fewer than eight different shrines in that county. In the will of Lady Cecily Gerbridge, dated 1418, ten marks are bequeathed for a pilgrim to visit Rome, and Bishop Gardiner of Norwich left twenty marks for a like purpose. In some cases the executors of a will were directed to give certain sums of money to all pilgrims who were willing to undertake an assigned pilgrimage for the deceased. A few extracts from these wills may be given from the volumes of " York Wills," published by the Surtees Society :—

1400. Roger de Wandesford, of Tereswell, in the county of Nottingham, left money to support a pilgrim "to visit the glorious confessors there resting," to whom he made a solemn vow when he was tossed about in the greatly troubled sea, between Hibernia and Norway, and nearly drowned.

1404. Matilda, wife of John Holbeck, citizen and merchant of York, left a silver-gilt necklace, set with gems, to be hung on the tomb of St. John of Bridlington.

1466. Wm. Boston, of Newark, chaplain, buried before the altar of St. Stephen in the parish church of Newark, ordered his tomb to be covered with a marble slab, on which should be placed a marble figure of his father, and another of himself. He also left 26s. viijd. for a priest to make a pilgrimage for him to Bridlington, Walsingham, Canterbury, and Hales.

1472. Wm. Ecop, Rector of the parish church of Heslerton, in the East Riding, ordered a pilgrim to visit the shrine of St. John of Bridlington, and seventeen other holy places named, and for the pilgrim to pay fourpence at each holy place visited.

1485. Dame Margaret Pigot, daughter of Wm. Sywardby, Esq., of Sywardby, left "my Table of Gold to St. John of Bridlington."

In several of these wills the soul of the testator is bequeathed " to our Lord Jesus, to our Lady Saint Mary, to Saint John of Bridlington, and to all the saints in heaven."

Judging from the number of bequests left to it, the shrine of St. John of Bridlington would appear to have been one of the most popular in Yorkshire.

The performance of religious duties and penances by proxy was, no doubt, largely resorted to by many members of the community. There is a popular story to the effect that a certain man had followed his wife to confession, and when she retired behind the altar to receive corporal discipline, he cried to spare her, for she was very tender, and he would take the punishment in her place ; whereupon, as he bowed himself to the rod, she cried, " Strike hard, father, for I am a great sinner ! "

There is little reason to doubt that when pilgrimage became the fashion the scrip and staff were as frequently assumed for the purpose of committing new sins as for the performance of penance for old ones. The holy well in its secluded and leafy bower, the hallowed shrine in the dimly-lighted cathedral, were excellent places of assignation, to reach which a pilgrimage formed a convenient and a plausible excuse. What proportion such impious pilgrims bore to their more devout companions we have few means of ascertaining, but we have considerable evidence that in quite early days the monkish custodians of shrine and relic were much perturbed by this abuse of pilgrimage, and they have not failed to record the fate that overtook the transgressors.

" PERPAVCÆ ENIM SVNT CIVITATES IN LONGOBARDIA, VEL IN FRANCIA AVT IN GALLIA, IN QVA NON SIT ADVLTERA VEL MERETRIX GENERIS ANGLORVM, QVOD SCANDALUM EST TVRPITVDO TOTIVS ECCLESIÆ."

So wrote a continental bishop of the period, and we have every reason to believe that the conduct of the dames of other lands were just as bad, if not rather worse, as the example of Eleanor, the divorced wife of Louis VII., goes to show.

It was in vain that the more pious fathers of the Church preached and wrote against the abuse of pilgrimage. Their pleadings fell on deaf ears, their eloquence was in vain, and availed but little to stem the growth of the many abuses. Pilgrimages had, in

common parlance, come to stay, and to many folk
going on pilgrimage was

> "A nostrum famous, in old popish times,
> For purifying souls that stunk with crimes;
> A sort of apostolic salt,
> That popish parsons for its power exalt,
> For keeping souls of sinners sweet,
> Just as our kitchen salt keeps meat."

"Jerusalem," wrote St. Jerome, "is now made a
place of resort from all parts of the world, and there
is such a throng of pilgrims of both sexes that all
the temptation, which you might in some degree
avoid elsewhere, is here collected together."

A few years after the death of Beda, Winfrid, an
English missionary in Germany, wrote to Cuthbert,
Archbishop of Durham, to say that there "was great
need to check the practice of pilgrimages, for many,
both men and women, only go abroad for the purpose
of living licentiously, without the restraint they would
find at home, or are tempted by the vices of the cities
in France and Lombardy to fall from the paths of
virtue." According to the testimony of Winfrid there
were few cities on the way to Rome where such
persons were not to be met with, and the historian
Gibbon tells us that "the roads were covered with
multitudes of either sex, and of every rank, who professed their contempt of life so soon as they should
have kissed the tomb of their Redeemer. Princes and
prelates abandoned the care of their dominions, and
the members of these pious caravans were a prelude
to the armies which marched in the ensuing age
under the banner of the cross."

During the eleventh century in particular the belief
in the merit and even the obligation in the sight of

Introductory

God of a pilgrimage to Jerusalem were as firmly impressed on the mind of every nominal Christian, whatever his rank or station, as are the necessity and advantage of a pilgrimage to the Kaaba of Mecca in the creed of the followers of Mohammed at the present day.

Each year saw the number of pilgrims augment, and all persons were strictly enjoined to hold a pilgrim in great respect and veneration, as an especial favourite of the Almighty, inasmuch as he had been admitted by Him to the glorious privilege of visiting the sacred places, and had retained, it was thought, a portion of their sanctity.

In all pilgrimages of real devotion the practice of walking was common, and it was usual for the pilgrim to make his journey barefoot. It was thus that Richard I. made his journey from Sandwich to Canterbury. In one of the Paston letters, dated 1471, the Duke and Duchess of Norfolk are mentioned as making a pilgrimage together in this manner from Framlingham to Walsingham. Henry VIII., in one of his numerous pilgrimages to Walsingham, walked barefoot from Barsham, a distance of three miles, and Henrietta Maria's pilgrimages from St. James's to Tyburn were similarly performed.

The returning Crusaders brought into this country from Palestine a large number of relics, to some of which we owe the founding of such shrines as that of the True Blood, at Hayles Abbey, in Gloucestershire, in which the sacred material had been imported by the Crusaders.

The papal assertion that relics possessed the power of self-reproduction was inevitable in the days when churches were so many and genuine relics so few, especially as bishops were threatened with deprivation of office should they dare to consecrate churches void of relics. Calvin, in his interesting little black-letter volume, printed in 1561, declares, with excusable exaggeration, that the portions of the true cross shown in the European churches were enough to load a large ship. The relics purporting to be those of our Lord's Passion—the holy blood, the seamless garment, fragments of the crown of thorns—were almost as numerous, as indeed were the relics of the Virgin. Her shift was shown at Aix-la-Chapelle, her combs at Rome and Besancon, and her wedding-ring at Perugia. The most popular relic, however, of the Virgin was her milk, such as that exhibited in England at Walsingham, and in many churches on the Continent.

The multiplicity of holy relics was not free from certain disadvantages, notwithstanding that their exhibitors could plead to sceptical and well-travelled pilgrims the papal decree that *all* holy relics had the Divine gift of self-multiplication. There is an old story told of a visitor making a tour of the various French shrines in the early years of the sixteenth century, to the effect that when shown the skull of John the Baptist at a certain monastery, the pilgrim remarked that the skull of the same saint had been exhibited to him only the day before at another abbey. "Maybe," the monkish custodian is said to have replied, "that was the skull of John the Baptist when a young man, whereas this in our possession is his skull after he was fully advanced in years and wisdom."

A full list of the relics still treasured in the continental churches would be indeed a surprising document.

With regard to the present-day attitude of the

Introductory

Church of Rome towards such relics, and the miracles
performed by their aid, the words of the late
Cardinal Newman may be quoted as authoritative,
unquestioned, and canonical :—

" Certainly," he wrote, " the Catholic Church, from
east to west, from north to south, is, according to our
conceptions, hung with miracles. The store of relics
is inexhaustible, they are multiplied through all lands,
and each particle of each has in it at least a dormant
—perhaps an energetic—virtue of supernatural opera-
tion. At Rome there is the true cross, the crib of
Bethlehem, and the chair of St. Peter, portions of
the crown of thorns are kept at Paris, the holy coat
is shown at Trèves, the winding sheet at Turin. At
Monza the iron crown is formed out of a nail of
the cross, and another nail is claimed for the Duomo
of Milan, and pieces of Our Lady's habit are to be
seen in the Escurial. The Agnus Dei, blessed medals,
the scapular, the cord of St. Francis, all are the media
of Divine manifestations of grace. Crucifixes have
bowed the head to the suppliant, and Madonnas
have bent their eye upon assembled crowds. St.
Januarius's blood liquefies periodically at Naples, and
St. Winifred's Well is the scene of wonders in an un-
believing country. Women are marked with sacred
stigmata, blood has flowed on Fridays from their
five wounds, and their heads are crowned with a
circle of lacerations. Relics are for ever touching
the sick, the diseased, the wounded, sometimes with
no result at all, at other times with marked and un-
deniable efficacy. Who has not heard of the
abundant favours gained by the intercession of the
Blessed Virgin, and of the marvellous consequences
which have attended the invocation of St. Anthony
of Padua? These phenomena are sometimes reported

37

of saints in their lifetime as well as after death, especially if they were evangelists or martyrs. The wild beasts crouched before their victims in the Roman amphitheatre, the axe-man was unable to sever St. Cecilia's head from her body, and St. Peter elicited a spring of water for his jailer's baptism in the Mamertine. St. Francis Xavier turned salt-water into fresh for five hundred travellers, St. Raymond was transported over the sea on his cloak, St. Andrew shone brilliantly in the dark, St. Scholastica gained by her prayers a pouring rain, St. Paul was fed by ravens, and St. Frances saw her guardian angel. I need not continue the catalogue. It is agreed on both sides ; the two parties join issue over a fact ; that fact is, the claim of miracles on the part of the Catholic Church ; it is the Protestants' charge, and it is our glory."

Faith-healing is, of course, as old as the hills, for before there was religion there was magic, and wherever there was magic faith-healing was largely practised.

In writing of the so-called miracles of healing which have taken place at numberless shrines and holy wells, and which have been inscribed on papal bulls by the thousand, one must speak with caution. No one in his senses now believes that an application of the reputed blood of Becket mixed with water will reset a fractured pelvis, or that a twisted limb can be straightened by dipping it into the waters of a holy well. At the same time we must remember that the Mediæval Period was an age of infinite faith, and therefore one of immense possibilities with regard to the relief, if not the cure, of diseases which may be, to a certain extent, controlled by the mind. That many of the reputed miracles of the Middle Ages were

Introductory

not genuine, and were feigned to bring fame to
some particular shrine, is certain. The great mass
of pilgrims had minds which, though constrained by
faith, the most biassed lover of the mediæval system
could not call scientific, so that the mere exercise
of walking from shrine to shrine, coupled with a
plain, wholesome diet, effected many cures of minor
ailments, which were hailed by the monks as cases
of miraculous healing.

It is the fashion to-day to regard the mediæval
miracle with scepticism. Yet the fact remains that
remarkable cures, bearing much similarity to the
old-time miracle, are effected at the present day.
Such a statement requires proof, which is furnished
by a paper on " Modern Miracles of Healing," which
was read only last year (1910) before the North
Wales Branch of the British Medical Association,
when several of the medical men present bore testimony to certain cases of healing at St. Winifred's
Well being of undoubted authenticity, an extraordinary testimony to the power of faith-healing in
this eminently scientific age, and one which helps us
to realise that many of the mediæval miracles were,
in a sense, quite genuine.

With the rise of the domestic shrine in England
the foreign pilgrimage declined, for who but the most
devout would make a perilous journey overseas for
benefits that could be more easily procured at home,
especially as the edict went forth that two pilgrimages
to a great shrine like that of St. David, in Wales,
equalled in merit one made to Rome? When the
occupation of showing genuine or assumed relics to
an ever-increasing number of visitors became a source
of profit, great inducements of various kinds, such as
indulgences, were held out to attract pilgrims, with

the result that pilgrimages degenerated until they became, for the majority of those attending them, mere holiday jaunts.

And what were the sentiments, one may ask, which animated these countless hordes of pilgrims—knights, nobles, kings, ladies, priests, clerks, gentles, and yeomen—and urged them to undertake so frequently such long and perilous journeys? The majority of such wayfarers, in the earlier days at any rate, may be regarded as devout and pious persons who honestly believed in the efficacy of their arduous pilgrimage.

To quote Mr. J. J. Jusserand [1] : "Arrived at the end of the journey, all prayed ; prayed with fervour in the humblest posture. The soul was filled with religious emotion when from the end of the majestic alley formed by the coloured twilight of the nave, the heart divined, rather than the eye saw, the mysterious object of veneration for which such a distance had been traversed at the cost of such a fatigue. Though the practical man galloped up to bargain with the saint for the favour of God, though the emissary sent to make offering in the name of his master might keep a dry and clear eye, tears coursed down the cheeks of the poor and simple in heart. He tasted fully of the pious emotion he had come to seek, the peace of heaven descended into his bosom, and he went away consoled. Such was the happy lot of simple, devout souls."

It is doubtful if a more charming description has ever been penned of the devout and genuine pilgrim than that quoted above; but there were others, in the later days especially, who were merely pleasure-seekers or holiday-makers, accompanied by a con-

[1] "English Wayfaring Life," J. J. Jusserand (T. Fisher Unwin).

Introductory

siderable number of adventurers, minstrels, dancers, and camp followers, living on the credulity or bounty of their wealthier fellow-travellers. Each may have had his quiet and devotional moment before the hallowed relic, as, the world forgetting, he confessed his sins or sought the intercession of the Blessed Virgin.

At the same time, it would be ridiculous to affirm that all who went on pilgrimage during the Middle Ages were actuated by devotional motives, or concerned their minds very much about the spiritual benefits to be derived from their journey. J. R. Green tells us that restless workmen made use of pilgrimages when seeking a new situation, and a statute of Richard II. attempted to put a stop to the practice. Thus we find that a small band of devout pilgrims would be joined by those to whom a pilgrimage was but a pretext for some other objective ; the merchant taking his goods to a distant town, the artisan in search of work, would, in many cases, join one of the numerous bands of pilgrims who were journeying in the desired direction.

We have a curious picture of the manner in which certain of our home-pilgrimages were prosecuted in the early years of the fifteenth century, when William Thorpe was tried for heresy by the Archbishop of Canterbury in 1407. Thorpe had been accused by Archbishop Arundel of having asserted that " those men and women who go on pilgrimages to Canterbury, to Beverley, to Walsingham, and to other such places, are accursed and made foolish, spending their goods in waste. Such persons as these spend much money and time in seeking out and visiting the bones or images of this or that saint, do that which is in direct disobedience to the commands of God,

41

inasmuch as they waste their goods partly upon innkeepers, many of whom are women of profligate
conduct, partly upon rich priests, who have already
more than they need."

"Ungracious lousel!" replied the Archbishop,
"thou favourest no more truth than a hound. Since,
at the road at the north door at London, at our Lady
at Walsingham, and many other divers places in
England, are many great and praisable miracles
done, should not the images of such holy saints and
places be more worshipped than other places and
images where no such miracles are done?"

With the increase of shrines all over the country,
it was inevitable that pilgrimages should tend to
become mere pleasure parties, in which the spirit of
real devotion and austerity was conspicuous by its
absence. A troop of pilgrims was never wanting
in the elements of humour, and so mixed a company
was bound to afford an opportunity for fun and
frolic. So much was this the case that as early as
the days of Charlemagne we find the pilgrim's badges
denounced as the insignia of imposture and deceit.
We have many contemporary records to show that,
as they trudged or cantered along the highways and
byways, they relieved the tedium of the journey with
songs, legends, and stirring tales of adventure, while
the notes of flutes, bagpipes, and other musical instru-
ments gave an additional gaiety to the scene. The
popular songs of the day were certainly broadly
humorous, if not something rather worse, for, as
Sir Thomas More observed, "there be cathedral
churches into which the country come with procession,
and the women following the cross with many an
unwomanly song."

Another passage from one of the early State

Introductory

trials may be quoted. The dialogue occurs between
a disciple of Wycliffe, *temp.* Henry IV., and Archbishop Arundel of Canterbury. "Also, sir," says
the disciple, "I know well that when divers men
and women will go after their owne wills, and finding out a pilgrimage, they will order to have with

The Canterbury Pilgrims, from an Illuminated MS, Reg 18, D. ii.

them both men and women that can sing wanton
songs ; and some other pilgrims will have with them
bagpipes, so that every towne they come through,
what with the noise of their singing and the sound of
their piping, and with the jangling of their Canterbury bells, and with the barking out of dogs after
them, that they make more noise than if the king

Pilgrim Life in the Middle Ages

came that waye, with all his clarions and minstrells. And if these men and women be a month in their pilgrimage, many of them shall be half a year after great jinglers, tale-tellers, and liars."

To this somewhat severe accusation the Archbishop replied that " Pilgrims have with them singers and also pipers, that when one of them which goeth bare-foote striketh his toe upon a stone, and maketh it to bleed, it is well done that he and his fellows begin then a song, or else take out of his bosome a bag-pipe, to drive away with such mirthe the hurte of his fellow. For with such solace the travaile and weari-nesse of pilgrims is lightly and merrily brought forth."

There were, however, more serious charges brought against the pilgrims and their followers than the foregoing. In Sir Thomas More's " Dyalogue on the Adoracion of Images " the interlocutor observes that " the most part [of pilgrims] that cometh, cometh for no devotion at all, but only for good company to babble thitherward, and drinke dronke there, and then dance and reel homeward."

According to Chaucer the pilgrims of whom he has given us so vivid an account in the " Canterbury Tales " were little more than a merry band of revel-lers, all decked out in their gayest garments, and exhibiting no sign of their austere profession in either appearance, behaviour, or spirit.

> " Every man in his wise made herty chere,
> Telling his fellows of sportes and of cheer,
> And of mirthes that fallen by the waye,
> As custom is of pilgrims, and hath been many a daye."

However hard they may have prayed at the end of their journey, they appear, during Chaucer's time

44

Introductory

at any rate, to have given themselves up to enjoyment on the way, and when they raised their eyes to heaven it will generally be found that they did so in order to take aim at it with the end of a bottle.

It is not difficult to understand why the " Wife of Bath," who, besides doing many of the lesser tours, had been three times to Jerusalem, longed to go on more journeys, and why the knight Geoffroi de la Tour Landry, in the treatise [1] he wrote on morals and behaviour for the use of his daughters, warned them against pilgrimages as against the plague. At the same time, these remarks must be taken as more applicable to the customary, fashionable, and regular pilgrimages than to those undertaken spontaneously by individuals or small bands of penitents from some strong religious impulse or motive, and how different the early Christian was from the " Canterbury " pilgrim the " Canterbury Tales " unfold.

There is a general impression that the custom of making pilgrimages had fallen into abeyance, had, in fact, died of inanition, long before the Reformation swept shrine and relic to the winds. Such was possibly the case with the smaller domestic shrines, for long before the close of the fifteenth century pilgrimage had ceased to be an important factor in the religious life of the country. At the same time, we know that Henry VIII. himself made more than one pilgrimage and gave the customary gifts to several shrines ; and the little black-letter volume entitled " Informacion for Pylgrymes unto the Holy Land," printed by Wynkyn de Worde about 1498, ran

[1] Harleian MSS., No. 1,764. Printed under the title of "The Knight of the Tower," by Caxton, in 1484.

Pilgrim Life in the Middle Ages

through three editions. The beautiful Pilgrims' Inn at Glastonbury was erected about 1475 to accommodate those visiting the holy places of St. Joseph of Arimathea and the relics of St. Dunstan; and although the daily resort to shrines for devotional purposes had practically ceased, the Jubilees of St. Thomas of Canterbury, the last one being kept in 1520, were attended by such vast crowds of people that special provisions were made for their accommodation. In 1533 Hugh Latimer wrote to his friend Master Morice, from his rectory of West Kineton (Kington West), in Wiltshire, saying: "I dwell within a mile of the Fossway, and you would wonder to see how many they come by flocks out of the West Country to many images—to our Lady of Worcester, &c., but chiefly to the Blood of Hayles, which they believe to be the very blood of Christ, and that the sight of it puts them in a state of salvation."

Spring was the favourite season for English pilgrimages to domestic shrines, particularly in the days when the delights of a holiday trip were tempered with the sense of performing a religious duty. As these latter-day pilgrims started on their journey well provided with money, and clad in rich garments, they were worth plundering. Country roads were unsafe for solitary or small bodies of pilgrims who could not afford the luxury of an escort of armed servants; so for mutual convenience and protection, for safety and better entertainment on the way, they formed themselves into companies of sufficient strength to defend themselves if attacked on the ill-kept highways that led to Hayles, to Walsingham, or to Canterbury.

For better or worse the days of devotional pilgrimages in this country are over, except for the Roman

Introductory

Catholics, and on every side the Pilgrims' Ways are
strewn with the wreckage of mediævalism. No
longer does Chaucer's merry cavalcade ride forth
in the fresh spring morning, a motley company

"From every shire's end
Of England, to Canterbury they wend
The holy blissful martyr for to seek,
That them hath helpen when that they were sick."

Yea, verily, the days of devotional pilgrimages
are over, and as they have no equivalent in our land
it is imagination alone that will awaken the thought
that they once played an important part in the social
and religious life of our ancestors.

No longer does the wooden Christus hanging on
the oaken rood-tree bend the head to the penitent
suppliant ; and vanished utterly from our Protestant
churches is the bejewelled and glistening Mary and
her little company of angels. Long still and gone
are all these things, and only the reverence of a
reverie remains.

"Whence and whither, jolly Pilgrims, whither ride ye forth to-day,
That like kings ye canter, canter, canter on the King's highway ?
What your quest, and what your token ?   Be they bells or blooms
ye wear ?
Proud and princely are your trappings—can ye do the deed
ye dare ?
  .   .   .   .
Nay, but who be ye that ask us ?   Up and with us as we ride !
And may God not help the laggard that shall wait for time or tide !
We be Pilgrims of the Ages, with a world to win or lose !
Gentle, simple, up and with us! We can stay not while ye
choose !
We be Canterbury Pilgrims in a world we mean to win :
All the true of all the Englands—all the free of English kin,
All the brave of fifty kingdoms, all whose sires were Men of
Kent,

47

Pilgrim Life in the Middle Ages

Riding onward past the landmarks on the ways our fathers went ;
And we canter, canter, canter east and west and south and
    north
With a Canterbury gallop forth and forth and ever forth !
Far and fast our fathers cantered by the highways of the sea
When they rode with hempen bridle on the horse of oaken tree :
Sound of heart the stout old horse is though his mate be steed
    of steel ;
Bone and sinew tempered metal, stronger frame and swifter
    heel ;
Lady's hand can guide and curb him though the foam be on
    the reins,
And the lightning of the tempest be the life-blood in his veins.
Not a haven, not a headland but hath heard his bridle ring,
As we canter, canter, canter by the highways of the King.
What the tokens ? They be tokens of the bells of white and
    blue
In the mother garden-island, in the Kentish morning dew.
Blue for Hope, and white for Honour, let them bloom there
    spring to spring,
As we canter, canter, canter on the highways of the King !
Saintly relic, shrine and hallow ?—nay, hath pilgrim need of
    these,
Brothers' dust the ground we tread on, and the ooze of all the
    seas ?
Nobler promise hath our token. Hearken, Hearken ! In the
    sky
Ye can hear the Yule bells pealing from the belfry, low and
    high :
Bells of promise, pealing, pealing of an England free, and One
In the league of all the Englands ere the pilgrimage be done.
Peace and Freedom ! Peace and Freedom ! This the tale
    our token tells ;
And the world looks up to listen to the Canterbury bells."

Anon.

CHAPTER II

GENERAL REMARKS ON RELICS AND SHRINES

BEFORE considering in detail the religious customs and observances which the Protestant peoples have long regarded as "superstition," if not something rather worse, it may be well for us to bear in mind that just as men have given their lives to uphold the honour of their country, to defend that honour as symbolised in a few square yards of bunting, so men gave the labour of their lives to create fitting resting-places and shrines for the glorification of a hallowed and saintly relic. If we eliminate all such portions of the great architectural creations of the Middle Ages as were due to or influenced by religious sentiment and devotional superstition, the greater part of the personal appeal made by the material fabric vanishes. On every side, in this country as on the Continent, we find evidence of the immense pains and labour the monkish craftsmen took to enshrine in the most beautiful manner they knew some assumed fragment of the True Cross or a reputed phial of the Holy Blood ; and around these religious *motives* sprang up those beautiful architectural creations which, even in their ruin and decay, compel our wonder and stimulate our imagination. Not only, however, are these buildings to be regarded as architectural creations, for many of them are literally

49

Pilgrim Life in the Middle Ages

" prayers in stone," whereof every brick is an Ave Maria and every piece of carving a Paternoster. Thus it is that so many of our mediæval churches and cathedrals possess a plainly felt but indescribable atmosphere that permeates the material fabric, and which, by some mysterious and subtle influence, transforms the material house of man into the spiritual house of God, surely the highest and noblest ideal within the domain of architectural expression.

Relics formed the real wealth of the mediæval Church and the demand for some form of miracle-working relic was due in a large measure to a decree of the second Nicene Council (A.D. 787), by which bishops were threatened with deprivation of office should they consecrate churches without relics, a decree that holds good in the Roman Catholic Church at the present day. The natural consequence was that when no genuine relics could be obtained every kind of fraud was perpetrated.

It is really astounding the extraordinary value the clergy put upon relics, and the great efforts they made to secure them. No means were considered too low to obtain them, and a regular trade was done in saintly relics.

The graves of the saints and martyrs became so ransacked, we are told by contemporary historians, that not so much as a finger-nail with any pretence to occult power remained unappropriated. With the authority of the Church to back him the relic-hunter was early abroad, awaiting his opportunity to purloin some arm, leg, or other portion of a saint's anatomy while such was being transferred to a new shrine.

It is related of one Stephen, chanter to the monastery of Angers, that he walked barefoot through France and Italy all the way to Apulia, for the sole

Remarks on Relics and Shrines

purpose of stealing an arm of St. Nicholas, the miraculous power of which had brought untold wealth and glory to the Abbey of Bari ; but he did not succeed in his attempt.

A considerable business, too, was done in " faked " relics, for the clergy, unless they could procure genuine ones, were obliged to be content with imitations, with which we may be sure the market was flooded.

Thus it came to pass that after a while the bogus or mechanical-working relic was in danger of ousting the genuine article, for if the relic could not be saintly it could easily be extraordinary.

So one monastery would exhibit the plume of a phœnix, presented by one of the popes ; another treasured the mark Cain bore on his forehead ; while a third would proudly call attention to the tip of Lucifer's tail, lost in conflict with a Syrian hermit.

Henry Stephens, the famous French printer, mentions that in the sixteenth century there was exhibited in a French monastery a phial of glass containing some of Christ's tears, and in another church a glass containing some of His breath.

A very favourite device was the image or picture containing some hidden mechanism, which was worked with gratifying results. The more popular of these mechanical contrivances were representations of the Virgin shedding real tears and the Crucifix exuding blood. At Breslau the good fathers, with a touch of inventive genius, showed their astonished congregations a carving purporting to be a representation of " the devil carrying his grandmother on a wheel-barrow " !

It must not be forgotten that from very early days there had always been within the Church a considerable number of iconoclasts, men who thought that religion could be taught and preached without the help of pictorial symbolism or sacred imagery.

In 726 Leo published a long edict against the growing use of relics, shrines, and images of all descriptions, when his decrees met with such fierce opposition that a civil war resulted. Leo's son, Constantine Copronymus, renewed his father's edict, and in 754 convened at Constantinople a Council, at which the use of images and relics was condemned. These decrees were warmly welcomed by the Eastern churches generally, but were utterly rejected at Rome.

Among the Latins the most eminent iconoclast was Claudius, Bishop of Turin, who, in 823, ordered all images, and even the Cross itself, to be cast out of the churches and burned. He treated relics with the utmost contempt and ridiculed the virtues ascribed to them. He also censured the frequent pilgrimages to the Holy Land and to the tombs of the saints.

As one would expect, the relics most eagerly sought, apart from the bones of saints and martyrs, were pieces of the wood of the Cross, drops of the Holy Blood, phials containing portions of the Virgin's milk, the nails and similar memorials of the Crucifixion.

St. Jerome states (" Epist. ad Eustachium ") that the column to which our Lord was fastened for the scourging existed in his time in the portico of the Holy Sepulchre, and that it retained marks of the blood of our Saviour.

Beda places this column within the church, and Gregory of Tours dilates on the miracles wrought by it.

The number of nails by which the Saviour was

Remarks on Relics and Shrines

fastened to the Cross has always been a matter of dispute. Nonnus affirms that three only were used, and in this he is preceded by Gregory Nazianzen. Cornelius Curtius, an Augustine friar who wrote a treatise, " De Clavis Dominicis," insists on the use of four nails, and in this he is supported by the earliest representations of the Crucifixion, in which four nails are always shown. The upraised arms and the three nails belong to a comparatively late period of pictorial religious art.

Of the four reputed original nails the Empress Helena is said to have thrown one into the Adriatic during a storm, which at once ceased. The early history of the second nail is obscure, and authorities differ as to whether it was inserted by Constantine in his helmet, his crown, or in one of his statues at Constantinople. However, this nail was afterwards found, considerably mutilated, in the church of St. Croce-in-Gerusalemme, at Rome. The Cathedral of Milan claims to possess the third original nail, which Eutropius states was fixed through one of our Saviour's hands, and which, we are told by Rufinus (" Ecc. Hist.," iv.), was used by Constantine as a bit, in accordance with the prophecy of Zechariah (xiv. 20), " In that day shall be upon the bells [bridles] of the horses, *Holiness unto the Lord*." The fourth and last nail, said to have been the one driven through our Saviour's right foot, is shown at Trèves, where is also the seamless garment.

The wood of the Cross is stated by Lipsius to have been such as happened to be nearest at hand, in which case it would probably be oak, as this grew plentifully in Judæa ; and what are claimed to-day to be authentic pieces of the original Cross bear much resemblance to fine-grained and dark oak.

Pilgrim Life in the Middle Ages

Beda states that the wood of the Cross on which the Saviour suffered was—the upright of cypress, the cross-piece of cedar, the head-piece of fir, and the *suppedaneum* (footpiece) of box. This differs from the Eastern tradition, which substitutes olive and palm for the fir and box.

Be this as it may, the Cross, like so many of the popular relics, had the faculty of gracing two or more shrines at the same time. It existed in a complete state at Constantinople, and in fragments all over Europe.

The discovery, or invention, of the true cross by the Empress Helena is assigned to A.D. 326, the twenty-first year of the reign of her son Constantine. Briefly the tradition is to the effect that this devout princess, in her seventy-ninth year, inflamed with holy ardour, resolved to visit the scenes of our Lord's Passion. The pagans had obliterated all the marks of the hated Christians, Calvary had been piled up with stones and earth, on the summit of which was erected a temple of Venus. The Empress, however, hearing of a Jew who knew where certain memorials had been hidden, forced him to disclose the secret. The spot he named was carefully excavated, with the result that within it three crosses were found, and lying beside them the title-board which Pilate had written as the superscription for that on which our Lord suffered. St. Ambrose affirms that this title was attached to one of the crosses, but other historians assert that Helena herself had no guidance as to which was the *true* cross, until, by the suggestion of the Bishop of Jerusalem, certain sick and infirm persons were touched by all three, when, as only one produced miraculous cures, there no longer remained any doubt as to which was the authentic one.

Remarks on Relics and Shrines

Over the hallowed spot a church was built by Helena, or St. Helena as she afterwards became, and within it the real Cross was deposited, after a considerable portion had been sent to Constantinople, to be inserted by Constantine into the head of one of the statues representing himself.

At a later date the remaining portion of the Cross found its way to Rome, where the Church of St. Croce-in-Gerusalemme was built specially for its reception.

A festival to commemorate the Invention of the Cross was ordered to be celebrated annually on May 3rd, and on Easter Sunday the Bishop of Jerusalem exhibited the great object of devotion to thousands of devout pilgrims.

Small portions of the holy wood, set in gold and gems, were distributed to those who could afford to purchase them, while to make the supply equal to the extraordinary demand, it was boldly asserted that the holy wood had a miraculous power of self-reproduction, and could never be diminished however largely it was distributed.

St. Cyril, Patriarch of Jerusalem, affirms the miraculous nature of the holy wood, which he likens to the five small loaves with which five thousand people were supplied. From the time of Heraclius we hear but little about this more or less complete Cross, the discovery or invention of which was severely criticised by Jortin ("Remarks," vol. iii.). It may have been destroyed by the Saracens when they conquered Jerusalem in 637, but nothing is definitely known about it. The wooden title-board, however, is still preserved at Rome, where it was sent by Constantine and placed in a leaden chest above the vaulted roof of St. Croce Church, the whole being walled in and its position indicated by an exterior mosaic inscription. This had become illegible from lapse of time, but while some repairs to the church were being carried out during the pontificate of Innocent VIII., A.D. 1492, the window through which the sacred relic was viewed became broken, and the holy title was discovered. Such is the history recorded on a wall of the church, encircling a stairway leading to the Chapel of St. Helena. Moreover, this discovery and the truth of the find were authenticated four years later by a papal bull of Alexander VI.

The Crouched, or, more correctly perhaps, the crutched or crossed Friars, were founded in honour of the discovery of the Cross by St. Helena. According to Chaucer, to crouch is to make the sign of the cross. They appear, also, to have been called *crosiers* for the same reason. They were fairly numerous on the Continent, and came to England in the thirteenth century, when they founded friaries at London, Oxford, and Reigate. In the Greek Church *Crouched-mass Day* is held on the 14th of September, and on that day the ecclesiastical year commences.

F. A. Gasquet, in his " English Monastic Life," writes : " The Crossed Friars are said by some to have taken their origin in the Low Countries, by others to have come from Italy in very early times, having been instituted or reformed by one Gerard, prior of St. Maria di Morella at Bologna. In 1169 Pope Alexander III. took them under his protection and gave them a fixed rule of life. These friars first came to England in the year 1244.

" Matthew Paris, writing of that time, says they appeared before a synod held by the Bishop of Rochester, each carrying a stick upon which was a

Remarks on Relics and Shrines

cross. They presented documents from the Pope and asked to be allowed to make foundations of their fraternity in England. Clement Reyner puts their first establishment in this country at Reigate, in 1245, and their second in London, in 1249. This second foundation is the better known, as it has given the name of Crutched Friars to a locality in the City of London. They had a third house at Oxford, and altogether there were six or seven English friaries. Besides the cross upon their staves, from which they originally took their names, the friars had a red cloth cross upon the breasts of their habits."

There were two classes of miraculous pictures, one comprehending those which are said to have had a miraculous origin, like the Veronical portrait ; the other, a far more numerous class, include those which have caused miracles to be performed, such as the picture of the Virgin at St. Giovanni e Paolo, near Rome, which was seen to shed real tears when the French armies invaded Italy. One of the best known pictures of this class is in St. Peter's at Rome, and is important for the authentication of the miracle. It consists of a picture of the Virgin with a mark under the left eye, and this inscription : "This picture of the Most Holy Virgin Mary, which stood between the pillars of the porch of the ancient Basilica, having been struck by an impious hand, poured forth blood on the stone which is now protected by a grating." Another of the famous relics at St. Peter's, and one that is rarely shown, is the Veronical present-ment of our Lord, said to have been painted from life by some unknown person, Veronica, who took it to Rome, where an altar was erected in its honour. The Veronical handkerchief, on which is the impress of our Lord's face, is also at Rome. St. Veronica, however, is a purely mythical person, the term being a corruption of *vera icon*, a true image.

It may be mentioned that the majority of the above-mentioned relics and images, together with hundreds of others, are still to be seen in Roman Catholic churches.

To give a list of the wonderful relics in the Italian churches alone would fill many volumes, but the following are only a few to be seen in the church of St. Croce :—

1. Three pieces of the cross, presented by Constantine.

2. The title of the Cross with inscriptions in Hebrew, Greek, and Latin.

3. One of the holy nails with which Christ was crucified.

4. Two thorns from the sacred crown of thorns.

5. The finger of St. Thomas the Apostle which touched the most holy rib of the risen Lord.

6. One of the pieces of money received by Judas Iscariot.

7. The cord by which our Lord was bound to the Cross.

8. The sponge.

9. A piece of the seamless garment.

10. A portion of the veil and some of the hair of the Virgin Mary.

11. Some earth from Calvary saturated with holy blood.

12. A phial of the milk of the Blessed Virgin.

13. A phial of our Lord's blood.

14. Some of the manna with which God fed the Israelites in the Wilderness.

15. A portion of the rod of Aaron that budded.

Remarks on Relics and Shrines

16. Part of the head of John the Baptist.
17. A tooth of St. Peter.
18. Bones of Mary Magdalene.
19. Relics of Saints Bridget, Galian, Felicite, Catherine, and Margaret.

Previous to the Reformation these relics were nearly, if not quite, as numerous throughout the British Isles.

In Glasgow, for example, mention is made of a gold phial containing part of the coat of St. Kentigern, also the mouth of St. Ninian in a gold casket, part of the girdle of the Virgin Mary and a phial of crystal containing her milk, a portion of the manger in which our Lord lay, and a small bag containing some of the sweat of St. Martin.

The relics in the various English cathedrals, churches and abbeys showed a great similarity ; for it was only the favoured few, like Durham, Shaftesbury, Canterbury, Gloucester, and Edmundsbury, that could boast of the possession of a martyr's sacred remains with which to draw the ever-wandering bands of pilgrims who perambulated the country for pleasure, health, or devotion.

The following list of relics in Wimborne Minster, before the Reformation, may be taken as typical of those possessed by other religious houses, and one cannot fail to notice their close analogy with the continental examples to which attention has already been called.

1. A piece of the Cross.
2. Part of our Lord's robe.
3. A large stone from His sepulchre.
4. A piece of the altar upon which our Lord was lifted up and offered by Simeon.
5. Some hairs of our Lord's beard.

6. A piece of the scourging pillar.
7. Part of the alabaster box.
8. A shoe of St. William.
9. Part of the thigh of the Virgin Agatha.
10. Some bones of St. Catherine.
11. Part of St. Mary the Egyptian.
12. Part of our Lord's manger.
13. A thorn from His crown.
14. One of St. Philip's teeth.
15. Some blood of St. Thomas à Becket.
16. The hair shirt of St. Francis.

The authorities of St. Mary's Church, Warwick, enticed pilgrims from all parts of the Midlands in order to show them such marvels as the manger of our Lord, part of the burning bush of Moses, the chair of the patriarch Abraham, some of the Virgin's hair, and part of the face of St. Stephen.

In 1762, during some repairs to the capstone and the addition of a new copper vane to the fine spire of Salisbury Cathedral, the workmen discovered a wooden box containing a round leaden one, $5\frac{1}{2}$ inches in diameter and $2\frac{1}{4}$ inches deep. Within this inner box was a piece of woven fabric considered to be a relic of the Virgin Mary, the patron of the church, which had been deposited as a charm to guard the spire from danger. The relic and boxes were enclosed in a copper cylinder and replaced where they had been found.

It was usual for relics to be enclosed in a small chest, box, or casket ; and depositories of this kind were practically universal in all European churches before the Reformation, and exist in large numbers in Roman Catholic countries at the present day. The reliquary was made of wood, stone, iron, gold, or silver, and was frequently lavishly decorated with

Remarks on Relics and Shrines

precious stones. Personal reliquaries, in the form of a brooch, were often worn as a charm against harm or disease. A good example is furnished by an ancient brooch, which was made in the reign of Elizabeth, and once belonged to a Highland chief, Maclean of Lochbury, in the Isle of Mull, being formed of silver found on his estate. It is of circular form, scolloped, and surrounded by small upright obelisks, each set with a pearl at the top ; in the centre is a round crystalline ball, considered a magical gem ; the top may be taken off, showing a hollow in which sacred relics were placed. On the reverse of the brooch are engraved the names of the Three Kings of Cologne, and the word " consummation." This was a consecrated brooch, and worn not only for the purpose of fastening the dress, but, like the pilgrims' signs of earlier days, as an amulet.

The wills of clerics and ecclesiastics often reveal the bequest of relics to some church or convent. William of Wykeham, the founder of St. Mary's College, Winchester, and of that other " Saint Maries College," or New College, Oxford, bequeathed to Winchester Cathedral, where he lies within his beautiful chantry, a golden cross, encased within which was a piece of the " Tree of the Lord."

Among some documents discovered in an old parish chest at Tavistock in 1885 was a very interesting Warden's Roll (1385-6), which is considered to be the earliest document of this character in existence. The record in Latin and engrossed on parchment is headed : " Account of Reginald Strepa, Warden of the light of the Blessed Eustachius of Tavistock, from the feast of the Invention of the Holy Cross in the year of the Lord 1385 to the same feast in the next following 1386." The box also yielded

Pilgrim Life in the Middle Ages

a number of churchwarden's rolls of the fifteenth
and sixteenth centuries. From one of these we gather,
that in 1471 the treasure of the church had received
the following additions : " one beryl set in silver,
and with a chain of silver to hang the aforesaid to the
pix with the body of Christ on the principal feasts ;
one cross of silver-gilt with the figures of St. Mary,
the Virgin and St. John the Evangelist to the same
belonging ; one box, in which the hair of St. Mary,
the Virgin and St. Mary Magdalene are contained ;
one cup of silver ; one little cross, the legacy, of John
the Hermit ; one censer of silver."

Not only did parish and small conventual
churches compete with the great cathedrals and
abbeys in the matter of relics, but even the little
chapels attached to hospitals and almshouses were full
of similar things. In early days when these hospices
were used by the poorer class of pilgrims, for whom
the custodians of the wealthy shrines had no great
love, relics found their way into these charitable
institutions to attract the wealthier pilgrims who had
alms to dispose of.

St. Bartholomew's Hospital, just outside Oxford,
was once an important charity of which the chapel
and a few portions of the secular buildings remain.
Many relics were kept in this chapel—the comb of
St. Edmund, the skin of St. Bartholomew, the bones
of St. Stephen, and a rib of St. Andrew the apostle.
Such as were troubled with continual headaches were
cured by using the comb of the saintly Edmund.
These relics attracted so large a number of pilgrims
that the Fellows of Oriel College conveyed them
to their Church of St. Mary, Oxford, where they
remained until the reign of Elizabeth.

When a woman was taken to St. Bartholomew's

Remarks on Relics and Shrines

Hospital, London, with her tongue so swollen that she could not close her mouth, Rahere, the founder of the charity, applied his remedy :—

" And he reuolvynge his relikys that he hadde of the Crosse, he depid them yn water and wysshe the tonge of the pacient ther with and with the tree of lyif, that ys with the same signe of the crosse upon the same tonge. An yn the same houre all the swellynge wente his way, and the woman gladde and hole went home to here owne " (" Mediæval Hospitals of England ").

The Maison Dieu of Dunwich benefited by the alms of pilgrims who went to see its holy cross, which, like that at the hospital at Colchester, was reputed to be a portion of the true Cross. To nearly all these hospitals where relics were exhibited indulgences were granted to the pilgrims who should visit them and contribute to the charities.

We learn that : " In the midst of the *Feretory* of St. Cuthbert his sacred shrine was exalted with most curious workmanship, of fine and costly green marble, all lined and gilt with gold ; having four seats or places, convenient underneath the *shrine*, for the pilgrims or lame men, setting on their knees to lean and rest on, in the time of their devout offerings and fervent prayers to God and Holy St. Cuthbert, for his miraculous relief and succour ; which being never wanting, made the *shrine* to be so richly invested that it was esteemed one of the most sumptuous monuments in all England, so great were the offerings and jewels bestowed upon it ; and no less the miracles that were done by it even in these latter days."

Still to be seen is the shrine of the Three Magi at Cologne, one of the most celebrated and splendid ever erected. The value of the jewels alone with which it is ornamented is estimated at £300,000. Magnificent shrines may be seen also at Aix-la-Chapelle, while another almost as good is preserved in the Museum of Mediæval Antiquities, at Rouen.

The pilgrims who wended their way to the Holy Sepulchre at Jerusalem would find all along the route, in church or monastery, an immense number of curious relics to excite their wonder and appeal to their devotional instincts.

Some of these marvels are described by the chaplain who accompanied Sir Richard Torkyngton and a party of pilgrims to the Holy Land, in the sixteenth century. Of Lyons he writes : " Ther ys a Cuppe of an Emerawde stone, wherof ower Savyor Crist drank at hys Mawndy." Of Milan : " Ovyr the hye Auter in the Roff or toppe of the Churche ys a syne of a sterr of golde, and in the mydys of the sterre ys on of the naylis that ower Savyr Crist was crucifyed w^t. Ther breune lampes abowth it that ye may se it p' f' ghtly." At Padua, among other things, he mentions " the tong of Seynt Antony yett ffayer and ffressh with which tong he convertyd myche peple to the ffeythe of Crist." At Padua also, in a Franciscan abbey, " we see the ffynger of Seynt Luke that he wrote the holy gospell w^t," and in the Church of St. John, at Rhodes, lay " the ffynger of Seynt John that he shewyd ower Sav^r whaune he seyd *Ecce Agnus Dei!* "

They would also pass the Isle of St. Nicholas, with its famous iron tools that never lost their edge owing to the miracle wrought by this saint, one of the seven islands of Rhodes, where dwelt a daughter of Hippocrates in dragon-like form, who could only be restored to her proper shape on receiving the

Remarks on Relics and Shrines

kiss of a soldier who was a virgin. Such were a few of the piquant wonders and surprises with which the mediæval pilgrim was beguiled throughout the length of his journey.

The practice of making valuable presents to shrines, though by no means always associated with pilgrimages, was akin to them in spirit. Offerings to shrines were made either annually, or at other periodical intervals, by great numbers of people.

From the household book of the Earl of Northumberland, we find that he gave donations every year to several popular shrines, and kept a candle burning constantly before some of them, with an allowance of money to the priest who should attend it. Edward I. made periodical gifts to over a hundred shrines, and his queen is recorded to have given twelve florins of gold, for herself and her son, to the several shrines of Becket at Canterbury, with three florins more for the child which her Majesty was then expecting.

During sickness it was common for the invalid or his friends to tempt the intercession of a saint by vowing to present quantities of corn, bread, or wax at his shrine, the precise quantity being frequently determined by the weight of the patient. The most valuable offerings were those made by bequest. Ladies, at their death, often bequeathed their richest dresses and most costly jewels to the shrine of their favourite saint, and it was in this way, as much as by the gifts of pilgrims, that immense wealth was accumulated by the churches.

One reason why gifts were made in this form rather than in money was to insure their permanent attachment to the particular shrine to which they were bequeathed. At famous shrines like that of

Pilgrim Life in the Middle Ages

Becket many of the offerings would be preserved, but at many of the lesser ones the priests claimed the gifts as their own. At the celebrated image of our Lady in St. Paul's, even the candles set up by the devotees were not allowed to burn, but were regularly taken down and carried to a room below the Chapter House, where they were melted as a perquisite of the canons. The same appears to have been the custom prevailing at most of the London shrines, and from the loss of this source of revenue the value of many of the livings in the city was sensibly diminished at the Reformation.

The immense popularity of numbers of small shrines, and wells of water sanctified by some pious hermit, was due in no small measure to the mediæval belief that everything, from a cut finger to a great calamity, was directly attributable to the Great First Cause—the will of God. Implanted in the mind of every man and woman was a real belief in the actual personal presence of God in every joy or success that befell them, and an equally firm conviction that the devil was personally responsible for every accident or piece of misfortune. Secondary causes had not yet been studied, by the masses at any rate, so that the mediæval mind possessed an earnest faith in the supernatural, and a firm belief that the universe was controlled by the Divine and by satanic forces respectively. The result was that the Church assigned a tutelary deity for every situation of life, and so filled the country with an endless number of shrines, each of which possessed some specific virtue. The custom is aptly ridiculed in Sir Thomas More's "Dyalogue": "We set every saint in his office, and assign him a craft such as pleaseth us. Saint Loy we make a horse-leech, and because one smith is

Remarks on Relics and Shrines

too few at the forge, we set Saint Ippolitus to help him. Saint Appollonia we make a tooth-drawer, and may speak to her of nothing but sore teeth. Saint Sythe women set to seek their keyes. Saint Roke we appoint to see to the great sickness, and with him we join Saint Sebastian. Some saints serve for the eye only, St. Germain only for children, and yet he will not once look at them but if their mothers bring with them a white loaf and a pot of good ale. And yet is he wiser than St. Wylgeforte ; for she, good soul, is, as they say, content to be served with oats, peradventure to provide a horse for an evil husband to ride to the devil, for that is the thing she is so sought for, insomuch that women have changed her name, and, instead of St. Wylgeforte, call her St. Uncumber, because they reckon that, for a peck of oats, she will not fail to uncumber them of their husbands."

This list might be carried much farther, for there was scarcely a single ill to which the mediæval flesh was heir that was not regulated and governed by some saint. From the same local and specific efficacy many of the lesser and uncanonised shrines enjoyed a reputation but little inferior to those which could boast of a celestial patron.

Prominent among the European shrines that drew such multitudes from these shores was the Virgin's house at Loretto. According to legendary lore this " Santa Casa " is the identical dwelling in which our Lord was born, and in which Mary was born, betrothed, and married. It is said to have been discovered by St. Helena three centuries after the Incarnation, on its original site, from which, in 1291, it was carried by angels through the air and set down in Dalmatia, where it did not rest for long, as three

years later, in December, 1294, some shepherds saw
it flying over the Adriatic towards Italy, where it
was eventually deposited at Loretto. The building
is of stone, and measures thirty-two feet long,
thirteen feet wide, and eighteen feet in height. On
the right hand of the altar is an effigy of the Virgin,
" black as a negress, and liker a Proserpine than a
Queen of Heaven." A bull of Pope Paul II. sets
forth in detail the " infinite miracles " that have been
wrought at this shrine, which is bedecked with votive
offerings of vast value from all parts of the world.

"Our Lady of Loretto " once had a chapel at
Musselburgh, near Edinburgh, which possessed a
famous image of the Virgin. To this shrine, an
immensely popular one, James V. of Scotland made a
pilgrimage from Stirling in 1536. Lyndsay, an old-
time satirist, sang thus of its pilgrims :—

> " I have sene pass ane marvillous multitude
> Young men and women, flingand on thair feit,
> Under the forme of frenzeit sanctitude,
> For till adore ane image in Laureit;
> Mony came with thair marrowis for to meit."

The shrine of the " Three Magi " at Cologne is one
of the most popular attractions this ancient German
city has for the modern tourist. This is another of
those shrines due to the wonderful discovering powers
of St. Helena, who, having detected the burial-place
of these kings in the Far East, removed their bodies to
Constantinople, where they remained in the Church
of St. Sophia until the reign of the Emperor
Emmanuel, who allowed them to be removed to the
Cathedral of Milan. With the fall of Milan, in 1164,
the relics were given by the Emperor Frederick to
Raynuldus, Archbishop of Cologne, whose successor,

Remarks on Relics and Shrines

Philip von Heinsburg, placed them in the magnificent reliquary that reposes in what is probably the most remarkable shrine in the world. The relics consist of three skulls, reputed to be those of the Magi, but so enveloped in velvet and heavily jewelled embroideries, that only the upper part of each skull is visible.

The holy coat of Trèves, or, more correctly, perhaps, the seamless garment, reputed to be that worn by our Saviour at his crucifixion, and mentioned by St. John (xix. 24), was given to the ancient episcopal city on the Moselle, by St. Helena, who is said to have converted her palace at Trèves into the cathedral which she endowed with this treasure. Notwithstanding that quite a score of other churches claim to be the possessors of a similar garment, the genuineness of the Trèves relic has been affirmed by a papal bull and attested by many miracles wrought at the shrine.

Many of the more famous relics of the Church of Rome are shown only at intervals of five, ten, or twenty years ; and at one time the seamless garment was exhibited once only in every hundred years, and then stored in some secret hiding-place, and so securely hidden that its existence was considered to be very doubtful. However, on July 6, 1844, Bishop Arnoldi, two years after his appointment to the see, announced a centenary jubilee, at which the holy coat would be exhibited. The official circular was to the following effect : " That, in consequence of the urgent request of the clergy and body of believers in the bishopric of Trèves, the only relic preserved in the cathedral, being the coat without seam worn by our Saviour, will be exhibited for six weeks, from the 18th of August following, that the wish of all

Pilgrim Life in the Middle Ages

who have the pious intention of making a pilgrimage
to Trèves to behold and venerate the holy garment
of our Divine Redeemer may be fulfilled, and each
may gain the entire remission of his sins, granted
by Pope Leo X., under date of July 26, 1514. The
said Pope—namely, with the wish that the Cathedral
of Trèves, which has the honour of preserving the
seamless coat of our Lord Jesus Christ, and many
other holy relics, may be distinguished by suitable
grandeur of establishment and splendour of ornament—gives, according to the words of the aforesaid
bull, a full remission of sins in all future time to all
believers who go on pilgrimage to the exhibition
of the holy coat at Trèves, sincerely confess and
repent of their sins, or at least have a firm intention
to do so, and who, moreover, contribute with a liberal
hand to the suitable decoration of the cathedral as
recommended by the holy father, but which still
remains imperfect from the end of last century."
This epistle, containing the promise of one of the
most extraordinary indulgences ever issued, naturally
drew an immense concourse of pilgrims to Trèves.
" Pilgrims came from all quarters, many in large
bands, preceded by banners and marshalled by their
village priests. It was impossible to lodge the great
mass of footsore travellers, and they slept on inn-
stairs, in outhouses, or even in the streets, with their
wallets for their pillows." With the opening of the
cathedral doors the crowds flocked to the shrine,
where, prostrating themselves before the relic, they
exclaimed : " Holy coat, to thee I come ! " " Holy
coat, to thee I pray ! " until in the course of six
weeks some millions of people had gone through the
ceremony, and left behind them an immense sum
of money for the decoration of the cathedral.

Remarks on Relics and Shrines

Many contemporary prints were issued of the relic, and these all depict a loose garment of simple form and wide sleeves, entirely without seam or decoration.

With the closing of this remarkable exhibition, controversy at once began, and Johann Ronge addressed a letter to the Bishop of Trèves denouncing the resuscitation of the superstitious observances of the Middle Ages. Although supported by Czerski and many priests, Ronge's letter excited much wrath at Rome, and he was excommunicated. He continued to lead a considerable number of followers, who denied the supremacy of the Pope, much to the alarm of the German Governments, and in 1850 his following was suppressed and he himself expelled from Germany. He eventually found a home in London, where he gained a livelihood by teaching.

The Scala Santa, or Holy Stair, is in a chapel of the church of St. John Lateran, at Rome. It consists of twenty-eight white marble steps, and is affirmed by its custodians to be the stair which Christ ascended when He appeared before Pilate. It was carried by angels from Jerusalem to Rome. To-day, as for centuries, thousands of pilgrims creep up its steps on their knees, with rosaries in their hands, and kissing each step of the holy stairs as they ascend. A similar Scala Santa, also claimed to be the genuine and original one, may be seen at Bonn. In addition to the holy stair, the church of St. John Lateran possesses a wonderful headshrine of St. Peter, and the extraordinary relic of the Holy Blood, said to have resulted from our Lord's circumcision.

CHAPTER III

HERMITS, ANCHORETS, AND RECLUSES

"At the close of the day, when the hamlet is still,
   And mortals the sweets of forgetfulness prove,
When nought but the torrent is heard on the hill,
   And nought but the nightingale's song in the grove—

. . . .

'Twas then by the cave of a mountain reclin'd,
   A hermit his nightly complaint thus began;
Though mournful his numbers, his soul was resign'd,
   He thought as a sage, tho' he felt as a man."

                                        BEATTIE.

ALMOST every form of religion appears to have had
adherents who correspond more or less to our general
idea of a hermit. Among the Jewish sects we have
the Essenes, of whom De Quincey wrote with such
eloquence and learning ; and Buddhism is not without its solitary dwellers.

Of the Essenes, Spanheim gives the following
particulars ("Eccl. Ann." ix.) :—

" They admitted only grave or aged men into their
society ; had a community of goods and provisions ;
practised celibacy ; lived an austere life, enduring
much fatigue, and using coarse food and clothing ;
they exercised no trade or art by which mankind

72

could be injured or vice cherished ; observed stated
periods for prayer in a prescribed form ; observed
the Sabbath somewhat superstitiously ; were eminently zealous in piety, beneficence, and hospitality ;
loved solitude and contemplative silence ; required
of their disciples a probation of four years ; punished
delinquents with severity ; avoided lawsuits, con-
tentions, and disputations, and therefore were not
troublesome to our Lord."

To whom the honour of being the first Christian
hermit belonged was a much discussed question as
early as the fourth century after Christ, at which time
the issue was narrowed down to the respective claims
of Paul the Hermit and the much tempted St.
Anthony. In the Epistle to the Hebrews we are
told how those of whom the world was not worthy
wandered in the desolate places of the earth, and
lived in the dens and caves of mountainous regions ;
and there is little doubt that among these early cave-
dwellers is to be found the earliest Christian hermit
—such an one, for example, as Paul, who, when the
Decian persecution raged in his native land of
Thebaid, in Upper Egypt, withdrew to a grotto in
a remote mountain. A palm-tree growing near his
cave is said to have furnished him with both food
and raiment ; and in later and happier times, when
the persecutions of the Christians began to cease,
habit had so endeared him to his primitive way of
living, that he was unwilling to break his enforced
retirement.

Shelley, in his " Alastor," has depicted well a fitting
home for the Spirit of Solitude, and the imagination
of the poet has given us an exquisite yet a realistic
description of the scenic properties of the abodes of
the first hermits :—

Pilgrim Life in the Middle Ages

"The eternal pyramids,
Memphis and Thebes, and whatsoe'er of strange
Sculptured on alabaster obelisk,
Or jasper tomb, or mutilated sphinx,
Dark Ethopia in her desert hills
Conceals. Among the ruined temples there
Stupendous columns and wild images
Of more than man, where marble demons watch
The Zodiac's brazen mystery, and dead men
Hang their mute thoughts on the mute walls around."

In every case we find that the habitations of these early hermits were entirely secluded from all other abodes of men, although at times they appear to have fixed their dwellings in the neighbourhood of each other, when their cells were called by the collective name of *laura*. Even in such instances, however, they always lived personally separate ; and thus the *laura* was distinguished from the *cænobium*, or convent, where the inmates formed themselves into a society and held everything in common.

To Paul the Hermit the distinction is usually assigned of having first devoted himself to this kind of solitude, and it is recorded of him that he said three hundred prayers a day. A little heap of pebbles by his side served to tell him how he progressed in his devotions, perhaps the first instance of beads, for the word *bede* or *bead* means literally *prayer*, the name afterwards being applied to the small globular bodies used for telling beads—*i.e.*, counting prayers.

When these hermits began to foregather into a society we have the institution of Anchorets or monachism, in which they acknowledged the authority of some common Superior. The next step in a natural gradation was that great turning-point in

74

the history of Christianity, the development of monastic life, for there is little doubt that it was in the peaceful seclusion of the cloister that Christianity, from being intensely practical and objective, became more meditative, introspective, and mystical.

The temptation of St. Anthony by the devil is a very familiar story, and one for which there is historic groundwork, as may be gathered by him who peruses the Life of this saint, by Athanasius. Here we are told how St. Anthony gave all his goods to feed the poor, and frequented only the society of the ascetic. He was the great hermit who was the father of monasticism. He withdrew to a grotto in a rock which had been used for the purpose of a tomb, where, by excessive fasting and exhaustive spiritual conflicts with the Evil One, he worked himself into a morbid and highly excited state of mind. In later life he retired to a very distant mountain, where he spent twenty years among the ruins of a dilapidated castle.

Another famous hermit who flourished towards the close of the fourth century was St. Simeon Stylites. Having passed a long and severe novitiate in a monastery, this devotee contrived within the space of a small circle of stones, to which he was confined by a heavy chain, to ascend a column raised gradually from nine to sixty feet in height, on the top of which, without descending from it, he passed thirty years of his life, and at length died of an ulcer in his thigh. Crowds of pilgrims from Gaul and India are said to have thronged around his pillar, and to have been proud to supply his necessities.

Those acquainted with the " St. Simeon Stylites " of Tennyson will not fail to perceive how carefully and gradually this noble poem has been developed,

Pilgrim Life in the Middle Ages

and how faithfully the historical character has been preserved.

> " O my sons, my sons,
> I, Simeon of the pillar, by surname
> Stylites, among men ; I, Simeon,
> The watcher on the column till the end ;
> I, Simeon, whose brain the sunshine bakes ;
> I, whose bald brows in silent hours become
> Unnaturally hoar with rime, do now
> From my high nest of penance here proclaim
> That Pontius and Iscariot by my side
> Show'd like fair seraphs. On the coals I lay,
> A vessel full of sin : all hell beneath
> Made me boil over. Devils pluck'd my sleeve ;
> Abaddon and Asmodeus caught at me."

The images of St. Simeon were regarded with an intense veneration, and Theodoret tells us that they were set up as protecting amulets at the entrances of the shops in Rome.

We are all familiar with the story of Peter the Hermit, who, barefooted and penniless, inveighed against the atrocities of the Turks to Christians at Jerusalem, and exhorted the warriors of the Cross to take up arms against the infidels. His impassioned eloquence inspired all Europe with enthusiasm, and enlisted many followers in the cause. In those days the sword was the title by which estates and countries were won, and by which they were held. The passion of the age was for religious warfare, peril, and adventure, especially as fighting for possession of the sepulchre was a more agreeable method of doing penance than the wearing of sackcloth in a village church or mortifying the flesh with many strokes. The first Crusade set out on its wild career, a motley company of knights, spendthrifts, barons, beggars, women, and children. Then came the second, the

Hermits, Anchorets, and Recluses

third, and the fourth Crusades, which differed but little in personnel from that which had inaugurated the movement. Crusading was the amusement and hobby of two centuries, while two millions of Europeans, among them the flower of the armies of England, France, and Germany, perished before the cause was abandoned.

Turning to our own country, we find that the first Christian hermit of whom we have any definite and authentic records was St. Dunstan, afterwards Abbot of Glastonbury, and seventh Archbishop of Canterbury (A.D. 960), and the first of the seven primates of all England who hailed from the great Abbey of Glastonbury. He was one of those master-spirits of whom it is almost impossible for a late posterity to form a correct judgment. His great powers of learning and his varied accomplishments are almost the only points upon which his numerous biographers are agreed. His enemies ascribed his gifts to magic, the unlawful knowledge of which, said they, lay buried in the Somerset marshes, in the mystic island of Avalon, and in Glastonbury where St. Dunstan is said to have occupied a cell, or *destina*, which, according to his biographer Osbern, was not more than five feet long, two feet and a half in breadth, and barely the height of a man.

There appear to be very few of our early bishops and saints who did not prepare themselves for a religious life by dwelling in solitary state in some rocky cave or primitive hermitage.

There are few counties in England to which history or tradition does not assign the abode of a hermit, while Durham perhaps is exceptionally rich in such cave dwellings.

St. Jerome was one of the first to point out the

dangers of a life of this kind. " Pride," says he, " soon steals on a man in solitude. If he has practised fasting for a short time, and has seen nobody, he begins to think he is a person of consequence, and forgets himself, who he is, and whence he comes, and whither he is going."

With regard to the extraordinary visions seen by the early hermits, we have been told that " the body, when not fed with a sufficiency of wholesome food [and the hermits sometimes mixed their flour or pottage with wood-ashes and burnt herbs] deludes the senses with strange dreams by day or night, and the quick vigour of the understanding is lost in wandering imaginations." Be this as it may, St. Jerome and St. Benedict had strange visions, as also did Walter, a hermit who is thought to have lived on or near Flamborough Head, and whose strange dreams were recorded by Alcuin of York. One of the most interesting of these visions is that of Drycthelm, who, having " been some time dead, rose again to the life of the body, and related many remarkable things which he had seen," [1] and who, after his vision, took the monk's habit at Melrose Abbey, and retired to a hermitage.

Alcuin of York has also recorded the visions of Guthlac of Croyland, who inhabited a hermitage in the swamps, and who was always doing battle against foul fiends. Etha of Crayke was a dweller on a hill so thickly shut in by trees that, according to tradition, a squirrel could reach York by hopping from bough to bough. " Here in the depth of the wilderness," says Alcuin, " he led an angelic life."

There is little reason to doubt that many, if not all, of these hermit visions were the result of severe

[1] Beda's " Eccles. Hist.," Bk. 5, chap. xii.

Hermits, Anchorets, and Recluses

and prolonged fasting. Physicians know as a fact that lack of bodily nourishment, coupled with solitary confinement, stimulates rather than checks the sensuous imagination.

When the youthful St. Jerome fled into the desert of Chalcis, and lived among the hermits, he confessed that the physiological effect of the severest starvation was to give intensity to the desire for sensual indulgence. " Oh, how often," he exclaimed, " set in the desert and in that vast solitude which, scorched by the fierce rays of the sun, afforded to monks a horrid dwelling-place, how often did I find myself amid the sensuous delights of Rome ! I was alone and filled with bitterness. My limbs were rough with sackcloth ; my body squalid as an Ethiopian's with fasting. Day by day I wept and groaned and denied myself sleep, and if, overborne with weariness I sank upon the ground, my bones rattled like those of a skeleton. Yet while from fear of hell I had made myself a companion of scorpions and wild beasts, my imagination rioted among luxurious dances. My face was pallid with hunger, my soul was heaving with concupiscence." In " Piers Plowman " we read about the " eremites " who worked until they discovered that those in friar's garb had fat cheeks. Those who feigned religion for the sake of its worldly advantages Langland called " lollers."

> "As by English of our elders, of old men's teaching,
> He that lolleth is lame, or his leg is out of joint,
> Or maimed in some member, for to mischief it soundeth.
> And right so soothly such manner eremites
> Lollen agen the Belief and Law of Holy-Church."

Milman, in his " Latin Christianity," tells us how

79

Pilgrim Life in the Middle Ages

in the time of Pope Innocent IV. (1240), all the hermits, solitaries, and small separate confraternities, who lived under no recognised discipline, were registered and incorporated by a decree of the Church, and reduced under one rule, called " the Rule of St. Augustine," with some more strict clauses introduced, fitting the new ideas of conventual life. Innocent died before his reforms could be fully carried out ; but, with the aid of a miracle, they were completed by his successor in the Papacy, Alexander IV. ; to whom, when he was most needed, St. Augustine himself appeared, clad in a long black gown, tattered and torn, in sign of poverty, bound round his waist with a leathern girdle and buckle, with a scourge in his right hand. He told Alexander that the contumacious hermits, who had refused to adopt the uniform rule and dress, were forthwith to accept the Augustine rule and habit, and to submit to monastic discipline. Notwithstanding St. Augustine's miraculous appearance, it was not until 1284 that these scattered hermits and independent communities were brought within the monastic " trade union," under the name in England of Austin Friars.

Closely allied to pilgrimages, and often, indeed, the *raison d'être* of such, were these hermitages, anchorholds, and recluse cells ; all of which were both recognised and regulated by the mediæval Church, and indulgences were granted to those who should visit them. Authentic relics of the canonised saints and martyrs were limited in number and safely guarded, but the rags and tatters of the wayside hermit, and of the ascetic recluse, were eagerly sought for the cure of ills and the other miraculous properties ascribed to them. It is an almost forgotten

Hermits, Anchorets, and Recluses

fact that the churchyard of mediæval days contained many buildings in addition to the church itself ; such as charnel-houses, chantry-chapels, church-houses for storing the church ales, stables for the horses of the nobility while they were attending Divine service, and hermitages and anchorholds for those who had given themselves up to a life of religious seclusion. Early in the seventh century the councils began to notice, modify, and control this kind of life. " Those who affect to be anchorites," say the Trullan canons, " shall first for three years be confined to a cell in a monastery ; and if, after this, they profess that they persist, let them be examined by the bishop, or abbot ; let them live one year at large ; and if they still approve of their first choice, let them be confined to their cell, and not be permitted to go out of it, but by consent and benediction of the bishop, in case of great necessity."

There were two distinct classes of these solitary livers, both, however, under vows as strict and as binding as those that governed the communities attached to the great monastic foundations.

The principal difference between the hermit and the recluse was that whereas the former might wander from and change his abode at will, the latter was immured and " sealed " within the *reclusorium*, or anchorhold, for life. There appears to be no doubt that from the earliest days of Christianity in this country men and women embraced a solitary life at their own pleasure, and, living in a cave or bower, trusted literally to Providence for their little needs, if poor, or spent their wealth in charity, if rich.

These primitive rock hermits seem always to have had an eye for the picturesque when choosing their

Pilgrim Life in the Middle Ages

humble abodes, as can be seen by the hermit caves
remaining at Warkworth, Wetheral, Bewdley, and

Rock Hermitage, Warkworth

many another lovely spot to which tradition has
associated one of these solitary dwellers.

Certain of these hermits appear also to have dwelt

Hermits, Anchorets, and Recluses

near the high-roads, and especially by fords over
the rivers, and in the vicinity of wells of water, where,
in addition to their prayers and blessing, they
bestowed a frugal sort of hospitality to all needy
travellers and pilgrims. It was not long before the
orders of hermits and recluses developed into well-
established institutions under the jurisdiction of the
bishops, and they became quite as much religious
orders as were those of the Benedictines or the Franciscans. Just as a bishop to-day does not ordain a
deacon until he has obtained a "title," so the mediæval
bishop admitted no man into the order of hermits
until he had obtained a presentation to a hermitage.
Both hermitages and recluse cells were generally
endowed with lands or money to make them self-
supporting ; and the patronage of them was bought
and sold in the same way as other religious benefices.
In the case of recluses such endowment was essential,
otherwise a conscientious recluse might have been
in danger of starving had he or she been dependent
on the alms and offerings of pilgrims and passers-by.

We are not surprised, therefore, to learn that
the bishops took pains to ascertain that the
offerings and endowments accruing would be
sufficient for the maintenance of the inmates before
admitting any one to the respective orders.

The initiation into the order of recluses was, according to the late Rev. E. L. Cutts, a religious ceremony
of great solemnity. " The vows having been taken
at the altar, the habit was placed on the *includendus*
(the person to be enclosed), who was then given
a lighted taper and a procession was formed. First
the choir, then the *includendus*, then the priest,
abbot, or bishop, with the congregation following,
and all singing a solemn litany. When the cell was

83

reached the priest entered alone, and consecrated and blessed the little chamber, after which he led in the *includendus*, and blessed him. The *includendus* now became the *inclusus* (the enclosed one), and was sealed within the living grave never to cross the threshold during life."

During the " sealing " ceremony the choir chanted appropriate psalms, while all prayed for the *inclusus*. The procession then returned chanting, leaving the recluse cut off for ever from the assembly of fellow-creatures. That recluse cells and anchorholds existed in England in considerable numbers is proved by the frequency with which they are mentioned, and by bequests left to them, in the wills of the charitably-minded, during the twelfth, thirteenth, and fourteenth centuries.

Thus, St. Richard, Bishop of Chichester, left bequests to Friar Humphrey, the recluse of Pageham, to the recluse of Hogton, to the recluse of Stopeham, and to the recluse of Herringham. Walter de Suffield, Bishop of Norwich, left bequests to " anchores " and recluses in his diocese ; and especially to his niece Ela, in the anchorhold of Massingham. In the will of Henry II. we find bequests to the recluses of Jerusalem, England, and Normandy. Lord Scrope of Masham, in 1415, bequeathed to every anchoret or recluse dwelling in London and its suburbs 6s. 8d., and to every anchoret and recluse dwelling in York and its suburbs 6s. 8d., and special bequests were made to Robert, the recluse of Beverley (40s.), and 13s. 4d. each to the anchorets of Stafford, Kirkbeck, Warth, Peasholme, Kirby, Thorganby, Leek, Gainsborough, Kneesall, and Dartford. Also to Thomas the Chaplain, dwelling continually in the church of

Hermits, Anchorets, and Recluses

St. Nicholas, Gloucester ; [1] to Elizabeth, late servant of the anchoret of Hampole ; to the recluse in the house of the Dominicans at Newcastle, and to every anchoret and "anchoretess" that could be found within three months of his decease.

Of the anchorets above mentioned the most famous was Richard of Hampole, who wrote a book of devotion for the use of a nunnery about the beginning of the reign of the third Edward. His little manual contains, among other pious rules, the following " seven marks to know when the Spirit of God works in the soul " :—

1. It makes a man or woman to set the world at nought, and all the worldly worships and vanities therein.
2. It makes God dear to the soul, and all the delight of the flesh to wax cold.
3. It inspires both delectation and joying in God.
4. It stirs thee to the love of thy neighbour, and also to compassion of thine enemy.
5. It inspires all manner of chastity.
6. It makes to trust in God in all tribulations, and to joy in them.
7. It gives desire to will to be departed and to be with God, more than to have worldly prosperity.

This famous Hermit of Hampole was Richard Rolle, born at Thornton, Yorkshire, about 1290, and educated at Oxford. When nineteen years of age he was seized with a desire to become a hermit, and obtained from Sir John de Dalton a cell, with daily sustenance, at Hampole, about four miles from Doncaster, where he lived until his death, in 1349. In addition to many prose treatises he is the author of the " Prick of Conscience," and he translated the

[1] This "Thomas the Chaplain" is thought to have dwelt in a chamber over the porch (mentioned in the Corporation Records of 1440), no part of which remains.

Pilgrim Life in the Middle Ages

Psalms into English prose. "The Prick of Conscience" (*Stimulus Conscientiæ*) is in seven parts,
and the author gives his reason for the title.

"Therefore this treatise draw I would
In English tongue that may be called
'Prick of Conscience,' as men may feel,
For if a man it read and understand wele,
And the matters therein to heart will take,
It may be his conscience tender make ;
And to right way of rule bring it be live [quickly]
And his heart to dread and meekness drive,
And to love, and yearning of heaven's bliss,
And to amend all that he has done amiss."

A few of these old recluse cells may be found
in our churches to-day, although they are not in their
original condition, as the partition walls have long
since been removed, and the cells now form part
of the aisles or transepts of the churches in which they
are found.

In actual construction there was probably but little
difference between the anchorhold and the recluse
cell, but much is left to conjecture, as not one
example of a detached timber anchorhold has survived. These appear to have been built adjoining
the main walls of the church, and some authorities are
of opinion that what are known as "low-side"
windows, which occur in so many of our churches,
and have long been a *quæstio vexata*, may mark the
sites of such anchorholds. This window is generally
found in the south wall of the chancel, near the south-
west angle, a few feet above the ground, and often
immediately beneath a large window, as at Dallington
Church, Northants. These apertures have nearly all
been closed up with masonry, but many indications
go to show that they had no glazing, but were

Hermits, Anchorets, and Recluses

covered externally by an iron grating, with a wooden door opening inwardly, the hinges of which are frequently to be seen imbedded in the masonry, although few of the wooden doors have survived. Among the purposes for which these windows are conjectured to have been formed is that they were for confessional purposes, although the position of many of them would make an orderly confession impossible. From another supposition, that they were connected with mortuary services, they are frequently called *lychnoscopes*. The "symbolical theory," that the window represents the wound in Our Lord's side, is plainly one of those *impertinences* of symbolism which have always constituted the weakest side of symbolic art. The theory most in favour at present is that these windows were used for the purpose of ringing a hand sanctus bell at the elevation of the Blessed Sacrament.

The most usual type of recluse cell, in the earliest days of Christianity as well as during the mediæval period, seems to have been a small chamber about twelve feet square, with three windows—one towards the choir of the church through which the inmate received the Sacrament, another on the opposite side for food, and a third to give light to the cell.

The "Ancren Riwle" was the manual generally adopted by all recluses and anchoresses as the text-book for the regulation of their conduct. It was written originally for three sisters, who, at the time, were living the life of anchoresses at Tarrant Keinston, in Dorset. These young ladies afterwards embraced the Cistercian rule, when they took up their abode at the neighbouring Abbey of Tarrant Crawford. This episode of their having migrated from the minor order of recluses to the greater one of Cistercians may explain the reason for the erroneous statement so frequently met with that the " Ancren Riwle " was written for the guidance of *nuns*. The fact that the sisters became nuns in no way affects the question that the " Ancren Riwle " was written for them, as its title implies, while they were living the life of anchoresses.

The late Mr. Henry Moule, a well-known Dorset antiquary, told the present writer that he had seen in the chancel of the old parish church of Tarrant Keinston a recluse cell of the type above mentioned, and that it remained intact until the greater part of the church was rebuilt, some sixty years ago.

The authorship of the " Ancren Riwle " is generally attributed to Richard Poore, who held the See of Salisbury from 1217 to 1229, and possibly for the same community, or for another convent of women, the author of the " Ancren Riwle " wrote the beautiful homily called " The Wooing of Our Lord," of which the first paragraph may be quoted :—

" Jesu, sweet Jesu, my love, my darling, my Lord, my Saviour, my honey-drop, my balm ! Sweeter is the remembrance of Thee than honey in the mouth. Who is there that may not love Thy lovely face? What heart is there so hard that may not melt at the remembrance of Thee? Ah ! who may not love Thee, lovely Jesu? For within Thee alone are all the things joined that ever may make any man worthy of love to another."

A few extracts from the " Ancren Riwle " will doubtless help us to realise the arduous nature of a recluse's life, and the many difficulties which beset her. " Hold no conversation," says the Bishop, " with any man out of a church window, but respect it for the sake of the holy sacrament

which ye see there through, and take men and
women to the wicket in the parlour to speak when
necessary." They are also exhorted to be on their
guard against men, " even against religious men."
Also, says he, " first of all, when you have to go to
your parlour wicket, learn from your maid who it
is that comes, and when you must go forth, go forth
in the fear of God to a priest and sit and listen, and
not cackle." Again : " If any man requests to see you
[to have the black curtain drawn aside], ask him what
good might come of it, and if any one become so
mad and unreasonable that he puts forth his hand
towards the wicket cloth, shut the wicket quickly
and leave him, and as soon as any man falls into evil
discourse, close the wicket and go away with this
verse, that he may hear it : ' The wicked have told
me foolish tales, but not according to Thy law,' and
go forth before your altar and say the *Miserere*."
Another curious rule was that which prohibited the
keeping of any animals in their cells, except the
domestic cat.

In the church attached to a convent of Carmelite
nuns (recluses of the strictest kind), at Mawgan,
Cornwall, at the junction of the transept and chancel,
the walls are cut away to the height of six feet
from the floor, and to the width of five feet from
each wall. The upper parts of the walls rest on
flat segmental arches, carried by a short octagonal
pillar. A low diagonal wall is built across the angle
thus exposed, and a small lean-to roof is run up from
it into the external angle, thus enclosing a triangular
space within. In this wall the low side window is
inserted, the sill being four feet from the ground.
Two small screens running flush with the inner walls
of the transept and chancel would convert the space

into a cell, of which similar examples are said to
have existed at one time at Grade, Landewednack,
and Edington.

Other remaining examples of recluse cells in
England include a small stone building of fourteenth-
century date, adjoining the north side of Rettendon
Church, Essex. The structure is two-storied, and is
entered through an elaborately moulded doorway
from the chancel. The lower floor is now lighted
by a modern window, and is used as a vestry. On the
west side of this chamber is a stone stairway built up
in the nave aisle, which gives access to an upper
story that agrees very well with the description
of a recluse cell. On the south side are two arched
niches, one of which was pierced by a small window
now blocked up, and which formerly looked down
upon the altar. On the left of the chimney is a
small square opening filled with modern glass, but
the hook upon which the original shutter hung is
intact.

At Clifton Campville, Staffordshire, is a somewhat
similar cell. Beneath it is a chantry chapel with
two fine five-light windows, ornamented with cusps,
and inside there is a beautiful groined ceiling. The
cell is reached from the chancel (as was usually
the case), through a doorway in the north wall,
from which a winding stairway leads to the upper
room. The two-light window of this chamber (shown
in the accompanying drawing) is modern, but there
are very distinct remains of the two square openings
by which the cell was formerly lighted. Other
reclusoria pertaining to this type are found at Chip-
ping Norton, Oxfordshire, and Warmington, War-
wickshire. Surrey has several interesting examples,
as at Shere, at Compton, and possibly at Dunsfold.

Chantry Chapel at Clifton
Campville, with remains of
Recluse Cell above.

Pilgrim Life in the Middle Ages

In the north aisle of St. Mary's Church, Whalley, is a chantry dedicated to St. Nicholas, and in the south aisle one dedicated to St. Mary. These two chantries were founded in consequence of a dispute that arose out of the suppression of the Hermitage, a building that once stood at the western end of the churchyard. It was founded and well endowed by Henry, Duke of Lancaster, in 1361, but owing to the unsatisfactory conduct of the recluse and her women attendants, it was suppressed in 1444 by order of Henry VI. The revenues were given to provide these chantries, which were to be served by two priests, who were to say daily Mass for the repose of the soul of Duke Henry. On the screen of the north aisle chantry we read: *Orate pro anima Thome Lawe, Monachi*—" Pray for the soul of Thomas Lawe, Monk." Adjacent to this chantry is the grave of John Paslew, the last abbot of Whalley Abbey, who was executed for his participation in the Pilgrimage of Grace (1556-7).

Of Richborough Castle, Kent, Leland writes. "Withyn the castel is a lytle paroche chirch of St. Augustine, and an heremitage. I had antiquities of the heremite, the which is an industrious man. Not far fro the heremitage is a cave, wher men have sowt and digged for treasure." All traces of this " lytle paroche chirch," and of the hermitage, have disappeared. When the redoubtable Guy, Earl of Warwick, returned from a pilgrimage to the Holy Land during the reign of Athelstan (A.D. 926), he found the Danes besieging Winchester, and the Danish champion, Colbrand, prepared to decide the issue by single combat against any of the Saxons. Earl Guy, still wearing the palmer's garb, met and defeated the Danish giant, after which he made him-

Hermits, Anchorets, and Recluses

self known to the King, and having returned thanks
for his victory in Winchester Cathedral, he retired to
a hermitage beside the Avon,[1] and passed the closing
years of his life in the cave which still bears his
name, and in all probability contains his bones. He
is said to have received his daily dole from the hands
of his Countess until his death, in the year 929.

In ancient deeds and charters there are many
records relating to anchorholds and recluse cells,
as at Norwich, where, in the churchyard of St. Julian,
there were a succession of anchoresses, some of whose
names have been preserved—Lady Julian in 1393,
Dame Agnes in 1472, Dame Elizabeth Scot in 1481,
Lady Elizabeth in 1510, and Dame Agnes Edryge
in 1524.

A document preserved among the registers of the
Bishop of Lichfield shows that there was an anchorhold for several female recluses in the churchyard of
St. Romuald, Shrewsbury, and in it the Bishop directs
the Dean of St. Chadd, or his procurator, to enclose
Isolda de Hungerford, an anchorite, in the houses
of the churchyard of St. Romuald, where the other
anchorites live.

In the same register we find a precept dated
February 1, 1310, from Bishop Walter de Langton
to Emma Sprenghoose, admitting her an anchorite in
the house in the churchyard of St. George's Chapel,
Shrewsbury, and he appoints the archdeacon to enclose her.

Bishop Roger, in 1362, gave a licence permitting
Robert Worthin, on the nomination of Queen Isabella,
to serve God in the reclusorium built adjoining the
Chapel of St. John the Baptist, in the city of
Coventry.

[1] Guy's Cliff, near Warwick.

93

Pilgrim Life in the Middle Ages

In 1402 Robert Chard, a monk of Ford Abbey, obtained permission to immure himself as an anchorite in a " solitary house," or cell, beneath Crewkerne Church, and what are thought to be portions of the anchorhold may still be seen on the external walls of this beautiful structure.

Mr. W. B. Wildman, in his " History of Sherborne," writes : " Near the Chapel of our Lady of Bow in Sherborne Abbey, was the Ankret House, all traces of which have disappeared," and Dean Stanley, in his " Memorials of Westminster Abbey," tells us that " here as often in the neighbourhood of great conventual buildings dwelt, apparently from generation to generation, a hermit, who acted as a kind of oracle to the neighbourhood."

In olden as in more modern days, the hermit has always appealed to the makers of our English literature, while two of Albert Durer's celebrated woodcuts depict St. Anthony and St. Jerome in their cells. In the National Gallery hangs Fra Angelico's famous painting of a hermit clothed in rushes.

From the story of Thaysis, in the " Golden Legend," we learn that " she went to the place which the abbot had assyned to her, and there was a monasterye of vyrgyns ; and there he closed her in a celle, and sealed the door with led. And the celle was lytyll and strayte, and but one lytyll windowe open, by which was mynistered to her poor lyvinge, for the abbot commanded that they should give her a lytyll brede and water."

Spenser, in the allegory of the Red Cross Knight, makes his hero, with Una and the Dwarf, meet with Archimago, the devil, in the guise of a hermit, and Spenser, keenly combatant against what he held to be the corruptions of the Roman Catholic Church,

Hermits, Anchorets, and Recluses

regarded his Satanic Majesty as the founder of
Catholicism. The knight and his companions are
sheltered in Archimago's house.

> "A little lowly Hermitage it was,
> Downe in a dale, hard by a forests side,
> Far from resort of people that did pas
> In traveill to and froe : a litle wyde
> There was an holy chappell edifyde,
> Wherein the Hermite dewly wont to say
> His holy thinges each morne and eventyde :
> Thereby a christall streame did gently play,
> Which from a sacred fountaine wellèd forth alway.
>
>   *   *   *   *   *
>
> Arrivèd there, the litle house they fill,
> Ne looke for entertainement where none was ;
> Rest is their feast, and all thinges at their will :
> The noblest mind the best contentment has.
> With faire discourse the evening so they pas ;
> For that olde man of pleasing wordes had store,
> And well could file his tongue as smooth as glas :
> He told of Saintes and Popes, and evermore
> He strowd an *Ave-Mary* after and before."

We all remember Goldsmith's " Turn, gentle
Hermit of the Dale," but the " Hermit [1] " by
Beattie, a poem of eight verses, is now well-nigh
forgotten. Of the same kind is Parnell's story of
the hermit who, bewildered by the disorders of the
world, arraigns the moral government of God, but is
restored to his right mind by the angel who accompanied him, and who had been the instrument of
Providence in all the horrors he had witnessed.
Fielding makes his benighted travellers fall in with
a compassionate hermit of the hill, who gives them
entertainment, and tells them of his early life, and in
" Ivanhoe " we have that curious character of half
highwayman and half hermit, in the jovial clerk of
Copmanhurst.

[1] The first two verses are quoted at the beginning of this chapter.

CHAPTER IV

FLAGELLANTS AND DANCERS

ONE of the most extraordinary features of the Middle Ages, and the direct outcome of pilgrimages, were the wandering bands of penitents. These companies were numbered by hundreds, and each of them possessed some individual chàracteristic. Some were composed of the poor only, others were limited to men, while one or two were made up entirely of children. Occasionally a brotherhood would arise with membership extended mainly to those who held peculiar opinions. The great majority, however, were free to all Christians without distinction of age, sex, rank, or opinion, though each of them had some particular form of discipline for their adherents.

Thus every now and then these bands of people would journey from shrine to shrine, praying and mortifying as they went, and gathering recruits along the way. After exciting interest for a short time the larger number of these associations would dissolve as suddenly as they had appeared ; a few survived for years, while one or two underwent periodical revivals down to comparatively recent times.

The most persistent of these bands of fanatics were the dancers, the palmers, and the flagellants.

The dancers made their first appearance at Aix-la-Chapelle in 1373, when they were composed of a

ragged set of wanderers who made begging and
vagrancy a profession. They had a secret system
of initiation, at which it was said, as with most of
these secret initiations, they practised all kinds of
abominations. Wandering about in bands of thirty
or forty, their apparent poverty, their earnestness,
and their frantic fanaticism gave them an extraordinary hold on the multitude.

Wherever they went their singular reputation
caused large crowds to assemble to watch their per-
formances, and thousands who went as sightseers
became infected with the mania, which came to
be regarded in the nature of a contagious disease
that was even more dreaded than the plague.

Everywhere the dancers became the centre of a
writhing mass of humanity making violent motions
of worship, offering prayers in the form of convulsive
shrieks, and acting as though they would take heaven
itself by storm. Their hysterical ravings were regarded as prophetic. It was quite in vain that the
axe beheaded hundreds of these maniacs, or that the
gibbets broke down with the weight of their bodies.

The flagellants were unquestionably the strangest
of all these itinerants of faith as they were the most
tenacious of existence. Wherever the shrieks and
groans of the gloomy flagellants alarmed the ears,
those in the vicinity fled and hid themselves, for the
penitential torrent of blood and tears absorbed all
with whom it came in contact. There was no escape
for any, rich and poor alike ; resistance was vain,
remonstrance unheeded. Under the penalty of
having the flesh flogged from their bones those
who happened to cross their path were forced to
become flagellants until they were released at the
first celebrated shrine.

Pilgrim Life in the Middle Ages

It was in 1260, about the time when the enthusiasm for the Crusades was flagging, that public associations began to spring up in Italy for the purpose of discipline. Multitudes of people, of all ranks and ages, practised this mortification of the flesh along the open streets in the hope of obtaining Divine mercy for their sins.

Perugia is said to have been the first scene of this madness, and a hermit named Rainier the instigator. The custom, after practically dying out, was revived in all its fury during the fourteenth century, and for ten years the flagellants perambulated and agitated Europe. This revival is said to have had its origin during a plague in Germany in 1349, when from the first the Teutonic knights met it with fierce opposition. In 1351 these warriors assembled and set upon a body of flagellants, massacred thousands of them on the spot, and compelled the remainder to be re-baptized.

The flagellants propagated the extravagant doctrine that flagellation was of equal virtue with the Sacraments ; that by its administration all sins were forgiven, that the old law of Christ was soon to be abolished, and that a new law enjoining the baptism of blood administered by flogging was to be substituted in its place. They were not supported by the heads of the Church, and Pope Clement VII. issued a bull against them, with the result that many of their leaders were taken and burned at the stake. The custom, however, continued to crop up at intervals. At the beginning of the fifteenth century flagellants are again mentioned in Lower Saxony. They rejected every branch of external worship, and entertained some wild notions respecting the evil spirit.

Flagellants and Dancers

The infection, as in the former outbreaks, spread with great rapidity, and was only suppressed by the Kings of Poland and Bohemia expelling all flagellants from their territories.

As enthusiasm for these various sects began to decline active measures for their total abolition were adopted by the Council of Constance (1414-18), but a remnant of them continued in existence until the close of the century. Lastly came the palmers, a class of foreign pilgrims whose real history and condition are but little known. Their designation is thought to have been derived from the palms, branches of which they brought home from Palestine as evidence of their pilgrimage. The distinction between them and ordinary pilgrims was that the pilgrim had some home or dwelling-place, but the palmer had none. The pilgrim travelled to some specific shrine or holy place, but the palmer to all. The pilgrim journeyed at his own charges, but the palmer professed poverty and went upon alms. The pilgrim might give over his profession and return home, but the palmer must persist till he obtained his palm by death.

The profession of the palmer was originally voluntary, and arose from that rivalry of fanaticism so prevalent during the earlier years of the Middle Ages. During the tenth and eleventh centuries men were sometimes ordered to become palmers—to give up wife, family, home, and country—as a penance for their sins.

CHAPTER V

HOLY WELLS

It is, of course, easy for us to understand the importance of the well in all countries and at all times ; for " living water " is the spring of life, and as such is quite a feature in the narrative of Moses, brief as that narrative is. In Eastern lands not so bountifully provided with streams and fountains of water as are Britain and the European countries generally, the well has always been of great social, economical, commercial, and even political, importance. In the Orient it is to-day, as it was for centuries before the Christian era, the meeting-place of the citizens in the eventide, the gathering-place of the shepherds and herdsmen ; and the cool, limpid waters in the sandy desert must have been the silent witnesses of countless acts of religion, social and political compacts, and commercial transactions.

Here, at the well-side, one journey begins or another is regulated, and at the green oasis in the sandy waste the weary pilgrim may find refreshment and repose. All travellers and explorers are agreed that the lack of fresh water is the curse of a kingdom, as the prospect of it in abundance is the *desideratum* that helps forward the weary steps of a stranger when he enters an unknown territory.

" The well digged which they digged not " has

Holy Wells

a conspicuous place in the catalogue of God's bounties of which Moses reminded the Israelites. Then again, the well figures prominently in the language of Holy Scripture, and the simile, the illustration, the metaphor, and the symbol are still telling forth the great Eastern proverb that " of all things WATER is the first."

It is now generally accepted that both tree and well worship existed in Britain long before the Christian era, and were not introduced here by the Christian missionaries, who, finding both in vogue on their arrival, tolerated them at first and utilised them afterwards as they did with so many other pagan customs. The success of the early Christian missionaries in this country was due in no small measure to their willingness to compromise with many of the pre-Christian customs they were powerless to stamp out, and to the readiness with which they grasped every opportunity of grafting the new faith of Christianity on to the pagan forms of religious observance.

In this way the Church assimilated beliefs it could not destroy, and in many cases substituted its saints and angels for the gods and spirits of the heathen cults. We know from Beda that the Saxons assembled at certain sacred places for the celebration of religious rites. Trees, rocks, and wells marked their sacred places, and that such were venerated by the Saxons is not a matter of conjecture but of evidence.

A canon of the reign of Edgar enjoins the clergy to be diligent in withdrawing the people from the worship of trees, stones, and fountains. But the pagans could not be weaned from the old customs by canons, laws, or edicts, and this was recognised by the authorities. Pope Gregory's letter to Mellitus (Beda, lib. i., c. 30) directs him to *retain* the old temples and consecrate them, " that the nation, seeing their temples are not destroyed, may remove error from their hearts, and knowing and adoring the true God, *may the more familiarly resort to the place to which they have been accustomed*." In short, the policy of the Church was to make the transition from pagan error to Divine truth as easy as possible. In England, where St. Augustine and his successors obeyed the papal directions, the people would be gathered together in the places they held sacred— within the stone circle, in the leafy grove, by hoary rock or holy well. And we have evidence of it in stones once sacred to Druidical worship, marked with a cross ; in wells of water once sanctified by heathen ceremonies, placed under saintly invocation by Christian superstition; in old church sites whereon Woden and Fregg, and before them Jupiter and Venus, were worshipped.

It is, therefore, easy to understand how an archaic devotional custom gradually developed in course of time, in the case of some wells at any rate, into a more superstitious one, how some wells came to be called " wishing-wells " and others to be regarded as " prophetic." Ancient wells of water are still frequently to be found near stone monuments or churches which have replaced them, and in many instances it is highly probable that the existence of the spring of water determined the position of the cromlech, monument, or church. A considerable number of our old churches, and even a few of our cathedrals, appear to have been built on the sites of stone circles where wells existed, and in some cases still exist. Glasgow Cathedral is traditionally

Holy Wells

said to have been built on the site of the cell of St. Kentigern, which is stated to have been placed within a Druidical circle, and a well may still be seen in the cathedral. On the site of this Scottish hermit's oratory the cathedral was erected. The visitor is shown a narrow shaft formed in a circular enlargement of the stone bench which runs round the interior of the walls, just beneath one of the Early English lancet-windows, by which shaft one may still dip into the limpid waters which supplied the Druidical lustrations, and then the daily drink to the Celtic hermit and the baptismal element to his Pictish converts.

St. Chad's Well, by which that saint and bishop had his oratory, still exists in a little garden adjoining St. Chad's Church at Lichfield, although the relics and bones of the saint, which had been carefully hidden and preserved during the Reformation, have been enshrined in the altar of the Roman Catholic Cathedral of St. Chad, at Birmingham, one of the finest architectural creations of Pugin, as it is one of the least known. This little well at Lichfield was frequented in olden days by a vast number of pious devotees, and even to-day it is customary for the clergyman, attended by the churchwardens and a great concourse of children, to visit this well on Holy Thursday (Ascension Day), when it is adorned with boughs and flowers, and the gospel for the day is read. The water, which is quite milky in colour, is supposed to possess certain medicinal virtues, which may have helped to strengthen the belief in its miraculous powers of healing.

Sir John Floyer, a physician of Lichfield in 1702, published a curious essay "To Prove Cold Bathing both Safe and Useful," in which he gave a table

103

of the diseases for which the water of St. Chad's Well was beneficial. London has several associations with St. Chad, for on the east side of Gray's Inn Road, near King's Cross, stood St. Chad's Well, which was one of the favourite spas of the metropolis. The New River takes its rise from springs called Chad's Well, situated in the meadows between Hertford and Ware ; and the course of the river in the north of London gave name to Chadwell Street.

Devonshire has several holy wells, as at Ladwell orchard at Ashburton, the overflow from which unites with the Ashburn stream below the town. The well was formerly known as Our Lady's Well, now corrupted into Ladwell. A short distance to the west of Ashburton is a spring called Gulwell the water of which is still considered efficacious to wash weak eyes with. The name Gulwell is a contraction of St. Gudula's well, as this saint was the patron saint of the blind, and had a lantern for his attribute. A granite cross once stood over this spring, and portions of it may be seen at Gulwell Farm. Lidwell or Ladywell, near Dawlish, with its gruesome stories of the monk-highwayman, is too well known to be described here. Totnes has a very interesting well in Leechwell, which, Mr. E. Windeatt tells us, " consists of three oblong stone troughs of different lengths placed side by side, fed by water issuing out of three spouts. One spring has always been considered efficacious in cases of diseased eyes, and is still used for such. The centre trough, known as ' long cripple,' is much longer than the other two, and was supposed good for lameness, but some say for the bite of a *long cripple* or grass snake ; the remaining trough for skin disease, possibly leprosy, as the lazar-house and its ground adjoined the well."

Holy Wells

Father Wallace, in his "Life of Edmund of Canterbury," mentions St. Edmund's Well at Oxford as having been resorted to by people for the healing of wounds and maladies, until the practice was prohibited by Bishop Sutton, 1280, on the grounds of superstition.

Recent analysis has proved that the water of many of these old wells is medicinal, and they have, therefore, certain curative properties ; and it was quite in accordance with the spirit of mediæval days to put such wells under saintly invocations, and to attribute their virtues to the miraculous power of the saintly patron. Others appear to have had no inherent virtue beyond that which all pure cold water possesses, but were reputed to have a supernatural efficacy to the devout. To one or two, special virtues were attributed ; and the idea that the waters of certain wells had marvellous healing powers was not confined to the British Isles, but prevailed generally over Europe.

We shall hardly doubt, if we consider the strength with which heredity and custom operate, and the tenacity with which the people of this country still cling to their local superstitions, that some of our wishing wells and springs may be those to which a superstitious veneration was paid in heathen days. From Canute's enactments against worshipping at fountains and wells, it is evident that pagan rites used to be observed at them down to his reign. The crooked pins which the Irish and Cornish peasantry still drop into their " holy " wells, and the grotesque jargon they utter when doing so, are traces of an old custom that has continued to the present day. Brand, in his " History of Newcastle," refers as follows to a well still called Beda's Well, near Jarrow : " As

Pilgrim Life in the Middle Ages

late as 1740 it was a prevailing custom to bring children troubled with any disease or infirmity ; a crooked pin was put, and the well laved dry between each dipping."

As one would expect, the more famous of these springs of water became fashionable places of pilgrimage, and the bishops frequently granted indulgences to those who visited them. These pilgrimage wells were generally enclosed in a building or well-house for the convenience of pilgrims and the profit of the custodians. A chapel, too, was often attached, in which the seekers of the miraculous virtues of the holy well might offer prayers for its efficacy and deposit their offering. The well-house and the chapel were the pump-room and assembly-room of these ancient spas, where inns sprang up to lodge and entertain the pilgrims ; and a famous holy well was as great an attraction to our old towns as the possession of medicinal waters is to the Bath, Cheltenham, Harrogate, or Tunbridge Wells of to-day. The ecclesiastical romancers—the guide-book writers of other days—embellished the original legends, to invest the neighbourhood of wells with the added charm of poetical association. Thus with many of these ancient springs of water there is a curious blending of archæology, history, and romance, which last, though it has least to do with facts, may be more real than the other two.

If we look through the histories and life-stories of the numerous Celtic saints who founded oratories in England, Scotland, and Ireland, we shall find that a very large proportion of them lived the life of hermits, in which cases it was essential that the saint should build his cell or oratory near a stream or spring of water in order to be near that indispensable necessary

Holy Wells

of life. Near many of these early oratories still to be found in Ireland, Wales, the North of England, and Cornwall, the spring which supplied the hermit saint is existing, and is reputed, in many instances, to be a holy well. It was almost inevitable that when every relic of these holy men, down to the rags and tatters of their garments, was reputed to possess miraculous properties, the wells which they had used should bear their names, and share in the individual virtues attributed to them.

Wells Cathedral, as its name implies, is associated with abundant springs of water. Near the east end of the fabric there are three such wells, on a spot now enclosed by the Bishop's garden, while the overflow of water fills the moat that surrounds the palace. In the fifteenth century Bishop Beckington (1443-64) caused a conduit to be made to convey a supply of fresh water to the inhabitants by a deed in which he granted " to William Vowell, the brethren, fellow-citizens, and burgesses of the city of Wells, to have and to hold for ever a conduit, with troughs and pipes, above and underground, to be supplied from certain water within the precincts of his palace called St. Andrew's Well, the waste water to be for the use of the episcopal mills." In return for this bounteous supply of fresh water, Vowell and his fellow-citizens agreed to visit Beckington's tomb in the cathedral once every year, and to this day the city of Wells is watered by this overflow from the ancient spring. Tradition asserts that Ina founded a church about 705, beside St. Andrew's Well, and placed it under the care of a small band of secular canons. This foundation was given many privileges by succeeding kings of Wessex, until the place was selected as the seat of the new bishopric founded by

Edward the Elder for Somerset, when its first bishop was Athelm, Abbot of Glastonbury, translated to Canterbury in 914.

Wells are found in many other cathedrals, as at Carlisle, where they have been covered over, and Evelyn speaks of a spring of water he saw in the " vestrie " of York Minister.

We know that when Paulinus baptized Edwin at York, it was in a spring over which a wooden oratory was erected for the occasion, and that over this oratory the walls and roof of the cathedral were afterwards raised. The well now to be seen in the crypt is said to be the one in which Edwin was baptized. Some of these wells had become renowned at a very early period.

The term " holy well " is common all over the country, and has given name to several parishes in England and Wales, and the now vanished Holywell Street of London derived its name from the same source.

" Holywell," in Flintshire, is the best example we have of a holy well. It is dedicated in honour of St. Winifred, a noble British maiden, the daughter of Thewith, who was lord of that part of the country some time during the seventh century. Her uncle was St. Benno, a holy man who built an oratory on the site of the present parish church. The popular tradition is to the effect that a neighbouring prince, one Caradoc, became enamoured of the maiden's charms. One day he pursued her with violence, but being unable to overtake her, he drew his sword, and at one blow severed her head from the body. The head bounded down the hill, until it was near St. Benno's oratory, and lo ! where it rested there gushed forth from the earth a copious stream of pure water, which was soon found to possess miraculous properties. The stones which had been spotted with the virgin's blood retained the sacred stains, and yearly, on the anniversary of the event, they assumed fresh colours. The well became a great place of pilgrimage, and was visited for generations by great crowds of pilgrims. We are also told that St. Benno restored the young lady's head to her shoulders, when the only personal trace of the adventure that remained was a fine white circle about the neck, which served to authenticate the miracle.

At the present day the fountain is one of the finest in the country, and from it water flows at the rate of twenty-one tons a minute. The building or chapel in which it is enclosed is an architectural gem built by the mother of the seventh Henry towards the close of the fifteenth century. The well itself is in a square-vaulted crypt with an ambulatory, over which is a small chapel, contiguous to the parish church, and on a level with it, the entrance to the well being by a descent of some twenty steps from the street. The water is in a star-shaped basin in the centre of the crypt, ten feet in diameter, canopied by a graceful stella vaulting, and enclosed originally by stone traceried screens filling up the spaces between the shafts that supported the vaulting. In the roof of the chapel are a number of crutches, arranged in a decorative manner, which are said to have been left by grateful cripples who were cured by the miraculous power of the waters. In the valley by which the well is approached are a number of stones which are pointed out as the penitential stations, at each of which the pilgrim stayed to pray on his way to make his final supplication by the famous well of St. Winifred.

Pilgrim Life in the Middle Ages

The legend of St. Winifred was related by the monk Elerius in 660, and repeated with various embellishments by Robert of Salop in 1190. Early in the fourteenth century Pope Martin V. granted special indulgences to all pilgrims who should visit St. Winifred's Well. The Cottonian MS. in the British Museum records many miracles that took place there, and sets forth in detail how the pilgrims' withered and useless limbs, diseases, and deformities were all healed and cured by the waters of the well, where the dumb recovered their speech and the blind their sight.

A collection of the miracles of St. Winifred, printed by Hearne from a manuscript assigned by experts to the end of the fourteenth century, tells us how " in the towne of Schrowysbury setan iij^e men togedur and as they seton talkyng, an atturcoppe cum owte of the wowz [walls], and bote hem by the nekkus alle thre, and thawgh hit grevyd hem at that tyme but lytulle, sone aftur hit roncoled and so swalle her throtus and forset her breythe, that ij of hem weron deed, and the thrydde was so nygh deed that he made his Testament and made hym redy in alle wyse, for he hoped nowghte but only dethe." The " atturcoppe " which wrought such harm in the ancient town of Shrewsbury is thought to have been a kind of large spider, and it is satisfactory to know that the third man was cured by an application of the water in which the bones of St. Winifred had been washed.

What the numbers were of pilgrims who visited this well is impossible to estimate, but as late as 1629, at St. Winifred's feast, there was an attendance of some two thousand persons, and one hundred and fifty priests. It is said that " on the stones at

Holy Wells

the bottom of the well grow the *Bissus iolethus,* and a species of red *Jungermannia,* known vulgarly as St. Winifred's Hair and Blood."

The well at Binsey churchyard, about two miles from Oxford, has the same dedicatory saint as the parish church, which, although not unique, is rather unusual, as there are at least one hundred and twenty saints to whom, or in honour of whom, wells are dedicated in various parts of the British Isles.

With regard to the Binsey well, we learn from the "Beauties of England and Wales" that "several priests used to dwell here under the appointment of the Prior of St. Frideswide's, Oxon, to confess and absolve devotees, and it is said that Secworth, on the opposite side of the river, contained twenty-four inns for the reception of these pious travellers."

In the exterior of the west end of East Dereham Church, Norfolk, is an arch, beneath which St. With-berga is said to have been buried. A spring of water now rises from beneath it, flowing doubtless from the sainted body, as the holy well at Flintshire from the head of her sister, St. Winifred.

At St. Mary-le-Wigford, in the High Street of Lincoln, the spring under the churchyard wall is covered over by a delightful little perpendicular building in the form and design of a chapel.

Ordinary churchyard wells are of a rather different character from those above mentioned, and in any account of them attention must be called to the fact that a large number of our old churchyards are of far greater antiquity than the churches to which they form the courts. Long before the erection of parish churches the people would be gathered together around a cross of stone, or a portable one of wood or bronze (of which latter some excellent examples are in existence), generally near a well of water, the Sacrament being administered by means of a portable altar, such as the one discovered in a bishop's grave in Durham Cathedral in 1828. Simeon of Durham, in his account of the translation of the relics of St. Acca, about the middle of the eleventh century, tells us there was found upon the saint's breast a wooden table in the fashion of an altar, made of two pieces of wood joined with silver nails. Leland tells us that a portable altar, said to have been used by Beda, was preserved at Jarrow in his time.

The wells in our parish churchyards are often in a remarkable position under the churchyard wall, half in and half out of the churchyard, and often near one of its entrances.

Remembering that few stone fonts of proved Saxon date exist, and that some of the wells and streams attached to the old Celtic oratories were certainly used for the rites of baptism, and also bearing in mind the origin of the well in York Minster, it appears highly probable that these wells were intended to supply the baptismal element, and may have been in many instances the actual fonts of the early Saxon converts. There is a curious instance in Bisley churchyard, Gloucestershire, in which an erection, assumed to be a churchyard cross, is stated, on the authority of a MS. preserved in the Bodleian library, to have been built over the churchyard well. The MS. states that on one occasion " a man having fallen into the well, the churchyard was excommunicated for three years, and the inhabitants were obliged to carry their dead to Bibury." An examination of an engraving of this so-called cross, given in Grose's " Gloucestershire," makes it apparent that the illus-tradition is not of an unusual type of churchyard cross,

Holy Wells

but is an ornamental covering, bearing much resemblance to several well-known examples of font-covers.

These old churchyard wells exist in such numbers that it is not possible to refer to them all, for a full list would be, indeed, a surprising document. A service was held recently at Plemstall, near Chester, for the dedication of the well of St. Plegmund, friend and tutor of King Alfred. The Archdeacon of Chester, who conducted the service, reminded the congregation that, while living there as a hermit, Plegmund acquired so great a reputation for sanctity and learning that Alfred, in 890, appointed him to the archbishopric of Canterbury.

Holystone, in Northumberland, has a very ancient well, in the centre of which, rising up out of the water, is a stone inscribed with this legend :—

"In this place, Paulinus the Bishop baptized three thousand Northumbrians. Easter DCXXVII."

The wells of Cornwall form almost a class by themselves, not only by reason of the romantic traditions that have been woven about them, but also in consequence of the excellent condition in which they are found. Cornish folk are extremely superstitious, and they have always held the belief that great harm will befall those who destroy or mutilate, not only the sacred wells but any of the ancient monuments of the county. The result has been to preserve to a remarkable extent such monuments as crosses, cromlechs, stone circles, and ancient wells of water. It is difficult to find a Cornish village of any size that cannot boast of a holy well. The district around St. Germans is typical of many other portions of this outlying western county. It abounds in mysterious piles of rocks such as the Trethevy Stone and the Hurlers, while no less attractive to the student of folklore are the sacred wells of St. Keyne and St. Cleer. The latter was used in former days as a *bowssening* pool, and held in great repute for its efficacy in restoring the insane to *mens sana in corpore sano*. Near at hand is the interesting church of St. Neot's, where is one of the oldest wells in Cornwall. The original baptistery was destroyed, but another has been erected over the well, the legendary history of which is set forth on a remarkable series of old stained-glass windows within the church.

The road from Liskeard to Looe passes by St. Keyne, where the waters of the well possess a wonderful property, according to Thomas Fuller, who says, " whether husband or wife came first to drink thereof, they get the mastery thereby." The well has been immortalised in Southey's well-known ballad, " The Well of St. Keyne."

> "A well there was in the west countrie,
> And a clearer one never was seen,
> There is not a wife in the west countrie
> But has heard of the well of St. Keyne."

The ballad goes on to relate how a traveller, sitting beside the well, met a countryman, with whom he had a long chat about its tradition :—

> "'You drank of the water, I warrant, betimes,'
> He to the countryman said ;
> But the countryman smiled as the stranger spoke
> And sheepishly shook his head.
>
> 'I hastened as soon as the wedding was o'er
> And left my good wife in the porch ;
> But faith ! she had been quicker than I,
> For she took a bottle to church !'"

St. Keyne, or St. Keyna, the tutelary saint of this well, is said to have been a pious virgin, the daughter

Holy Wells

of Braganus, Prince of Brecknockshire, who lived about the year 490. She is also said to have made a pilgrimage to St. Michael's Mount and to have founded a religious establishment there.

Another famous Cornish well is that of St. Maddern, of which Mr. Haslam writes : " The oratory was built near a little stream which flows under its south-western angle ; here a well has been excavated which is continually fed by the clear stream as it passes onward. The well is enclosed by rude masonry, having an aperture to the nave about 4 feet in height and $2\frac{1}{2}$ feet in width."

Ireland is quite as abundantly supplied with wells as is Cornwall, and the Celtic saints who came in such numbers from the Emerald Isle to the land of Lyonesse during the earliest days of Christianity would find the legendary kingdom of King Arthur as full of holy wells as was their native land. Mr. Petrie, in his " Ecclesiastical Architecture of Ireland," mentions, in addition to a large number of other holy wells, one at Tobar-na-Druadh, near Sheepstown, County Kilkenny ; St. Brigid's Well, at the Faughard, County Louth ; and Lady's Well, near Dundalk, which have stone roofings over them exactly like oratories.

Prominent among the holy wells of Wales is the Fynnon Vair, at Wygfair, near St. Asaph, in which the neighbouring spring rises at the west end of the church, and was enclosed in a stella well of the same plan and style as that of St. Winifred, at Holywell.

The author of an interesting work on Ireland, published in 1873, criticises in no uncertain manner the ceremonies and rites that were then being still performed at the holy wells of that country. " Some Roman Catholics say that pilgrimages and ' stations ' are not now made at these wells. Let any one visit

Lough Derg, or any of the other holy sites, and they will know the truth of this matter. There are some diseases and ailments that may be benefited by change of air and by clean and cold water, but these natural remedies are not to be had ' without price ' at the holy wells. Amidst the wild tribes of Africa there are not more superstitious devotees than the poor Irish, who may be seen ' making the stations ' at the holy wells."

Further : " The waters of ' Our Lady's well,' Cross-haven, County Cork, are supposed to be endowed with special healing qualities, and peasant-pilgrims come from great distances to bathe their eyes and drink of the sacred waters, with devout worship and prayers to Mary. Mariolatry is taking the place of the nominal Christianity. Those who are too feeble to go or be brought to the well send by members of their household religious charms, or pieces of coloured rag which have been previously blessed by the parish priest. The fragments are tied upon the branches of the trees over the water, and by this means the miraculous virtue of the well is supposed to be transferred to the owners of the suspended charms."

Any one who possesses any enthusiasm for old English celebrations could become an accomplished well-dresser during the month of June by studying the methods employed at Wirksworth, Tissington, Buxton, and many another well-dressing centre. The modern well-dressing, or decorating with floral garlands, is usually a kind of competition for local prizes, but it is nevertheless a marked survival of the days when this ancient custom had a religious significance in the pagan ritual of the Romans, who decked their springs with flowers in honour of the

DRESSED WELLS AT TISSINGTON.

water-nymphs in the manner described by Milton
in " Comus " :—

> " . . . the shepherds at their festivals
> Carol her goodness loud in rustic lays,
> And throw sweet garland wreaths into her stream,
> Of pansies, pinks, and gaudy daffodils."

Derbyshire appears to lead the way in this ceremony, but wells are still dressed at various places
in Staffordshire, Shropshire, Westmorland, and
Lancashire. The usual method is to make a back-
ground of clay and moss, either around or at the back
walls of the well, the flowers forming effective designs
against the dark moss.

At Tissington, where there are some fine wells,
Ascension Day is selected for the carrying out of
the ceremony, and the accompanying illustrations of
these decorated wells give a good idea of the
effect produced by our modern well-dressers. The
Tissington ceremony has a peculiar significance, as
it originated as a thanksgiving service for a bounteous
supply of water from the wells during an exceptional
drought in 1615, recorded thus in the old parish
registers : " There was no rayne fell upon the earth
from the 25th day of March till the 2nd day of
May, and then there was but one shower ; two more
fell between then and the fourth day of August, so
that the greatest part of this land was burnt upp,
bothe corn and hay." There are five wells at Tissington, each having a distinctive name. The Ascension
Day service is held in the church at 11 o'clock,
followed by a second service at each of the wells,
consisting of a psalm or one of the lessons for the
day, and a hymn, the Benediction being pronounced
on the conclusion of the last service.

Pilgrim Life in the Middle Ages

Affixed to the parish church of St. James's, Clerkenwell, London, is a tablet bearing the following inscription :—

A.D. 1800.

WILLM. BOVND ⎱ *Church Wardens.*
JOSEPH BIRD ⎰

For the better Accommodation
of the neighbourhood
This pump was removed
to this spot where it now
stands.

The Spring by which it is
supplied is situated four feet
eastward and round it as
History informs us, the Parish
Clerks of London, in remote
ages annually performed sacred
plays. That custom caused it
to be denominated *Clerks'*
Well and from which this
parish derived its name. The
water was greatly esteemed
by the Prior and brethren of
the order of St. John of Jerusalem and the Benedictine nuns
in the neighbourhood.

This tablet which was
Formerly fixed on the site of
the Ancient Clerks' Well, viz.,
the pump house, No. 2, Ray
St., westward, was fixed here
as a memento of the Past in
1878.

W. J. HARRISON ⎱ *Church Wardens.*
GEO. BLACKIE ⎰

According to Stow there was once a holy well at Shoreditch, dedicated to St. John. Simpson, in his "Agreeable Historians," tells us that "at Muswell

Holy Wells

Hill was formerly a chapel, called Our Lady of Muswell, from a well there, near which was her image. This well was constantly resorted to by way of pilgrimage."

In 1628 a number of people, brought before the Kirk Session of Falkirk, were accused of going to Christ's Well on the Sundays during May to seek their health. They were found guilty and sentenced to repent " in linens " three several sabbaths. In the Session Records of June 2, 1628, we find it stated, with reference to this trial, that " it is statue and ordained that if any person, or persons, be found superstitiously and idolatrously, after this, to have passed in pilgrimage to Christ's Well, on the Sundays of May, to seek their health, they shall repent in *sacco* (sackcloth) and linen three several Sabbaths and pay twenty lib. *toties quoties*, for ilk fault ; and if they cannot pay it, the baillies shall be recommended to put them in ward, and to be fed on bread and water for aught days."

In 1657, several parishioners were summoned before the same session for resorting to a well at Airth, a village six miles north of Falkirk, on the banks of the Forth, and the whole of them were ordered to be publicly rebuked for their " superstitious carriage."

As a good example of how these old customs persist in the popular mind, and continually crop up in spite of laws and enactments passed against them, the following extract from the *Hibernian Magazine* for July, 1817, may be quoted : " At Stoole, near Downpatrick, in the North of Ireland, there is a superstitious ceremony, commencing at twelve o'clock at night on every midsummer eve. Its sacred mount is consecrated to St. Patrick. The plain contains three wells, to which the most extraordinary virtues are attributed. Here and there are heaps of stones, around some of which appear great numbers of people running with as much speed as possible. Around others crowds of worshippers kneel with bare legs and feet, as an indispensable part of the ceremony. The men, without coats, with handkerchiefs on their heads instead of hats, having gone seven times round each heap, kiss the ground, cross themselves, and proceed to the hill ; here they ascend on their bare knees, by a path so steep and rugged that it would be difficult to walk up. Many hold their hands clasped at the back of their necks, and several carry large stones on their heads. Having repeated this seven times, they go to what is called St. Patrick's Chair, which are two great flat stones placed upright in the hill ; here they cross and bless themselves as they step in between these stones, and while repeating prayers, an old man, seated for the purpose, turns them round on their feet three times, for which he is paid ; the devotee then goes to conclude his penance at a pile of stones called ' the altar.' While this busy scene of superstition is continued by the multitude, the wells, and streams issuing from them, are thronged by crowds of halt, maimed, and blind, pressing to wash away their infirmities with water consecrated by their patron saint ; and so powerful is the impression of its efficacy on their minds that many of those who go to be healed, and who are not totally blind or altogether crippled, really believe for a time that they are, by means of its miraculous virtues, perfectly restored. These effects of a heated imagination are received as unquestionable miracles, and are propagated with abundant exaggeration."

CHAPTER VI

PILGRIMS' COSTUMES, TOKENS, AND BADGES

IGNORING for the moment the dresses worn by Chaucer's merry band, we find that in early days the costume of a professional pilgrim consisted of a long, coarse, russet gown, with large sleeves, sometimes patched with crosses, a leather belt round the shoulders or loins, with a bowl, bag and scrip suspended from it, a large round hat decorated with scallop-shells, or small leaden images of the Virgin and saints ; a rosary of large beads, hung round the neck or arm, and a long walking staff (the *bourdon*),[1] hooked like a crosier, or furnished near the top with a hollow ball, or balls, which were sometimes used as a musical instrument. Sir Walter Ralegh writes :—

> " Give me my scallop shell of quiet,
>   My staff of faith to walk upon ;
>   My scrip of joy, immortal diet ;
>   My bottle of salvation ;
>   My gown of glory (hope's true gage),
>   And then I'll take my pilgrimage."

In the earlier and more austere days of pilgrimage

[1] " This sompnour bar to him a stif burdoun,
      Was nevere trompe of half so gret a soun."
                              (" Canterbury Tales.")

Pilgrim Life in the Middle Ages

the pilgrim received consecration, which was extended to the various parts of his attire. He repaired to the church, where, after prostrating himself before the altar, certain prayers and Masses were said, ending with the *Gloria Patri, Ad te, Domine, levavi,* and the *Miserere.* On rising, the officiating priest consecrated his scrip and staff, sprinkling each with holy water, and placed the former round the pilgrim's neck, the latter in his hand. Should the intending voyage be a transmarine one, to Compostella, Loretto, or Jerusalem, the crosses of his gown were sprinkled in the same way and then sewn on his garment before the eyes of the assembled congregation. On leaving his town or village the newly-enrolled pilgrim was led out of the parish in procession, with the cross and holy water borne high before him.

Apart from such general tokens as images of the Virgin and saints, there were many distinctive badges worn by pilgrims who had visited, either in body or in spirit, certain particular shrines. Thus the distinguishing badge of pilgrims to the shrine of St. James of Compostella was an escallop shell worn either on the cloak or hat.

In the " Friar of Orders Gray," an ancient ballad, the lady describes her lover as clothed, like herself, in " a pilgrim's weedes " :—

> "It was a friar of orders gray,
>   Walkt forth to tell his beades;
> And he met with a lady faire
>   Clad in a pilgrime's weedes.

> 'Now Christ thee save, thou reverend friar,
>   I pray thee tell to me,
> If ever at yon holy shrine
>   My true love thou didst see.'

Pilgrims' Costumes, Tokens, and Badges

> 'And how should I know your true love
> From many another one?
> O by his cockle hat and staff,
> And by his sandal shoone.
>
> But chiefly by his face and mien,
> That were so fair to view;
> His flaxen locks that sweetly curl'd,
> And eyne of lovely blue.'"

And so on through twenty-eight verses.

The word "weed," as used in this ballad, is said by E. W. Fairholt to be "used indiscriminately by the poets of the Middle Ages to signify a single coat or cloak, or the entire dress, as we still talk of a widow's weeds."

The author of an anonymous work called the "Eulogium," cited by Camden, in writing of the excess of men's apparel, says : "They have another *weed* of silk which they call a *paltock*." J. R. Planché considered the "weed" to have been of Spanish origin, and probably brought "into fashion by the knights in the service of John of Gaunt or Edward the Black Prince, whose connection and communication with Spain was so near and so frequent." The adoption of the scallop-shell was due, according to popular tradition, to the relics of St. James being conveyed in some miraculous fashion from Jerusalem to Spain in a marble ship, at the sight of which the horse of a Portuguese knight took fright and plunged into the sea with its rider. After being rescued by the sailors his clothing was found to be covered with scallop-shells.

Erasmus gives another version when he causes one of his interlocutors to remark to a pilgrim recently returned from abroad :—

"What country has sent you safely back to us,

123

covered with shells, laden with tin and leaden images, and adorned with straw necklaces, while your arms display a row of serpents' eggs? "

" I have been to St. James of Compostella," replies the traveller.

" What answer did St. James give to your professions? "

" None, but he was seen to smile, and nod his

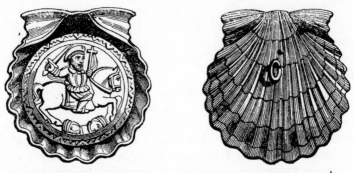

Sign of St James of Compostella

head, when I offered my presents, and he held out to me this imbricated shell."

" Why that shell rather than any other kind? "

" Because the adjacent sea abounds in them."

The adoption of the shell was due partly without doubt to its convenient form as either a drinking cup, spoon, or dish, a probability that is strengthened by the arms of the old English family of Dishington, who bear a scallop-shell as crest, one of those numerous instances we have in English Heraldry of *canting*, allusive, or punning arms, such as the *two trumpets* borne by Sir R. Trompington, and the *three bourdons* of Sir John Bourdon.

Pilgrims' Costumes, Tokens, and Badges

These *armes parlantes*, as the French heralds call them, form a fascinating study that is somewhat beyond the scope of this volume, as apart from the scallop-shell and the bourdon there is but one example that has even a remote connection with pilgrimages. This relates to the family of Mortimer, a family which few people associate, through the forgotten exploit of a Crusader ancestor, a *De Mortuo Mari*, with the *Dead Sea*.

If proof were wanted of the old-time popularity of pilgrimages from England to the shrine of Compostella, we have it in the fact that over twenty old English families bear scallop-shells on their heraldic charges. Boutell, in his " English Heraldry," writes, with regard to the *six escallops of silver on a red banner*, borne by Robert de Scales : " This beautiful charge, happy in its association with the pilgrims of the olden time, and always held in high esteem by heralds."

In " Piers Plowman " we read how a thousand men thronged together, crying upward to Christ and to His pure mother, that they might have grace to find truth. But not one knew the way until they met a Palmer in his pilgrim's weeds, with bowl, and bag, and vernicle, and asked him " whence he came? " " From Sinai," he said, " and from the Sepulchre. I have been to Bethlehem and Babylon, to Armenia, Alexandria, Damascus. You may see by the *tokens* in my cap that I have been to shrines of good saints for my soul's health, and walked full widely in wet and in dry."

All the more celebrated shrines had their special badges or tokens, generally made of lead, and the custodians of shrine and relic must have done a considerable business in disposing of them to devotees

Pilgrim Life in the Middle Ages

who had actually made a pilgrimage, or to those who wished the world to believe they had done so. These signs consisted of figures and devices of various kinds stamped in thin sheet-lead, and with pins at the back for fastening them to the garment. The most popular badge with pilgrims to the shrine of Edward the Confessor was one representing the head of the saint set on a long pin, the whole bearing much resemblance to a modern scarf-pin.

Chaucer tells us how

" They set their *signys* upon their hedes, and som oppon their capp,
And sith to the dyner-ward they gan for to stapp."

Giraldus Cambrensis, who was a young man when Becket lived, has described how he and his com-

Pilgrim's Signs from Amiens

panions, after the Primate's death, visited his shrine at Canterbury, after which they went to London " with the signs of St. Thomas hung about their necks," which shows how quickly these signs were hawked round the city.

The head of John the Baptist was the most famous relic in the Cathedral of Amiens, and at least two

Pilgrims' Costumes, Tokens, and Badges

tokens were struck for pilgrims. One of these, showing the full face of St. John, has inscribed round the margin :—

SAIN : IEHAN : BADDIDEN : DAMIES.

The other has the inscription :—

HIC EST SIGNUM : FACIEI BEATI IOHAVNIS BAVTISTE.

Curiously enough, among some other pilgrim signs

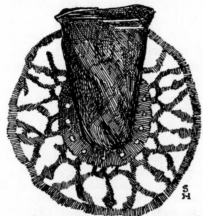

Canterbury Sign with Ampulla

dragged up from the River Stour, at Canterbury, half a century ago, was one representing St. John, nimbed, and bearing in his left arm the Holy Lamb. There was no inscription.

In England the signs and *ampullæ* (small flasks or vases) of the pilgrims to Becket's shrine were made in a variety of forms, one of the former, found in the Thames at London, being a small circular brooch, with the mitred head of Becket in the centre, and the words CAPUT THOME round the broad margin. The *ampullæ* were hollowed out so that they could hold a few drops of the celebrated "Canterbury water," which is said to have consisted of water mixed with the blood that had dripped from the martyr's wounds on to the pavement of the north transept where he fell. The Canterbury *ampullæ* were usually stamped with the figure of St. Thomas and the legend *optimus egrorum medicus fit Thoma bonorum*.

At first, we are told, small wooden receptacles were used for storing this precious blood, but were afterwards replaced by leaden *ampullæ*, for the reason that the sacred material possessed such vitality that the wooden flasks were split asunder when it was placed within them. Many marvellous cures are said to have been effected by an application of "Canterbury water."

The pilgrim in "Piers Plowman" had

"An hundred of ampulles on his hat set,
Signs of synay [Sinai] and shells of galice [Galicia],
And many a crutch on his cloak, and keys of Rome,
And the vernicle before, for men should know
And see by his signs whom he sought had."

One of the Canterbury signs shows Becket on horseback, a mitre on his head, and his hand raised in blessing, while the simplest form of all is a small disc of lead bearing the letter Ͳ. Several specimens of pilgrim signs may be seen in the Guildhall Museum, and others are in the British Museum. The Stour at Canterbury has yielded a few, but by far the greater number have come from the Thames, at either London or Blackfriars Bridge. Their occurrence in the Thames at London is rather peculiar, and has been stated to be due to the signs being lost from

Pilgrims' Costumes, Tokens, and Badges

the pilgrims' hats as they were crossing the bridges. As the great gathering-place for the pilgrims to Canterbury in London was on the south side of the river, at the famous Tabard Inn of Southwark, the explanation is not very convincing. The pilgrims to Walsingham wore several tokens, the most popular being a representation of the Annunciation, with the word " Walsynham " below. Free trade in pilgrims'

Canterbury Sign

tokens and badges was not regarded favourably by the papal authorities, and a bull threatened to excommunicate the unauthorised vendors who ventured to offer the pilgrim scallop-shells elsewhere than in Santiago or Compostella.

129

Pilgrim Life in the Middle Ages

Considering the immense number of these religious trifles that must have been struck when pilgrimages were at their height, the finds have been meagre, owing possibly to pilgrims' signs having been universally destroyed, together with other superstitious relics, at the Reformation. It is hopeless for the amateur to attempt to collect these " badges of devotion," for, small as is the number of genuine examples, the market is full of forgeries, and it is possible that some of those found in the Thames in the year 1836, and again in 1837, had never adorned

Canterbury Brooch

the cap of a mediæval pilgrim. Naturally the greatest number of these signs, badges, or tokens were struck for pilgrims visiting the shrine of St. Thomas at Canterbury, and were fashioned in many forms. One specimen is a full-length figure of St. Thomas in pontificals, with his right hand raised in the act of bestowing the Latin benediction. This had a long pin at the back so that the sign could be attached to the pilgrim's hat, or used as a brooch. Another form is circular, consisting of an outer ring inscribed with the words CAPUT THOME, and the head of St. Thomas in the centre, wearing a mitre. Small bells inscribed with the words *Campana*

Pilgrims' Costumes, Tokens, and Badges

Thome were very common, and were used either for attaching to the clothes of the pilgrims or possibly for the adornment of the horses on which the wealthier pilgrims performed their devotional journey.

A pilgrim's sign representing St. Thomas mounted

Canterbury Sign

on horseback is in the British Museum, together with the stone mould from which it was cast. Other moulds have been found at Walsingham and Lynn, in Norfolk, the former of which bear on one side a row of circular bands, each containing a six-pointed star, which encloses a medallion of the Annunciation. The Lynn example bears on one side the sacred monogram I.H.C., and on the other three concentric rings transfixed by an arrow.

Among many specimens in the British Museum are tokens representing St. Thomas, a Canterbury bell ; the Virgin and Child, from Walsingham ; the vernicle, with the head of Christ, from Genoa ; the axe of St. Olave ; the scallop-shell, from Compostella ; our Lady of Boulogne ; and many others.

As recently as April of this year (1911) some specimens of leaden pilgrims' tokens, hollowed out

Canterbury Sign.

to form *ampullæ*, were discovered at Thorpness, near Aldeburgh, in Suffolk, after an unusually high tide had washed away a portion of the cliffs.

It has been fittingly said that if Chaucer had had the good fortune to write in Latin or Greek, the English people and the English publisher would have taken great pains to interpret his meaning, but that, as he had the misfortune to write in English of an early period, he has comparatively few readers, notwithstanding the great educational work that has been and is still being done by the Chaucer Society, who have proved conclusively that Chaucer may be read fluently in his own language, without the

Pilgrims' Costumes, Tokens, and Badges

modernising aids of Dryden or of Pope. William
Morris and Professors Skeat and Wright, among
others, have pointed out, without much effect it must
be confessed, that it is mainly Chaucer's spelling
and obscurities of diction which frighten his would-
be readers, and that when read aloud intelligently
his language and meaning are clearly elucidated. Of
Chaucer the man but little is known, and his life is so
mixed up with the political history of his friend and
patron, John of Gaunt, that a life history of the one
would comprise that of the other.

The acknowledged facts in the poet's career are
delightfully brief—his education at Cambridge and
Oxford, his studies at the Temple, his admission as
page to the brilliant Court of Edward III., and his
there becoming a protégé of the Duke of Lancaster,
his dramatic and meteor-like rise in favour with the
monarch whom he served as ambassador to Genoa,
his rewards and pensions, his acquisitions of wealth,
his reduction to poverty by the deaths of his patron
and of his king, and finally, his own death in the
seclusion of the countryside.

By descent he was a Norman, and was thus able
to combine the speech of the Norman noble with
the Saxon poetry of the people, an epoch-making
accomplishment when we consider that for many
years after the Conquest two languages were spoken,
the Saxon and the Norman-French, and so long as
the Saxon spirit remained unsubdued, the two
languages remained unmingled until the coming of
Chaucer.

A few philologists like William Barnes have
deplored the introduction of Norman-French into the
simple Saxon speech of our ancestors ; and although
sentimentalists may regret the decay of a vernacular

133

speech, they cannot deny that the languages which are philologically purest lack the wealth of those that are hybrid. Be this as it may, the language of Chaucer, partly Teutonic and partly Saxon, may still

CHAUCER AS A CANTERBURY PILGRIM.
(*From the Ellesmere MS.*)

be heard in some counties where it has degenerated into a local dialect, although what is called modern education is rapidly obliterating the last traces of

Pilgrims' Costumes, Tokens, and Badges

the tongue with which our Norman-Saxon forbears rallied their troops in battle, and with which they prayed and worshipped.

It is generally admitted that it is by the Prologue of the "Canterbury Tales" (the author of the Epilogue is not known) that Chaucer has lived in the past, and will continue to live in the future, and this mainly in consequence of the wonderful way in which, by the sheer force of his art, he has made his heroes and heroines so individualistic within the rather limited range of qualities with which he has endowed them. In some, and by no means minor, respects Chaucer is the best fruit the English poetical tree has produced, his especial merit being that he was the first poet who drew individual character with truthfulness and discrimination. The great charm of the "Canterbury Tales" is that, in reading them, one can recognise each individual as a distinct personality, and it has been said of this original and highly unconventional poet that "he had all the merit of Montaigne, more than the wit of Swift, and Wordsworth's love of Nature as well." To this may be added that, however much the interest of his characters may vary, or his incidents turn from pathos to humour, we are conscious always of a remarkable power of observation, of dramatic and narrative skill.

With Chaucer the poet or with Chaucer the man—genial, honest, and diligent—we are not here concerned, and these few lines have been written for the purpose of showing that although so great an artist in poetry and so delightful a story-teller, Chaucer was singularly accurate in his descriptions of what many poets would consider to be insignificant details. To few imaginative writers, Shakespeare

always excepted, have modern archæologists gone
for their authority regarding the details of ancient
apparel ; but Chaucer is *the* authority for the
vestments and dresses as worn by his contemporaries,
and in two standard works on English costume,
those of Planché and Fairholt, there must be many,

THE SQUIRE.
(From the Ellesmere MS.)

probably in the two books some hundreds of references to the costumes so vividly described by this
father of our modern English literature. In this
" Prologue " we find all the various types of pilgrims
making company together—the merchant, the miller,
the reeve, the clerk of Oxenford, the pardoner, the
knight, the cook, the yeoman, Alisoun (the notorious
Wife of Bath), Harry Bailey (the Host of South-

Pilgrims' Costumes, Tokens, and Badges

wark), and many others, who, having completed their pilgrimage, ride away homeward as the sun begins to draw upward. The costumes of the more prominent of this merry band—there were thirty-one of them until they were overtaken by a canon's servant and his master—may be referred to briefly.

THE SERGEANT-AT-LAW.
(*From the Ellesmere MS.*)

The *Squire* was an accomplished gentleman, for

"Wel coulde he sitte òn hors, and faire ryde.
He couldé songés wel make and endite [recite],
Juste (joust) and eek daunce, and wel purtray and write."

He is described as wearing a short gown, with " sleeves long and wide," and

"Embrowdid was he, as it were a mede
Alle full of fresshe flowres white a red."

137

Pilgrim Life in the Middle Ages

His locks, too, "were crull as they were laid in presse."

The dress of the *Franklin*, or country gentleman, is not described ; he is merely stated to have worn an anelace or knife, and a gipciere, or purse of silk, hanging at his girdle.

The *Sergeant-at-Law* had on a medley coat, with

THE PRIORESS.

(From the Ellesmere MS.)

a silk girdle, decorated with small bars or stripes of different colours.

> "He rood but hoomly in a medlee cote,
> Gird with a seynt [girdle] of silk, with barrés smale,
> Of his array tell I no lenger tale."

Of the *Nonne*, a Prioress, we are told that :—

> "She was so charitáble and so pitóus,
> She woldé weepe if that she sawe a mous
> Caught in a trappe, if it were deed or bledde."

Pilgrims' Costumes, Tokens, and Badges

Her jewellery consisted of :—

> "A piere of bedés gaudid al with grene;
> And thereon heng a broche of gold ful shene,
> On which was first y-wretten a crowned A,
> And after, *amor vincit omnia.*"

The *Yeoman* was clad in "a cote and hoode of grene," his horn was slung in a green baldrick, a silver image of St. Christopher was on his breast, and a gay bracer on his arm. From one side was suspended a sword and buckler, and from the other side hung a dagger. Tucked beneath his girdle was "a shefe of arrowes bright and kene," with heads of peacocks' feathers, and in his hand he carried "a mighty bow."

The *Miller*

> "... was a stout carl for the nones,
> Ful big he was of braun, and eke of boones."

His beard was as red as a fox and as broad as a spade, and he was clad in a white coat and a blue hood, with a sword and buckler by his side. We are also told that

> "He was a jangler and a golyardeys (buffon or jester),
> And that was most of synne and harlotries."

The *Reeve*, the "sclendre colerik man," was arrayed in a long blue surcoat, "and by his side he bar a rusty bladde."

His beard was closely shaven, his hair cut close round the ears, and docked on the top of the crown like a priest's, or, as Chaucer has it :—

> "His top was dockéd lyk a preest biforn."

Pilgrim Life in the Middle Ages

The *Pardoner*—

> "No berd hadde he, ne never sholdé have,
> As smothe it was as it ware late i-schave;
> I trow he were a geldyng or a mare."

On his hat he wore a vernicle, a small piece of linen with a face on it, said to have been copied from the Veronical portrait of Christ, impressed on the kerchief given Him by St. Veronica with which to wipe His face as He passed her bearing the cross. When the

THE PARDONER.

(From the Ellesmere MS.)

kerchief was returned to her it was impressed with the image of the Saviour's face. The kerchief was given to St. Clement, and is still at Rome, although it is one of those relics that are rarely shown. There is a similar relic in Spain, and one in Jerusalem,

Pilgrims' Costumes, Tokens, and Badges

among other places, and they are all regarded as genuine from the circumstance that the image was, by folding, miraculously tripled or quadrupled, as the case may be.

As a badge the vernicle was also worn by the palmers. To attend to their creature comforts—

> "A cook thei haddé with them for the nones,
> To boyle the chiknes with the mary bones,
> And poudre marchaunt tart and galyngale.
> Wel coulde he knowe a draught of Londone ale.
> He coudé roste and sethé, broille and frie,
> Maken mortereus, and wel bake a pye."

The *Doctor of Physic* was attired " in sangwyn and in pers," or, in more modern parlance, blood-red and dark blue, lined with taffeta and sendal. He appears to have been a very good physician, for

> " He knew the cause of every maladye,
> Were it of hot or cold, or moyst or drye,
> And where thei engendred, and of what humóur;
> He was a verray parfit practisóur."

Alisoun, the *Wife of Bath*, who, since her twelfth year, had greeted five husbands at the church door, and was ready to welcome the sixth when the fifth should die, had already been three times to Jerusalem ; and had visited Rome, Bologna, Compostella, and the three kings of Cologne. St. Paul, said she, counselled virginity, but God bade man increase and multiply.

She was a very fine lady, and wrathful indeed if any wife in the parish walked before her to the offering of Mass.

The fine coverchiefs with which she attired her

head on Sunday weighed a pound, her hose was scarlet, and her shoes were new. For travelling she attired herself in a wimple, a hat as broad as a target, and a mantle. The *Carpenter's Wife* wore a girdle, " barred all of silk," and a white " barme-cloth," or apron, full of gores. The collar of her shift was embroidered before and behind with

THE WIFE OF BATH.
From the Ellesmere MS.)

black silk, and fastened by a brooch as big as the boss of a buckler. Her head was adorned with a white " volupere," or cap, tied with tapes, and a broad silk fillet. From her girdle hung a leather purse, ornamented with buttons and silk tassels ; her shoes were laced high upon her legs.

The *Parson* has a twofold lamentation concerning

Pilgrims' Costumes, Tokens, and Badges

the " sinful costly array of clothing." First he tells
of " the sin in superfluity of clothing, which maketh
it so dear, to the harm of the people, not only to
the cost of the embrouding, paling, winding, or
bending, and semblable waste of cloth in vanity ;
but there is also the costly furring in their gowns,
so much pounsoning [pouncing] of chisel to make
holes, so much dagging of shears, with the superfluity in length of the aforesaid gowns, trailing in
the dung and in the mire on horseback and eke on
foot, as well of man as of woman."

Secondly he makes complaint " upon that other
side, to speak of the horrible disordinate scanti-
ness of clothing as be these cut *slops* or *hauselines,*
that through their shortness and the wrapping of
their hose, which are departed of two colours, white
and red, white and blue, white and black, or black
and red, make the wearers seem as though ' the fire
of St. Anthony, or some other mischance, had
cankered and consumed one-half of their bodies.' "

Lydgate, in his poem " The Pilgrim," describes
two persons, one dressed as a widow,

> "The t'other, save a gambeson,
> Was naked to mine inspection."

In those days the clergy were attired like the
laity ; and the *Ploughman* rails at them for riding
glittering with gold on high horses, gayer than those
of any common knight, wearing golden girdles and
gowns of scarlet and green. Many priests, he says,
have mitres embellished with pearls, like the head of a
queen, and a golden staff set with jewels. Chaucer's
Monk is also dressed in open defiance of the regula-
tions of the Church. The sleeves of his tunic were
edged with *fur de gris,* his hood was fastened beneath

143

his chin with a curiously wrought pin of gold, and from the bridle of his horse hung many bells.

It would probably become tedious to trace these details of mediæval costume any further, but we may say with Fairholt : " Chaucer—the Shakespeare of the Middle Ages—has, in his immortal ' Canterbury Tales,' given us the best information connected with the costume of the different grades in English society during this reign " (Edward III.). Of the " Tales " in general Professor Henry Morley wrote : " The whole range of life is in them, from purest religious aspiration to the grosser humours of the flesh, but whoever reads ' The Canterbury Tales ' straight through is left with a most healthy sense of human fellowship, knit by a sense of the true beauty of womanhood and of the true source of strength in man."

We are not surprised to find Chaucer figuring in the *Index Librorum Prohibitorum*, with which is incorporated the *Index Librorum Expurgandorum*, from which latter title the publication obtained its popular but hardly correct name of *Index Expurgatorius*. The author of the Prologue to the " Canterbury Tales " is in good company, for although Dryden is a notable exception, he has with him Milton, Spenser, Dante, Petrarch, Addison, Swift, Goldsmith, Bacon, Robertson, Mill, and Gibbons, to name but a few of the immortals on whose works the shadow of the Vatican has fallen. Curiously enough, although Henry VIII. is one of the prohibited authors, an exception is made in favour of an early tract he issued against Martin Luther.

After the Reformation, when Protestantism showed signs of becoming as intolerant as the creed it had displaced, and the setting up of a press censorship

Pilgrims' Costumes, Tokens, and Badges

was anticipated, Milton, in the " Areopagitica," used all his powers of argument to dissuade the English authorities from adopting the practice of the Romanists, " who acted," said he, " as if St. Peter had bequeathed them the keys of the Press as well as of Paradise."

The woodcuts of some of the " Tellers of the Canterbury Tales " that illustrate this chapter are from the sketches of Chaucer's Pilgrims which illustrate the famous Ellesmere MS., a folio on vellum, in handwriting of the fifteenth century, with illuminated capitals, and a coloured drawing of each of the Pilgrims in the dress of the period.

CHAPTER VII

PILGRIM ITINERARIES

WE have already called attention to the early account
of the Holy Land, written by Adamnan, Abbot of
Iona, at the dictation of Bishop Arculf, who had
spent nine months at Jerusalem. Beda abridged
this narrative into a textbook, the forerunner of
the long series of English records of travel and
adventure to which the impulses of religion prompted
the inmates of monastic houses.

King Ina had reigned over Wessex for nearly
forty years, had defeated the South and East Saxons
in battle, had conquered and dethroned Geraint, the
King of Devon and Cornwall, and had magnificently
restored the tomb of King Arthur, and so caused
Glastonbury to become a sanctuary where Britons
and Saxons could forget their racial antipathies and
worship at the same shrine. The " Dooms of King
Ina " have come down to us in their splendid integrity
as unimpeachable evidence of the wisdom of this
great king and of his zeal for the spiritual and
temporal welfare of his subjects. Yet in 726, with
Ethelburga, his queen, he renounced his kingdom
and journeyed to Rome, where he spent the remainder of his life in penance. Here he founded
a kind of almshouse or hospice for members of
English nationality, where the young could be

146

educated, pilgrims entertained with food and lodging, and the sick nursed back to health. This *Schola Saxonum*, as the hospice was called, was near the Vatican, on the site now occupied, appropriately enough, by the Hospital of Santo Spirito. The endowment was transferred to the English College in the sixteenth century. Near the hospice was a cemetery, in which, when he died, King Ina was laid to rest.

There is a general impression that the tribute known as Peter's Pence was instituted by King Ina for the purpose of providing funds for the maintenance of his English school at Rome. This, however, is quite unsupported by evidence, for this Róm-feoh, as the Saxons called it, was a papal exaction, which, from the beginning of the tenth century, became a regular tax of a penny on every hearth. It is now thought to have originated in the tribute paid by Offa of Mercia for the papal authorisation of his new and short-lived archbishopric of Lichfield. In time the tax became commuted for an annual payment of £201 9s. from the whole kingdom, and was recognised and paid by William I. In 1306 Pope Clement V. tried unsuccessfully to abolish the commutation and return to the original levy of a penny a hearth. In 1336, when John's tribute to the Pope was repudiated, Peter's Pence was also held back for a time.

In 737 St. Boniface, the great apostle of Germany and a native of Crediton, in Devon, went to Rome to confer with Pope Gregory III. upon the best means of repairing the condition of the Church, which had been desolated by the inroads of the Saracens. To Boniface the Pope gave extraordinary powers, and in Rome he saw in some of the pious English monks and pilgrims the material he needed for his work of reformation. Here St. Wunebald not only prepared to follow his uncle into Germany, but persuaded his younger brother, Willibald, and several of his relations and friends, to place themselves at the disposal of the great Devonshire saint, whose Life was written by his nephew Willibald, a great pilgrim, as may be gathered by those who peruse the " Hodœporicon, or Itinerary of St. Willibald," published by the Palestine Pilgrim Text Society.

The notes and itineraries of these early pilgrims are of the utmost value with regard to the topography of the Holy Land, and they had a large, although rather an indirect, share in the advancement of civilisation. Willibald was born about the year 701, and possibly in Devonshire, and it is from a Saxon nun of Heidenheim, St. Walburga's Convent, a kinswoman (in all probability a sister) of Willibald, that we have the most authentic account of the family history, the first work that we know to have been written by an English lady.

We have already seen how the spirit of adventure which urged the Saxons to leave their native forests and swarm over Britain still fired the imagination of their monkish descendants. Some, like Boniface, felt drawn to missionary work in heathen countries, others became pilgrims, when Rome and Jerusalem were the chief objects of their ambition. Willibald's motives are disclosed thus :—

" He began to ponder how he could most effectually leave the world with its riches and possessions, his parents and relations, country and home, by making a pilgrimage in a strange land. He opened his secret to his father according to the flesh, and besought him with earnest entreaties not only to grant his sanction to the request, but himself also to accompany him in pilgrimage. At first, when he thus urged his father to forsake the uncertain riches of the world and to enter into the service of the heavenly warfare, leaving home and family, and seeking the glorious threshold of Peter, the prince of the apostles, he would not, but said that it was dishonourable and cruel thus to desert his wife and young children, and leave them defenceless to the care of others. But the eager soldier of Christ continued to plead in behalf of the austere religious life ; oftentimes urging the motives of fear and terror, and then again the soothing promises of eternal life, the sweetness of Paradise, and the love of Christ ; until he so wrought upon his mind that in the end he prevailed, and his father and brother Winibald gave their promise to set out on the path he had adopted and proposed to them."

Thus the father, St. Richard, and his two sons, Willibald and Winibald, and a band of young nobles set out for Southampton, then called Hamlemuth, from the River Hamble that joins Southampton Water a few miles below Southampton (" *Hamalea-mutha, juxta illud mercimonium, quod dicitur Hambich* "). Here they crossed the Channel, and, according to the biographer, pitched their camp near Rouen (" *In ripa fluminis, quod nuncupatur Sigona, juxta urben quæ vocatur Rotum* ").

It was the summer of 721, and the country was much disturbed in consequence of the Saracen conquerors of Spain having invaded France, but the pilgrims do not seem to have been molested. Proceeding on their way, they visited the shrines of many saints until they came to what the biographer

Pilgrim Life in the Middle Ages

calls the " Gorthonic land," a place that has not
been definitely identified, but is probably Piedmont.
Continuing their journey, they came to the city of
Lucca, where St. Richard became ill, died, and was
buried by his sons in a tomb at the Church of St.
Frigidian, an Irish saint who was Bishop of Lucca
in 556. Many miracles are recorded as having
occurred through the intercession of St. Richard, one
of them being described thus :—

" A monk named George, who served the daily
Mass at this altar (dedicated in honour of St.
Richard), lay in a hopeless state of suffering from
a pulmonary disease. As he slept a form with a
majestic beard and bright angelic countenance
appeared to him, wearing a royal crown, and
holding a sceptre, and bade him go for relief to
the altar at which he had so continually served in
Holy Offices. He obeyed the vision and was cured "
(*vide* " Historia Lucensis," by Canon Franciotto).

In the seventeenth century this altar was still to
be seen, beneath which was the following epitaph :—

" HIC REX RICHARDVS REQVIESCIT SCEPTRIFER ALMVS,
REX FVIT ANGLORVM, REGNVM TENET ISTE POLORVM,
REGNVM DIMISIT, PRO CHRISTO CVNCTA RELIQVIT,
ERGO RICHARDVM NOBIS DEDIT ANGLIA SANCTVM.
HIC GENITOR SANCTÆ WALBURGÆ VIRGINIS ALMÆ,
ET WILLIBALDI SANCTI SIMVL AC WINIBALDI,
SVFFRAGIVM QVORVM DET NOBIS REGNA POLORVM. AMEN."

By the Bollandists this inscription is assigned to
the twelfth century. It was in 1151 that the monks
of Eichstadt wished to remove the relics of St.
Richard to the church where St. Willibald rested ;
but the people of Lucca refused to give up the
remains of the Saxon prince, but after great per-

suasion they allowed a small quantity of his dust
to be removed.

In a very interesting pamphlet on " Saint Richard
the King of Englishmen," Mr. Kerslake deals with
the localisation of a personage who has hitherto
been isolated from the stream of history, with St.
Richard's title as king and his territory in the
neighbourhood of Exeter.

To return to St. Willibald and his brother
pilgrims, we find that after attending to the
obsequies of their father they hastened over the wide
regions of Italy, and arrived safely at Rome and
stood before the glorious Basilica of St. Peter, the
great apostle.

The two brothers suffered greatly from fever at
Rome, where they remained until the spring of 723,
when, with one companion, they set out for " the
delectable and desirable city of Jerusalem." Their
journey lay by pleasant paths and sunlit valleys,
—rich in religious and historical associations—by
Terracina, Gaeta, and Naples, spending three days
in Sicily, and crossing the Adriatic to Albania, and
thence by Chios and Samos to Ephesus.

From here " they walked two miles along the
coast to a town of great size called Figila. They
were there one day, and having begged some bread,
went to a fountain in the midst of the city, and
sitting beside it on the margin of the basin they
dipped the bread in the water and so ate of it."

The journey was continued on foot along the coast
to Patara, where the winter was passed ; then crossing over to Tortosa, they visited Ortha, where they
attended a service officiated over by a bishop of
the Greek Church. Proceeding to the tower of
Emessa, they would enter territory in the occupation

of the Saracens, on whom they appear to have made a favourable impression. From Emessa they set out for Damascus, where they visited the scene of the conversion of St. Paul :—

"And having prayed there, they went on their pilgrimage into Galilee, until they came to the place where Gabriel first came to Blessed Mary with the salutation, 'Hail, full of grace!' A church now stands there, and the village in which the church is is Nazareth. The heathen would many times have destroyed the church, but the Christians so often ransomed it. There having commended themselves to the Lord, they walked on, and came to the village of Chana, where the Lord turned water into wine. A great church stands there, and in the church an altar, composed of one of the six water-pots which the Lord commanded to be filled with water which He turned into wine, and of that wine they partook."

This interesting itinerary is too long to be described in detail, but St. Willibald at length arrived at Jerusalem. After visiting all the famous shrines of Jerusalem he proceeded to Bethlehem, seven miles distant. "The place of the Nativity was of old a cave beneath the ground, and is now a house in form four-square, cut out of the rock, and the earth dug away round it and removed. . . . The church over the grotto is a glorious building cruciform."

The next place of call was the monastery of St. Saba, where a large community of Greek monks still reside. On setting out again he passed through Lydda and Jaffa, and thence along the seashore to Tyre and Sidon.

After crossing the Lebanon to Damascus and many other places he eventually reached Constan-

tinople, where he and his companions resided for
two years, and Willibald had a cell allotted to him
in the precincts of the great church of St. Sophia,
near the tomb of St. John Chrysostom.

After seven years of pilgrimage Willibald settled
down to the ordinary routine of a monk's life at the
monastery of Monte Casino, under the rule of Abbot
Pertinax, a strict Benedictine.

In 737 St. Boniface arrived at Rome with an
immense company of converts, and here he was met
by his nephew Willibald, who, when asked to be the
solace of his old age, followed his uncle to the banks
of the Rhine. As long as Boniface lived Willibald
was his Chancellor, and was consecrated bishop.
After the martyrdom of his famous uncle, in 754, St.
Willibald took a foremost place among the bishops
of his day, and he lived to see Saxony converted to
the Christian faith by the labours of his kinsman
Willihad, and another Englishman, St. Lebuin. He
died over eighty years of age, and his body rests in
his own cathedral church of Eichstadt. " Such was
this English prince who, in abandoning his claim
to an earthly kingdom, gained for himself, and for
thousands of others, a place in the eternal kingdom,
and an imperishable name in the records of the
English saints." So wrote Bishop Brownlow in his
interesting papers on Boniface and Willibald, to
which I am indebted for much information concerning the lives of these saints.

Almost as famous as St. Willibald were his brother
St. Wunebald and his sister Walburga. In 757
Wunebald made a pilgrimage to the shrine of his
uncle, St. Boniface, when he was so infirm that he
nearly died at Fulda, but rallying, and by slow
stages, was able to reach his monastery of Heiden-

heim. From here he sent to Willibald at Monte Casino to say he wished to travel thither, but he was persuaded not to undertake so long a journey. He was joined at Heidenheim by his brother, and the Saturday before Christmas Eve, in the year 761, he gave a long address to Willibald and the monks, and " then, lifting up his eyes to heaven, he said, ' Into Thy hands, O Lord, I commend my spirit ' ; and sitting up as he was in the bed, he gave up his soul. His monks clothed his body in his sacerdotal vestments, and laid him as he had directed in a stone coffin, which he had hewn out for many years, and they chanted their psalms all night long beside his remains."

We have not quite done with St. Willibald, for fifteen years after the above-named event he set about rebuilding the abbey of Heidenheim. Three years were occupied in the task, but the chapel intended for the shrine of St. Wunebald was completed at an early date, and when it was ready his tomb was opened for the translation of his remains to the shrine in the new building. Bishop Willibald, in the presence of his sister Walburga and his clergy, raised the stone and dug down to the coffin, which was placed on a bier and carried to the shrine, " and when the solemnities were over they gave thanks to God and the blessed St. Wunebald."

Walburga did not long survive the translation of her brother's relics. She died about 776, and once more St. Willibald came to Heidenheim and laid her body by the side of Wunebald. Numerous miracles are said to have taken place at her tomb, and, if we are to believe the heads of the Roman Church, there is distilled, to the present day, in a miraculous manner from her bones, a clear, colourless dew called the

Pilgrim Itineraries

"oil of St. Walburga." Be this as it may, the late Cardinal Newman wrote thus of it : "The oil still flows ; I have had some of it in my possession ; it is medicinal ; some think it so by a natural quality, others by a Divine gift. Perhaps it is on the confines of both. I may add that I have some of it in my possession now."[1]

In post-Conquest days the first great pilgrim to follow the Crusaders to the Holy Land was Sæwulf, a merchant whose confessor was Wulstan, Bishop of Worcester. He eventually gave up his business to escape from its many temptations, and joined the monks of Malmesbury Abbey. A full account of his entrance into the Holy Land, and his journey to Jerusalem, then in the hands of the Crusaders, will be found in "Early Travels in Palestine," edited, with notes, by Thomas Wright, F.S.A. The book comprises the narratives of Arculf, Willibald, Bernard, Sæwulf, Sigurd, Benjamin of Tudela, Sir John Maundeville, de la Brocquière, and Maundrell.

It may be of interest to note that William of Malmesbury, the author of "The Life of St. Aldhelm," "History of the Kings of England," "History of English Prelates," &c., was Sæwulf's contemporary, though a younger man.

The following curious law was enacted during the reign of Richard I. for the government of those going by sea to the Holy Land : "He who kills a man on shipboard shall be bound to the dead body and thrown into the sea ; if the man is killed on shore, the slayer shall be bound to the dead body and buried with it. He who shall draw his knife to strike another, or who shall have drawn blood from him, to lose his hand ; if he shall have only struck with the

[1] "Apologia," Appendix, p. 44.

155

palm of his hand without drawing blood, he shall be thrice ducked in the sea."

Sir John de Mandeville may not inaptly be called the father of the modern English traveller ; for in 1332 he started on a tour to the East and the Holy Land, when he traversed almost the identical ground that had been covered in the previous century by the celebrated Venetian, Marco Polo, whose account of his travels is not so loaded with the mass of incredible stories which run riot in the descriptions of Mandeville. Marco Polo is justly considered the founder of the modern geography of Asia, and in later days his original statements were confirmed by Oderic, who visited India and China in 1320 ; by Schiltberger of Munich, who accompanied Tamerlane in his expeditions through Central Asia ; by Pego-letti, an Italian merchant who went through the heart of Asia to Pekin in 1335 ; and by Clavijo, the Spanish Ambassador to Samarcand, in 1403. On September 29, 1332, Sir John Mandeville left England for Egypt, where he took service with the Sultan and fought against the Arabs. He then went to the Holy Land, and wandered through Asia until he reached the dominions of the great Khan of Tartary, under whom he again took military service. Returning to England after an absence of thirty-four years, this knight-errant wrote an account of his adventures, which he dedicated to Edward III. From this time but little is known about him, and his latter days are involved in obscurity. He is thought to have died at Liège in 1372, and to have been buried in a convent of the Belgian town. A fourteenth-century MS. account of his travels may be seen among the Cottonian manuscripts in the British Museum. The first printed edition was issued

Pilgrim Itineraries

by Wynkyn de Worde in 1499, and during the succeeding century the work enjoyed great popularity. It was translated into several languages, and regarded as second only to Marco Polo's account as an authority on Eastern travel, countries, and customs.

George Augustus Sala has related that he once saw in a library at Seville a copy of the "Voyages of Marco Polo," with annotations by Columbus of sentences like these : "lie," or "a great lie," or "a wicked lie"; "but modern researches have proved that Marco Polo was not an Italian Baron Munchausen" (*Sala's Journal*, August 27, 1892).

There is no reason to doubt that the organisation of bands of pilgrims for transmarine voyages was a well-established business ; during the eleventh and twelfth centuries in particular the sight of these well-filled pilgrim ships must have been almost as familiar to the coast-town dwellers as are the excursion steamers to the present generation.

In 1428, 7th Henry VI., licences were granted to various English ports for captains of vessels to carry devout persons, being the King's subjects, to St. James's shrine at Compostella, provided that they would first swear "not to take anything prejudicial to England, nor to reveal any of its secrets, nor carry out with them any more gold or silver than what would be sufficient for their reasonable expense."

In 1455, 23rd Henry VI., James Butler, Earl of Wilts, had licence to visit the shrine of St. James of Compostella, with a suite of thirty persons, "yn ye shyppe caullid ye Saynte Jago of Waymuthe," provided they took an oath similar to that already mentioned. The following are the numbers of pilgrims who embarked in 1428 from the favoured

Pilgrim Life in the Middle Ages

ports which were granted special licences for this
traffic :—

Port.						Number of Pilgrims.
London ...	...	...	...	...	...	280
Weymouth	...	...	...	...	...	122
Yarmouth ...	...	...	...	...	...	60
Plymouth ...	...	...	...	...	...	40
Liverpool ...	...	...	...	...	...	24
Bristol ...	...	...	...	...	...	200
Dartmouth	...	...	...	...	...	90
Jersey ...	...	...	...	...	...	60
Exeter ...	...	...	...	...	...	30
Ipswich ...	...	...	...	...	...	20
			Total Pilgrims	...		926

The names of some of the vessels appear to have
a direct reference to what an old writer calls " their
occupation in this holy adoration."

The following is a list of the more prominent ships
employed in this profitable business about the middle
of the fifteenth century: —

Ship.					Tonnage.
Ye Katherine ...	...	...	...	...	140
Ye Galliotte ...	...	...	...	...	150
Ye Marye Batte ...	...	...	...	...	100
Ye Little Nicholas	...	...	...	...	120
Ye Pylgryme ...	...	...	...	...	100
Ye Holy Ghoste ...	...	...	...	...	90
Ye Saynte Marye	...	...	...	...	110
Ye Adventurer ...	...	...	...	...	100
Ye Dorcette ...	...	...	...	...	100

These records are highly interesting, as they show
that the traffic was an important one. In Rymer's
" Fædera " are many allusions to the granting of
licences for the embarkation of pilgrims, but they
are very similar to the examples given above.

Pilgrim Itineraries

By a law of 9 Edward III. English pilgrims were compelled to embark and return by way of Dover, " in relief and comfort of the said town "; and in 13 Richard II. (1389), at the request " of the Barons of Dover," who alluded to this ordinance, the King commanded that all pilgrims and others, excepting soldiers and merchants, should embark either at Dover or Plymouth; but at no other port without the special licence of the King. It has been suggested that these restrictions arose partly from a desire to check the practice of smuggling, at which certain pilgrims are said to have been adepts.

In the Bodleian Library two precious manuscripts are preserved recording the two pilgrimages made to the Holy Land, at rather an advanced age, by William Way, Fellow of Eton, who, having visited Compostella in 1456, made his first journey to the Holy Land in 1458 and his second in 1462. It was largely from these MSS. of William Wey that Wynkyn de Worde, Caxton's apprentice and successor in the business, compiled the pilgrim's Baedeker, or " Informacion for Pylgrymes unto the Holy Londe," of which we shall have something to say a little later.

To return to the Fellow of Eton, we find that his first journey occupied a period of thirty-nine weeks only, which must have been a marvel in those days; and out of these thirty-nine weeks only thirteen days were spent in the Holy Land. His second pilgrimage, made when he was fifty-five years of age, was of even less duration, as it occupied thirty-seven weeks and three days, one week only being pased at Jerusalem. We have it on the authority of Wood that William Wey (1408-76) was

Pilgrim Life in the Middle Ages

a Devonian. His original MS. (in prose and verse) was printed in 1857, under the title of "The Itineraries of William Wey." There is no account of his journeys in Wright's "Early Travels in Palestine," but they are mentioned, together with an account of Wey, in Bishop Tanner's "Bibliotheca."

On April 8, 1506, Sir Richard Guildforde and John Whitby, the Prior of Guisborough, set out for the Holy Land from Rye, in Sussex, and although they were both stricken with illness and died during their first week at Jerusalem, an account of their journey was published five years later, in 1511, by Richard Pynson. This account was doubtless given to Pynson by the chaplain who accompanied them. The climate was very trying for English travellers and a considerable number of them left their bones in Palestine. William Wey had warned his compatriots against any indiscretion of diet or exertion that might bring on the "flyxe." These bands of comparatively well-to-do pilgrims appear to have so timed their departure that they could witness some of the great ceremonials of Venice, the wealthiest and most beautiful city on the route. William Wey arranged his second journey so that he could witness the celebration of the Vigil and Feast of Saint Mark, which was held towards the end of April. Sir Richard Guildforde and his companions spent many weeks at Venice, where they saw the Espousal of the Adriatic on Ascension Day, and the Procession of Corpus Christi, "which," writes the chaplain, "exceeded all other that ever I sawe so moche that I cannot wryte it."

This Espousal of the Adriatic was an aquatic ceremony symbolical of Venice in the days when she surpassed all her rivals in the splendour of her

Pilgrim Itineraries

buildings and in the extent of her maritime commerce. Pope Alexander III. sent to the Doge the famous nuptial ring, with which, in assertion of his naval supremacy, "to wed the Adriatic." The ceremony was performed from the deck of the *Bucentaur*, or state-galley, with all the pageantry of a pageant-loving age. The galley was crowned with flowers like a bride, and amid the harmonies of music and the acclamations of the spectators, the ring was dropped into the sea. Thus the Republic and the Adriatic were wedded, and to make the union indissoluble the ceremony was repeated from year to year.

The pilgrims with whom Guildforde sailed from Venice were detained in the ship for seven days off Jaffa, waiting, as Professor W. Minto tells us, "the leisure and good pleasure of the lords of Jerusalem and Rama." On landing they were subjected to so many discomforts that, in the words of the chaplain, "bothe my mayster and mayster Pryor of Gysborne, were sore seke," a circumstance due in part no doubt to the whole company having been forced to occupy an old cave, where they "lay in the same grotte or cave Frydaye all day, upon the bare stynkynge stable grounde, as well nyght as daye, right euyll intreated by the Maures."

At Rama, the favourite halting-place for pilgrims going from Jaffa to Jerusalem, was a hospital for their reception, founded by Philip of Burgundy, but according to the chaplain's testimony it was in almost as bad a condition as the filthy den at Jaffa.

After the deaths of Guildforde and the Prior at Jerusalem, the chaplain, whose name appears to be quite unknown, set out on his homeward journey. After another night in the Jaffa cave he set sail

161

Pilgrim Life in the Middle Ages

for Venice, a voyage that usually occupied a month ; but on this occasion, owing to storms and contrary winds, the nameless one, who in the absence of a definite cognomen must be known merely as the chaplain, was nearly eighteen weeks on his homeward voyage.

As Professor Minto says: " Pilgrims were often, like most modern tourists, indifferent sailors, and the earliest naval ballad in our language is a humorous description of the sufferings of these landlubbers between England and Spain.

> "'This meanëwhile the pilgrims lie,
> And have their bowlis fast them by,
> And cry after hot malvoisie
> Them help for to restore.
>
> And some would have a salted toast
> For they might eat n'er sodd ne roast,
> A man might soon pay for their cost
> As for oo day or twain.
>
> Some laid their bookis on their knee,
> And read as long as they might see,
> "Alas ! mine head will cleave in three,"
> Thus saith another certain.'"

The narrative of Robert Blackadder, of Glasgow, a notable pilgrim who died in 1508, is, says Mr. Gordon Duff, " preserved among the Venetian State Papers," and as far as the present writer has been able to ascertain, has never been printed or described; so that any one who has access to these documents might be doing a real service by examining the narrative of this Glasgow pilgrim. In 1517 Sir Richard Torkyngton, Rector of Mulberton, in Norfolk, went to the Holy Land. He travelled alone to Venice, but on his homeward voyage from Jaffa

Pilgrim Itineraries

he was joined by five English priests, and a London "pewterer," who died on the voyage. Two MS. accounts of his journey are in the British Museum, and one has been printed in recent years for the first time, with an Introduction by Mr. W. J. Loftie. It consists mainly of extracts from the earlier itineraries, and contains little information that had not been previously published.

The "Informacion for Pylgrymes" was a guide-book for the devout tourists, and although three editions are known to have been printed, only one copy of each is in existence at the present day. These editions are frequently spoken of as having been issued and printed by Caxton, but this is erroneous, as they were all issued by Wynkyn de Worde, the first about 1498, the second in 1515, and the third in 1524. Wynkyn de Worde was Caxton's apprentice and succeeded to the latter's business on his death, in 1491. Succeeding the title is a table of routes and distances, measured in leagues and miles, to all those places visited by pilgrims ; and after that a statement of "change of money for England to Rome and to Venice." Then follow directions concerning provisions, modes of travel, contracts with patrons and masters of vessels, a list of havens to be touched at between Venice and Jaffa. Then comes a short itinerary of the pilgrimage to Jerusalem, and an account of several visits which were made round the city to other sacred spots, as the Mounts of Olive and Zion, the Valleys of Jehoshaphat and Siloam, the cities of Bethlehem, Bethany, and Nazareth, and the River Jordan. In 1824 the Roxburghe club issued a facsimile edition limited to thirty-four copies, and the remarkable little book remained practically unknown to the multitude, in

Pilgrim Life in the Middle Ages

its original dress, until 1893, when Messrs. Lawrence and Bullen published a wonderfully good facsimile of the 1498 edition, with a very able introduction from the pen of Mr. W. Gordon Duff. The following extracts have been taken from this 1893 edition, and they show that although continental travel in the fifteenth century left much to be desired as judged by the luxurious standards in vogue to-day, these mediæval pilgrims could, if they were possessed of sufficient money, make themselves fairly comfortable in both mind and body by following the advice given in their guide-book. The original spelling has been retained, otherwise one could hardly believe the book was printed for a fifteenth and not a twentieth-century pilgrim.

The vessels or galleys were evidently not under the supervision of a port sanitary authority: —

" And chose you a place in the sayd galey in the ouermest stage, for in the lowest under it is ryght euyll & smouldryng hote and stynkynge. And ye shall paye for your ship freyghte, and for meet & drynke to port Jaffe and agayn to Venyse 5 [?] dukates, for to be in a goode honest place and to have your ease in the galey and also to be cheryshed."

The chamber or cabin was to be

" as nyghe the myddes of the shippe as ye may, for there is leest rollynge or tomblinge to kepe your brayne and stomache in tempre. And in the same chambre to kepe your thynges in saufgarde. And bye you at Venyse a padlocke to hange on the doore when ye shall pass in to yᵉ londe."

A bond was entered into with the patron.

" Also, whan ye shall make your covernaunt take good hede that the patron be bounde unto you alle before the duke of Venyse in a M [thousand] dukates

Pilgrim Itineraries

to kepe all manere covenauntes wyth you. That is to wyte, that he shall conduce you to certen hauens by yᵉ way to refresshe you & to gete you fresshe water & fresshe brede and flesshe."

The pilgrims were also advised to see that " the sayd patron serve you euery day hote meete twyes at two meeles. The fore noon at dyner and the after noon at supper. And that the wyne that ye shall drynke be good and the water fresshe & not stynkyng ; if ye come to haue butter, & also the byscute."

This severely practical information gives the traveller hints as to his sleeping.

" Also ye shall bye you a bed besyde Saynt Markys churche in Venyse, where ye shàl haue a fether bed, a matrasse, a pylowe, two payre shetes, and a quylte, & ye shall pay but thre dukates. And whan ye come agayn bryng the same bed agayn and ye shall haue a dukate & an half for it agayn though it be broke & woren."

As the returning stranger in a foreign city might experience some difficulty in tracing the vendor, he is advised to " marke his hous & his name that ye bought it of agenst ye come to Venyse."

" Also byie you a cage for half a dosen of hennes or chekys to haue wyth you in the shyppe or galey, for ye shall haue nede to them many tymes. And bye you half a busshell of myle sede at Venyse for theym."

There appears to have been a rush for comfortable quarters when the ship touched land.

" Also whan ye come to hauen townes yf ye shall tary there thre dayes, go betimes to londe, for then ye maye have lodgynge before a nother, for it woll be take up anone."

Pilgrim Life in the Middle Ages

English travellers were told to
" beware of fruytes that ye ete none for no thynge. As melons & suche colde fruytes, for they be not accordynge to our complexyon & they gendre a blody fluxe. And yf ony enghysshe man catche there that syknesse, it is a grete merueylle but yt he deye therof."

The advice given with regard to the mules which awaited the pilgrims at Jaffa shows the hand of the experienced voyager.

" Also whan ye shall take your asse at port Jaffe be not to long behynde your felowes, for and ye come betyme ye may chese the best mule or asse that ye can, for ye shall paye no more for the beest than for the worste. And ye must geue your asse man there of curteysye a grote of Venyse. And be not to moche before neyther to ferre behynde your fellowes for by cause of shrewes."

Except that ham sandwiches are not mentioned the dietary recommended on the way to the Jordan bears much similarity to that with which the modern tripper appeases his hunger.

" Also whan ye shall ryde to flume Jordan take wyth you out of Jerusalem brede, wyne, water, harde eggys and chese, and suche vytaylles as ye maye haue for two dayes. For by alle that waye there is none to selle."

" And if ye goo uppe to the place where our lorde Jhesu Cryste fasted xl dayes yt is passyngly hote and ryght hyghe. And whan ye come downe agayne for any thynge drynke noo water, but rest you a lytyll. And thenne ete brede & drynke clere wyne wythout water, for water after that grete heete gendreth a flyxe or a feuour, or bothe that many one have deyed therof."

Pilgrim Itineraries

Such are a few extracts from the " Informacion for Pylgrymes," which, however, was not the first book of travel to be printed, for that honour is usually accorded to Bernhard de Breydenbach's account of the transmarine pilgrimage to Jerusalem, a work to which all our pilgrim-authors were much indebted. Pilgrimages to the Holy Land were affected but little by the Reformation, and they have suffered no break in historical continuity. The modern tourist to the Jordan no longer carries with him " harde eggys and chese," for Mr. Cook is a more up-to-date organiser than were the " patrons " of the fifteenth century.

CHAPTER VIII

WINCHESTER TO CANTERBURY

BEFORE the death of Becket, and his canonisation as
a glorious martyr, Winchester, by its possession of
the bones of the great King Alfred, and the shrine of
his tutor, St. Swithin, was the first city of Britain
in popular esteem, and in the number of pilgrims who
visited it. Compared with the bones of St. Swithin
the Canterbury relics were meagre, although they
had been supplemented by the head of the Winchester
bishop. The monks of Christ Church [1] were intensely
jealous of the popularity of the Hampshire shrine,
which seriously threatened the ecclesiastical supremacy of Canterbury. Some writers go so far as to
say that the monks of Canterbury positively rejoiced
at the martyrdom of the head of their church, and saw
in the tragedy of his death the Heaven-sent means
by which they could make their city take precedence
of Winchester in the matter of holy relics. Be this
as it may there is no doubt that the fall of Becket
saw the rise of Canterbury, and however much the
monks of his order may have revered their great
primate while living, they reverenced his bones with
an intensity that was accorded to no other saint
in the history of Latin Christianity. The tragic
circumstances of his death, the most flagrant breach

[1] Christ Church Priory, Canterbury ; the present Cathedral.

168

of the privilege of sanctuary ever recorded in the annals of history, made Canterbury the most holy shrine in Christendom; and although that of St. Swithin continued to be highly esteemed by the masses, the city of Winchester became of secondary importance when St. Thomas of Canterbury was the most fashionable saint in Europe.

Notwithstanding that three books on this so-called Pilgrims' Road have appeared in recent years, the history of the ancient trackway, which is, in many parts, of far greater age than the earliest pilgrim, is still involved in obscurity. There are so many tracks the pilgrims may have taken, so comparatively few portions we know they actually did tread. There were innumerable detours from the direct course, robber-infested districts to be avoided, rivers and streams to be crossed, and visits of devotion to be paid to the numerous holy places that sprang up like mushrooms on either side of the main track. At the same time, if we use a little imagination and trust to the instinct of locality, it is possible to define what was the probable route followed by the majority of the wayfarers.

It is generally admitted, all writers are agreed on the fact, that the trackway itself is of greater antiquity than the events which give it the greater part of its present-day interest. The " holy road " to Canterbury was merely the renascence of an older highway that led in the same general direction; a harrow or hoary old road to which the feet of multitudes of devout pilgrims gave a new lease of life, just as in later days the ancient trackway was remembered and used by those who wished to avoid the payment of the tolls demanded on the newer and more direct highways. All that one is justified in

Pilgrim Life in the Middle Ages

saying with certainty is that the position of much of the road, on the shoulder some few hundred feet below the crest of the hill, stamps it as an early track-way, and that, finding it more or less in existence, the pilgrims from the shrine of St. Swithin at Winchester to that of Becket at Canterbury used such portions of it as suited their purpose.

With the archæology of the road we need not be much concerned, for antiquaries are far from agreed as to its earliest history. The late Grant Allen used to maintain that the older track was a British " tin " road along which this precious metal of mediæval days was conveyed from Cornwall to the ports of Kent, but this has been disputed by others. At the same time, there is abundant evidence that parts of the Pilgrims' Way, in Kent at any rate, are of very great antiquity, and Professor Boyd Dawkins confidently assigns the Kent track to a pre-Roman period, since it links together two such important monuments of the Stone Age as Kits' Coty House and Coldrum.

The multitude of pilgrims which came from Southampton journeyed up to Winchester to visit the shrine of St. Swithin, before setting out on their long road through the southern counties to Canterbury. Leaving the city by Jewry Street, through the north gate and Hyde Street, they passed through the picturesque string of " worthy " villages, the first on the route being Headbourne or " Hyde Bourne " worthy, which has an ancient and possibly pre-Conquest church dedicated to St. Swithin. On the original west wall was an external rood, or crucifix, and in the fifteenth century an additional wall was built for the preservation of the relic, which is now in a very mutilated condition.

Winchester to Canterbury

Should the ancient track across the water meadows be preferred, we leave the highway at Hyde Abbey to follow the raised bank known as the Monks' Walk, which brings us to the south porch of King's Worthy Church, beyond which the track joins the highway. This parish is now united to Abbotsworthy for ecclesiastical purposes. Still farther on we pass through Martyrsworthy, a very small village with a Norman church. The word " worthy " that distinguishes this string of villages is from the A.-S. *weorth*, a homestead, and is found, among other places, at *Worth* Maltravers and Ham*worthy*, in Dorset, and at *Worth*ing, Sussex.

From Martyrsworthy the road winds along the beautiful Itchen valley, passing Itchen Abbas and the finely-wooded uplands of Avington Park, to Itchen Stoke, where, having crossed the river, it leads on to Alresford, the manor of which place was given to the prior and monks of St. Swithin by a king of Wessex. To Alresford Bishop Lucy proved a great benefactor, for he practically rebuilt it in the eleventh century, and constructed a canal to connect the stream flowing through the town with the Itchen, thus opening up a trade route to Southampton to the great benefit of the inhabitants. The large pond remaining at Alresford was part of the scheme for supplying the canal with water. From Alresford the road goes to Bishop's Sutton, where was an episcopal palace. Local tradition has it that the pilgrims passed through the village of Ropley, and an old farmhouse, known as Pilgrims' Place, lends support to the statement. The village lies off the beaten track, so we must return to the road that leads by way of Chawton to Alton; thence to Holybourne, where a small stream rises in the

Pilgrim Life in the Middle Ages

churchyard and gives name to the parish. The church was a pilgrims' chapel, but has retained few features of interest. From here to Farnham the way lies through Alice Holt Woods, a favourite retreat in mediæval days for bands of outlaws and robbers, who attacked the caravans of the wealthy merchants as these passed from London to Winchester. At the time of St. Giles's Fair, Winchester, five mounted sergeants were sent by the wardens of the Fair to protect the valuable merchandise on its way through the woods.

Two miles beyond Bentley the way joins the almost forgotten Harrow Way, and immediately afterwards enters Farnham. Since 860 A.D., when Farnham was granted to Bishop Swithin, it has remained in the possession of the diocese of Winchester, and Farnham Castle is still the official residence of its bishops. From Farnham the Pilgrims' Way follows the main road for a short distance, and then keeps along the southern slope of the Hog's Back, leaving the new road to run along the crest of this narrow chalk ridge. Before long the little village of Seale is reached, with a fine church and an old manor-house named Shoelands, beyond which lie Puttenham and Compton. The latter is one of the prettiest villages on the route, and possesses a remarkable church dedicated to St. Nicholas. The chancel is divided from the nave by a Norman arch with chevron moulding, and the sanctuary is separated from the chancel by a low arch with dog-tooth moulding, surrounded by a wooden balustrade, coeval in date, which is considered to be the oldest piece of church woodwork existing in England. The sanctuary is of two stories, the lower one having a vaulted roof. The upper story was approached originally by

external steps, but these have been superseded by
an internal stairway. This upper room also contained an altar. It has been conjectured that it
served for a pilgrim chapel, and that the external
stairs were used by the priest to avoid entering the
body of the church; but a contrary opinion has been
expressed. Piscinas remain in both the upper and
lower portions of the sanctuary.

From Compton to Guildford the " Way " is chiefly
a sandy lane, very tiring to traverse in places. The
River Wey is crossed at St. Catherine's Ferry, which
takes its name from the little ruined chapel crowning
the summit of a neighbouring hill. For many years
this little building has been roofless. It has the
unusual number of five doors, two of which
have been converted into window spaces over
the north and south entrances respectively. Concerning these latter there has been much conjecture,
but Mr. Thackeray Turner, in a paper read at the
Archæological Institute, gave it as his opinion that
they opened originally on to an interior processional
gallery, used to enable the pilgrims to view the sacred
relics of the chapel. There were probably external
steps leading to the doors, one for entrance and the
other for exit, so that the devotees could circulate
round the gallery without inconveniencing each other.

The present chapel was built by Richard de
Wauncey, of Guildford, in 1317, on the site of an
older building. A spring at the foot of the hill was
reputed to have miraculous healing powers for
diseases of the eye, and the place was much visited
by pilgrims other than those who were proceeding
to Canterbury. After crossing St. Catherine's Ferry,
the old track passed through Shalford and Chantries
Wood to another hilltop capped by St. Martha's, or

Pilgrim Life in the Middle Ages

St. Martyr's Chapel, thus leaving Guildford a little to the north. The town itself does not lie in the direct course, but the pilgrims would find Guildford a convenient spot at which to break their journey. Guildford must have been greatly enlivened by the advent of the pilgrims, especially as the Festival Days of St. Thomas approached—December 29th, the date of the Martyrdom, and July 7th, the Feast of the Translation—when thousands of pilgrims and sightseers wended their way to the famous shrine.

Of the Guildford churches that of St. Mary is the most interesting. It terminated originally in three eastern apses, a most unusual construction which was unfortunately mutilated for the purpose of widening the road following a visit of George IV., who threatened never to visit the town again unless the streets were widened to prevent his carriage being obstructed by the traffic.

From St. Catherine's Ferry the track lies across the marshes. By the wayside is Ciderhouse Cottage, formerly a pest-house or hospital for pilgrims who fell ill on the journey, and so on to the summit of the hill where stands the Church of St. Martha, or more correctly, of the Holy Martyrs. The building, cruciform in plan, dates from Norman times. In the twelfth century a new chancel was built and dedicated to St. Thomas of Canterbury, expressly for the use of pilgrims on the way to his shrine. In later days it was restored by Bishop William Waynflete, Beaufort's successor in the see of Winchester, and the founder of Magdalen College, Oxford; and to all who should visit it and contribute funds for the work, or say there a Paternoster, Ave, and the Creeds, he granted an indulgence of forty days. The building lay in ruins until some seventy years ago, when it was restored for worship. A few old stone coffins are preserved, but the greater part of the fabric is modern.

In a little hollow of the hills nestles Tyting Farm, containing a small oratory, and possibly used at one time by the priest who served St. Martha's Chapel. On the southern side of St. Martha's Hill lies the once beautiful Chilworth Valley, now defaced by the powder-mills erected some three centuries ago. Of the Vale of Chilworth William Cobbett, still the truest and best of all possible guides to this part of the country, wrote : " This valley, which seems to have been created by a bountiful Providence as one of the choicest retreats of man, which seems formed for a scene of innocence and happiness, has been, by ungrateful man, so perverted as to be instrumental in effecting two of the most damnable of purposes ; in carrying into execution two of the most damnable inventions that ever sprang from the mind of man under the influence of the devil ! namely, the making of gunpowder and of banknotes ! Here, in this tranquil spot, where the nightingales are to be heard earlier and later in the year than in any other part of England ; where the first bursting of the buds is seen in spring ; where no rigour of seasons can ever be felt ; where everything seems formed for precluding the very thought of wickedness—here has the devil fixed on as one of the seats of his grand manufactory, and perverse and ungrateful man not only lends him his aid, but lends it cheerfully. As to the gunpowder, indeed, we might get over that. In some cases that may be innocently, and, when it sends the lead at the hordes that support a tyrant, meritoriously employed. . . . But, the banknotes ! To think that the springs which God has commanded to flow from the sides of these happy hills, for the comfort and delight of man—to think that these springs should be perverted into means of spreading misery over a whole nation ! "

Of this description Grant Allen, an ardent admirer of this son of the Surrey soil, wrote : " I do not know whether the English language has ever been more charmingly or more transparently written."

From St. Martha's the path descends a steep gully to Weston Wood and through Albury Park, where the old church was partially destroyed by the late Mr. Drummond, the Irvingite, who turned it into a mortuary chapel for the Drummond family. From Albury the road goes to Shere, a picturesque village with an interesting church. From Shere the track trends towards Gomshall without touching that place, but cuts across the fields to the left, and so to Hackhurst Downs beyond. Along the hill the path is studded here and there with large yew-trees, and just before dipping into the valley of the Mole four ancient yew-trees stand together in a group. At the foot of the Downs lies Dorking, half a mile away from which is Burford, where the pilgrims probably crossed the river, as here are some remains of a wayside shrine known locally as the Pilgrims' Chapel. Onwards along the southern slope of Boxhill the road winds until it reaches the summit of Colley Hill, overlooking Reigate, where a magnificent view is obtained of the surrounding country. The hill is now the property of the Borough of Reigate, and is used as a public park. A portion of the lower slope has been used for building, and the Committee of the National Trust Fund have recently issued an appeal for funds to purchase about sixty acres on the summit, that it may be preserved for the public as an

Winchester to Canterbury

open space of great historical interest and national beauty. Two tracks lead down the hill to Reigate, one known locally as the Old, the other as the Pilgrims' Road. The site of the Reigate shrine of Becket is now occupied by a market-house, but parts of its foundations were discovered some years ago when the adjacent prison was being enlarged. Other ancient chapels here were those of St. Laurence the Martyr and the Chapel of the Holy Cross, the latter attached to the Priory of Augustinian Canons founded in the thirteenth century by William of Warrenne, sixth Earl of Surrey. The priory has been replaced by a modern building, but has retained a few fragments of the older foundation.

From Reigate the road proceeds by way of Gatton Park to Merstham, the manor of which was given by Athelstan to the monks of Christ Church, Canterbury, in the tenth century. The church is of early foundation, although it now exhibits a variety of styles. It possessed a set of wall paintings representing incidents in the life of St. Thomas, but these, together with a wooden rood-screen, were removed during a " restoration " of the church about fifty years ago. From Merstham onwards the track is very indistinct, but is easily recognised again at Titsey Park, through which it passes. Just beyond Titsey village is an old house known as Pilgrims' Lodge Farm, and farther on at the cross-roads we leave Surrey and pass into Kent. Here, as one would expect, the Pilgrims' Way becomes more clearly defined, and crossing the Darent, we soon reach Otford, with its extensive ruins of an archiepiscopal palace, one of three such houses built between Otford and Canterbury. This particular palace at Otford was a favourite residence with the prelates, and was frequently visited by

Pilgrim Life in the Middle Ages

Becket. A spring of water behind the church is still known as St. Thomas's Well, where, according to local tradition, St. Thomas struck the earth with his staff, and water immediately flowed out.

The so-called " well " is thought to have been a swimming-bath attached to the palace. It is thirty feet long and ten or twelve feet broad, the floor paved and the sides lined with stone. We are also told how, Becket being " busie at his prayers in the garden at Otford, was much disturbed by the sweete note and melodie of a nightingale that sang in a bush beside him, and in the might of his holinesse commanded all birds of this kind to be henceforth silent." So the song of the nightingale was banished from Otford.

We next reach Kemsing, where there is a holy well dedicated to St. Edith, whose statue in the church-yard was an object of great veneration. Lambarde, who visited the neighbourhood in the reign of Elizabeth, wrote : " Some seelie bodie, brought a pecke or two, or a bushell of corne, to the churche after praiers made, offered it to the image of the saint. Of this offering the priest used to toll the greatest portion, and then to take one handfull or little more of the residue (for you must consider he woulde bee sure to gaine by the bargaine), the which, after aspersion of holy water and mumbling of a fewe wordes of conjuration, he first dedicated to the image of Saint Edith, and then delivered it backe to the partie that brought it, who departed with full per-suasion that if he mingled that hallowed handfull with his seede corne it woulde preserve from harme and prosper in growthe the whole heape that he should sowe, were it never so great a stacke."

The road from Otford is a narrow lane that leads

178

to Wrotham, with its ruins of another palace. Over
the chancel of the church is a peculiar passage in
the thickness of the wall, known as the monks' or
nuns' passage, which has windows looking down into
both nave and chancel. This has been described as
a "watching chamber." Another passage leads
beneath the tower, and may have been for the use
of processions from the palace. From Wrotham,
through Paddlesworth and Snodland, we reach the
Medway, although the exact spot where the pilgrims
crossed the river is a disputed matter. Many seem
to have gone by way of Maidstone, where Archbishop Boniface built a hospital for their reception
(see Chapter X). The greater number, however, may
be presumed to have crossed either at Snodland Ferry
or Cuxton, while others crossed at Aylesford, a mile
or so below. From Snodland a winding path leads
across the marshes, then goes towards the hills,
and past the megalithic monument known as
Kit's Coty House. All around the hillside on
which this interesting dolmen stands numerous
other stones lie scattered, some of them known
locally as the "countless stones," and at one
time an avenue of stones about six miles long connected the place with the dolmen at Addington. From
Kit's Coty House the Pilgrims' Way passes along
a lane which soon emerges into the Maidstone Road,
which it crosses, and then proceeds farther along a
lane that winds up a hill, passing the White Horse
Stone. Soon the village of Boxley comes into view,
nestling at the foot of the downs, where are the
scanty remains of the once famous Abbatia S.
Crucis de Gracias, the Abbey of the Holy Rood of
Grace (see Chapter XI.), which no good pilgrim
would pass unvisited.

Pilgrim Life in the Middle Ages

By Detling and Thornham the road reaches
Hollingbourne, with an inn known originally as
the " Pilgrims' Rest," but now hiding its ancient fame
under the sign of the " King's Head." The manor
of Hollingbourne was granted to the Archbishops of
Canterbury by Athelstan in 1015, and in Domesday
it is described as *Terra Monachorum Archiepi*.

The road now passes through the grounds of Stede
Hill, and then to Lenham, a delightful little town
with quaint houses and a church mainly of the
Decorated period, which still retains the sixteen oak
stalls for the monks, in the chancel. Near the church
are three large tithe-barns, originally the property
of St. Augustine's Abbey, to which the whole manor
was granted by Cenwulf, King of Mercia. From
Lenham the road goes to Cobham Farm and thence
by fields to Charing, a manor said by tradition to
have been given to the ancient British Church by
Vortigern. Even if this were not so, it was certainly
one of the first manors to be given to Augustine by
Ethelbert, King of Kent. Close by the church are
the extensive ruins of the third archiepiscopal palace
we have passed since we first stepped over the Kentish
border. The palace hall, part of which still remains,
was that in which Henry VII. was entertained, and
Henry VIII. and his Court were received on their
way to the Field of the Cloth of Gold. This portion
of the ruins now serves the purposes of a barn. The
church was visited by all pilgrims on account of
its famous relic of the block on which St. John the
Baptist was beheaded. Tradition says the relic was
brought from the Holy Land by Richard Cœur de
Lion, and was given by him to either Archbishop
Baldwin, who crowned and then accompanied Richard
on a crusade, or to Archbishop Hubert Walter. The

relic remained in the church until 1590, when it was probably destroyed by a fire which left nothing but the walls standing, and even the bells were melted by the fierce heat. At Charing begins the last fourteen miles of the journey, the road passing through Westwell, Eastwell, Boughton Aluph, Godmersham and Chilham, but this last portion of the Pilgrims' Way has become much intermixed with subsidiary footpaths and field tracks. From Boughton Aluph Church the path ascending the hill is undoubtedly the true way, thence to Godmersham, another of the numerous manors that belonged to the great priory of Christ Church. At Godmersham the priors had a fine manor-house, where they frequently resided, but nothing remains of the mansion except a thirteenth-century gable and doorway with a carved figure of a prior with his mitre and crozier. The church is an interesting one of Norman date, and some venerable yews are in the churchyard. It has been fittingly said that if the traditions of Chilham were authentic, it would be the most interesting village in the kingdom. The Roman foundations and Norman octagonal keep of the Castle may be seen on application. The church contains some extraordinary seventeenth-century monuments, among them life-size marble effigies of Temperance, Fortitude, " and other moral virtues which presumably departed this life in company with certain members of the Digges family." A large yew-tree in the churchyard is said to be coeval with the foundation of the church. At Chartham Hatch, a short distance beyond Chilham, the road becomes recognisable again. It passes through Howfield Wood, then climbs a hill, and strikes into Bigberry Wood. Continuing along a field-path through hop-gardens, the ancient way soon emerges into Watling Street, along which the large bands of pilgrims journeyed to Canterbury from London, the Midlands, and the north.

All these pilgrims entered the city by the West Gate, which so narrowly escaped destruction early in the last century, when, Mr. Wombwell's menagerie caravans being unable to pass through the gateway, the civic authorities proposed to remove the gate, the fate of which was only decided at the last moment by the casting vote of the mayor.

The Church of the Holy Cross stood originally on the West Gate itself. It was taken down and rebuilt on its present site, just without the walls, by Archbishop Sudbury in 1380.

At the West Gate the Pilgrims' Road from Winchester comes to an end. The reader whose interest in this historic trackway may have been awakened or strengthened by the brief notes given in this chapter will find a wealth of historical detail, architectural descriptions, and latter-day literary and other associations, in the three books dealing with this strip of rural England to which attention has already been called, namely, " The Old Road," by Hilaire Belloc, " The Pilgrims' Way " by Julia Cartwright (Mrs. Ady), and last, but by no means least, " The Pilgrims' Road " [1] by Mr. Frank C. Elliston-Erwood. As the last-named author says : " To those that determine to set out on the journey, I can promise much hard work, trudging across ploughed fields, through lanes ankle-deep in loose sand, through trackless—and, what is worse, tracked—woods, up to the crest and down into the valley, across grassy slopes scorched in the summer sun, along ancient and gloomy avenues, with shadowy hollows not yet pierced by

[1] The Homeland Pocket Books.

Winchester to Canterbury

the weak rays that filter through the closely-matted yew branches overhead. But all this has a reward. Whether you be painter, photographer, geologist, botanist, entomologist, archæologist, antiquary, historian, *littérateur*, or the amateur in a thousand and one strange learnings, you will find on the old road something that will interest you. In short, a holiday on the road will be a little cameo of life, and it will be strange indeed if, when the dark nights of winter drive you nearer your fireside, you cannot look back to one day, at least, when you felt that life was ' living ' on the Pilgrims' Road."

CHAPTER IX

THE SHRINE OF BECKET

WITH the murder of Becket in his own Cathedral of Canterbury commenced the most extraordinary series of pilgrimages ever recorded in the annals of our island story. All the concessions the Archbishop had striven for in vain during his life were yielded to his blood-stained corpse. Canonised as a glorious martyr, his shrine received hundreds of thousands of pilgrims, whose toes have worn those cavities in the stones which the visitors to Canterbury may still behold. The most celebrated pilgrim of them all was the proud Plantagenet himself, when, with bared back and streaming tears, the regale bowed before the pontificate, and so helped to rivet the English Church with a papal supremacy, until the light of scriptural truth broke out through Wycliffe's translation of the Bible, and increased in gathering strength until it culminated in the Reformation.

The news of Becket's assassination created extraordinary excitement. After his interment crowds of the afflicted repaired to the spot in the crypt of the cathedral where the lame recovered the use of their limbs, the blind received sight, the sick were healed, and many other notable miracles, as Gervase the monk informs us, were performed.

While the enthusiasm was at its height, messenger

The Shrine of Becket

after messenger arrived in Rome with tidings of the fresh wonders, and supplications that Becket might be made a tutelary saint for the blessing and protection of England. This favour was granted by the Pope, and the 29th of December —the day of his death—was assigned to Becket in the calendar.

With his canonisation, which took place two years

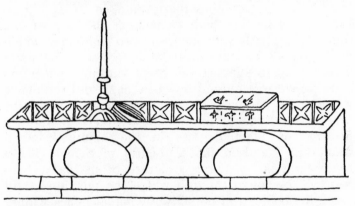

The Original Tomb of St Thomas, from the windows of Canterbury and Sens Cathedrals

and three months only after his death, Becket's shrine became, and for ages continued to be, the favourite resort of pilgrims of all countries and of all ranks.

The crypt of Canterbury Cathedral, where the remains of Becket were first laid hurriedly to rest, is a very noble one, of which each part has its own particular beauty and its own historical associations. The crypt beneath the choir was built by Prior Ernwulf, and remains practically unaltered since before the time of Becket's primacy. At the eastern

Pilgrim Life in the Middle Ages

end of this crypt, which dates from 1096, stood the altar of our Lady of Undercroft. Still farther eastwards is the crypt built since Becket's day, that extends beneath the Trinity Chapel and Becket's Crown. Against the end wall of the older crypt, which had a square and not an apsidal termination, were the altars of John the Baptist and St. Augustine, and in front of these two altars St. Thomas was buried the day after his martyrdom, in 1170. Here for fifty years his body remained, the site of his tomb being still indicated by two columns, which were placed at the head and foot of the tomb respectively to support the crypt vaulting, when the choir above was burned down in 1174 and rebuilt as we now see it during the next ten years. What the original tomb looked like we know from contemporary pictures on stained glass in the Trinity Chapel, Canterbury, and in the Cathedral of Sens. These representations depict a structure of masonry, with two oval openings through which the pilgrims could touch the coffin, and possibly the actual bones within, and it was through one of these oval openings that Henry II. thrust his head when he did his penance. On the tomb was placed a box, coloured green in the windows, which is thought to have contained the blood and brains of the saint which had been gathered up from the pavement in the transept where he fell. A tall candlestick is also shown, and a coil, which last has been conjectured to be a votive offering of wax.

For the fifty years that preceded the translation of his relics to a new shrine in 1220, there were but three " stations " at which pilgrims made their devotions. The first was in the north-west transept, where he fell, since called " the Martyrdom," from

"The Martyrdom"
Canterbury

the centre of which a column was removed so that a better view could be obtained of the hallowed spot. Here an altar was erected, called the "Altar of the Sword's Point," from the point of the sword which inflicted the last wound having been kept on it.

Here again we are fortunate in knowing what this altar looked like from a carved panel on the exterior of the south-west porch. At about the place in this transept where Becket fell a small square stone has been inserted, marking the spot where, according to tradition, a blood-stained fragment of pavement was cut out and sent to Rome as a sacred relic, but no satisfactory evidence to support the story has yet been produced.

The second station was the high altar before which the body lay all night, and the third was the tomb in the crypt. In later days, and for three centuries after his translation, there were four stations, in addition to the high altar, and possibly five if we include the sacristy, where certain minor and possibly assumed relics were shown.

The wardrobe accounts of 1299—1300, *temp.* Edward I., show that offerings were made in the King's name of 7s. at " the Altar before the image of Blessed Mary in the Undercroft, at the tomb where St. Thomas was first buried, at the Crown of the same saint, at the sword's point where the same saint underwent martyrdom, at the cloak [*clamiden*] of the same saint, and at the shrines of SS. Dunstan, Blaise, and Alphege."

The saint's body, as we have seen, was first buried at the east end of the crypt, but as money began to pour in, the monks were able to erect a more fitting shrine for so valuable a saintly asset, to which his remains were removed in 1220. The translation of the coffin was attended by the Pope's Legate, Pandulf, Cardinal of Milan, the Archbishops of Canterbury and Rheims, and an immense number of bishops and abbots.

The young King Henry III. was also present, and the reliquary or chest containing the relics was carried up the steps of Trinity Chapel by Archbishop Stephen Langton, the great patriot to whom we owe Magna Charta.

The archiepiscopal expenses were so heavy on this occasion as seriously to imperil the revenues of the see, for the primate entertained with a lavish hand " such an assemblage as never had been collected in any part of England before."

" Of bishops, and abbots, priors, and parsons,
  Of earls, and of barons, and of many knights thereto,
  Of sergeants, and of squires, and of his husbandmen enow
  And of simple men eke of the land—so thick hither drew."

Dean Farrar wrote : " The Archbishop had given two years' notice in a proclamation, circulated, not only throughout England but throughout Europe, and had given orders for maintenance to be provided for the vast multitude, not only in the city of Canterbury itself but on the various roads by which they would approach. Along the whole way from London to Canterbury hay and provender was given to all who asked, and at each gate of Canterbury, in the four quarters of the city, were placed tuns of wine to be distributed gratis, and on the day of the festival wine ran freely through the gutters of the streets."

During the two following centuries devotees to

the shrine of this most popular saint in the Romish
calendar increased daily.

> "And especially from every shire's end,
> Of Engle-land to Canterbury they wend,
> The holy blissful martyr for to seek,
> That them hath holpen when that they were sick."

Gifts and offerings poured in so fast that the shrine
became as famed for its riches as for its holiness,
and the oblations of gold and silver made by the
French pilgrims alone were incredible.

Erasmus, who visited the shrine in 1510, says :
" A coffin of wood, which covered a coffin of gold,
was drawn up by ropes and pullies, and discovered
an invaluable treasure. Gold was the meanest thing
to be seen there : all shone and glittered with the
rarest and most precious jewels of an extraordinary
bigness ; some were larger than the egg of a goose."

Beyond the Chapel of the Holy Ghost, erroneously
called Becket's Crown,[1] was to be seen " the whole
face of the blessed martyr, set in gold and adorned
with many jewels." From Erasmus we learn also
that when this glorious spectacle was offered to view,
the prior took a white wand and touched every jewel,
telling what it was, the value, and the donor of it,
for many were the gifts of great nobles and monarchs.

Louis VII. sent to this shrine the priceless jewel
called the " Regale of France," and here Edward I.
offered the golden crown of conquered Scotland.
Louis VII. also gave his cup of gold, with a yearly
rent of one hundred *muids* (hogsheads) of wine for
ever to the convent, confirming the grant by royal
charter, under his seal.

[1] The term Becket's Crown or Corona was applied to this relic,
and not to the chapel wherein it was exhibited.

The Shrine of Becket

One good result of these costly offerings was their appropriation for the rebuilding of much of the cathedral. Erasmus has also left us a description of the martyr's relics : " On the north door of the choir," he says, " the guides opened several doors, and the pilgrim beheld an immense collection of bones of all kinds—skull-bones, jaw-bones, teeth, hands, fingers, &c., which they kissed as they were severally taken out. In doing honour to the relics of Becket, they kissed the rusty point of the sword that split his skull and the fissure of the skull itself, exposed for that purpose in a silver case, and near the saint's monument were hung his hair-shirt, his belt, and clothes."

The floor of the chapel, laid down in 1220, when his remains were translated to the shrine, still remains, and is deeply worn into holes by the toes of the pilgrims who knelt on the first step of the shrine, which, together with the steps, has been completely swept away.

The martyrdom of Becket was celebrated by a jubilee every fifty years. There had been seven such jubilees before the Reformation, the last of them in 1520.

Among the more distinguished pilgrims who visited the shrine, apart from the particular penance of Henry II., were Richard I. and Louis VII. Philip, Earl of Flanders, came hither, as also did William, the great Archbishop of Rheims, and here, too, came Henry V. after his victory at Agincourt. Emanuel, Emperor of the East, and Sigismund, Emperor of the West, were also among the penitents, and here in 1520 Henry VIII. and the Emperor Charles V. knelt side by side, a striking contrast to Henry's edict of a few years later, when he appropriated the

Pilgrim Life in the Middle Ages

valuables from the shrine, caused Becket's remains to be torn from their resting-place, and his name erased from the service-books as that of a traitor.

The most remarkable event in the history of this shrine was the penance of Henry II., who, from St. Dunstan's Church, Canterbury, on July 12, 1174, set out, barefoot, and robed in the linen garb of the penitent, to seek forgiveness and absolution for his own share in the murder of the great archbishop. At the shrine of the martyr, then situated in the crypt, Henry, with his head partly thrust through one of the openings through which the actual coffin was visible, knelt and received five strokes from every bishop and abbot who was present, and three strokes from each of the eighty monks.

It is related that, as they beat him, he urged them to strike harder so as to make the penance very real, and each of them as the stroke descended, said, " As Christ was scourged for the sins of men, so be thou scourged for thine own sins."

The large patriarchal chair on which the Archbishops of Canterbury are enthroned is constructed of three large slabs of Purbeck marble, and, from the style of its ornament, is thought to have been first placed in the cathedral on July 7, 1220, for the great ceremony of the translation of Becket's remains from the crypt to the peerless shrine.

The fourth jubilee of St. Thomas, in 1370, was the occasion of a somewhat dramatic incident. Simon Sudbury, then Bishop of London, and later Archbishop of Canterbury, overtook on the London Road a vast concourse of pilgrims, whom he addressed in the following terms : " Plenary indulgence for your sins by repairing to Canterbury? Better hope might ye have of salvation had ye stayed at home

and brought forth fruits meet for repentance ! "
Thereupon a Kentish squire, Thomas of Aldon,
replied : " My lord Bishop, for that you have thus
spoken evil of St. Thomas and are minded to stir
up the minds of the people against him, I will forfeit
mine own salvation if you yourself die not a most
shameful death." With the beheading of Sudbury
on Tower Hill eleven years later the curse of Thomas
of Aldon was fulfilled. The head of Simon Sudbury
is still preserved in his native town of Sudbury,
while his body, with a leaden ball for head, lies in
a tomb on the south side of the cathedral choir of
Canterbury.

There appears to be little doubt that when the relics
of Becket were translated, only the body was placed
in the new shrine. The skull, always the most
venerated portion of a martyr's remains, was divided.
The crown of the skull was cut off and placed in
a very costly reliquary in the chapel popularly called
" Becket's Crown," the main portion being kept in
a silver reliquary that stood on the site of the place
of burial in the crypt ; and for over three hundred
years these two portions of the skull were kept in
separate shrines until they were brought together
again, when they were despoiled and the reliquaries
emptied of their contents.

The body shrine, which was famous throughout
Christendom for its magnificence, was in the Trinity
Chapel, above the crypt, the shrine being depicted
on a window of this chapel, the glass of which is
only a few years later in date than the structure
represented on it. The translation took place in
1220, while the glass is assigned to about 1230
by Mr. N. H. J. Westlake, in his " History of
Design in Painted Glass."

Pilgrim Life in the Middle Ages

When the shrine was despoiled at the Reformation, Stow tells us that " the spoil in gold and precious stones filled two great chests, such as six or seven strong men could do no more than convey one of them at once out of the church."

A strong military guard was sent to protect the treasure during its removal, and twenty-six carts were employed to take away the accumulated offerings. There is little reason to doubt that the treasure was paid over to the King, for John Williams, Master of the King's Jewels, in the November and February following the Dissolution, handed to him £13,553. The noted " Regale of France " Henry had mounted in his thumb-ring, and St. Thomas's staff came into his possession on April 27, 1540.

All those who would like to see what the original shrine of Becket was like should visit the modern Roman Catholic Church of St. Thomas at Canterbury, where the shrine placed over the altar, although it can hardly be an exact facsimile of the original, has been made up from a careful study of such early representations of it as are still preserved.

During some excavations near the site of Becket's tomb in January, 1888, some human remains were found which Dr. Farrer, the late Dean of Canterbury, considered to be without any doubt the remains of the murdered Archbishop. The coffin was discovered a few inches below the surface of the floor of the crypt, a few feet to the west of what was the original tomb of St. Thomas before his relics were enshrined.

By the character of the coffin in which they were found as well as by the place of burial, in the crypt, these remains were probably those of a saint ;

The Shrine of Becket

but that they were those of Becket is highly
improbable on a variety of grounds. If when his
shrine was despoiled the bones of St. Thomas were
gathered together and buried to save them from
insult, it is reasonable to assume that the relics would
have been hurriedly interred in some secret place, as
we know was the case with those of St. Chad, St.
Cuthbert, and a few other saints.

A coffin placed a few inches beneath so distinguished a burial-place as a crypt would seem to
indicate the interment of a saint whose burial there
was no need to hide, rather than a secreting of
such world-famed relics as those of the great Becket,
for so long as these remained in existence they would
always have been a thorn in the side of the
Reformers. Becket's position, or rather the veneration paid to his remains, was quite exceptional. He
was regarded as the Pope's champion, and his name
and the Pope's went together.

Had there been the slightest reliable evidence to
connect the more or less uninjured human bones
found in the crypt in 1888 with those of the saintly
Becket, the discovery would have been supported
by the Roman Catholic Church. As a matter of
fact it was a prominent member of this community,
the Rev. John Morris, S.J., the author of " The
Life of St. Thomas Becket," who was one of the
first to assail the theory of Dean Farrar and to
prove that although these remains may be, nay,
probably are, those of a saint (possibly St. Anselm),
they could not be the relics of the martyred Becket.
Another conjectured explanation was that the bones
were those of a monk of Christ Church, as when the
ground around the eastern end of the cathedral was
lowered some seventy years ago part of the old

cemetery of the monks was uncovered and several stone coffins exposed. The remains that were uncovered at this time are known to have been reinterred in the crypt ; but this theory has also been abandoned.

Mr. Morris furnishes an abundance of evidence, historical, religious, and surgical, some of the last named rather gruesome reading, to prove his negative—namely, that the bones were not those of Becket. We cannot follow this authoritative writer through his lengthy and minute examination of the medical evidence with which he supports his case, although a few extracts from his general arguments may be quoted at some length.

" First," he writes, " this skeleton [the one found in 1888] is very nearly entire, even the hands and feet are all there. If before this coffin was found any one had been asked whether, on the supposition that St. Thomas was buried and not burned [at the Reformation], and his bones were now to be found, it was to be expected that scarcely a bone should be wanting, the answer would have been that many places claimed to possess some relic of the body of St. Thomas, and that it would militate against any skeleton being his, if it were too complete."

" Next, any student of the history of Canterbury Cathedral would have said that if St. Thomas was buried, his bones would be found in an iron box and not in a stone coffin."

The medical examination of this assumed skull of Becket showed that although it was in several pieces the crown, except for a recent fracture, was practically uninjured, and had not been amputated.

All the early narratives describing the murder of

The Shrine of Becket

Becket agree in saying that one blow caused him to fall, and the next cut off the crown of the head.

Benedict says that "a large portion of the head was cut off." John of Salisbury records that "the crown, which was anointed with the holy chrism, was amputated." Grim tells us that "the crown, which was large, the blow so separated from the head that the blood was made white by the brain, and the brain was made red by the blood." Fitz-stephen says that "the blood and brain were drawn out by the sword from the cavity of the amputated crown."

We need not labour the point, as it is obvious that, if any reliance is to be placed on the chronicles of the above and other early writers, the head of St. Thomas, who died of these wounds, must have differed essentially from that discovered in the crypt and thought to be his.

We have already seen how the piece of bone that was cut off the top of the skull by the sword strokes was, from the time of the translation, accorded special honour in the chapel, which, possibly from the relic, was called "Becket's Crown." A fragment of the skull was sent to Rome, St. Augustine's Monastery possessed another portion, and a large number of churches all over the country claimed to possess genuine or "assumed" relics of St. Thomas of Canterbury.

Although a few contemporary writers state that Becket's remains were buried, and not burned as ordered, at the Reformation, the evidence in favour of burning is very strong, especially when we consider that neither on the accession of the Catholic Mary, nor at any other time, were the remains produced, as would have been the case if they had been in existence.

Wriothesley, Windsor Herald, says : " September, 1538. The bones of St. Thomas of Canterbury were brent in the same church by my Lord Cromwell."

Stow, whose first edition was published in 1565, says : " These bones, by commandment of the Lord Cromwell, were then and there burnt."

Holinshed, in his " Chronicles," first issued in 1577, has evidence to the same effect. " St. Augustine's Abbey," he says, " was suppressed, and the shrine and goods taken to the King's treasury, as also the shrine of Thomas Becket, in the Priory of Christ Church, was likewise taken to the King's use, and his bones, skull and all, which was there found, with a piece broken out by the wound of his death, were all burnt in the same church by the Lord Cromwell."

The proclamation ordering Becket's name to be erased from all missals and service-books was enforced with great severity, and the name was erased from the documents kept in the Canterbury archives. On December 20, 1540, Thomas Horton, *alias* Baker, Vicar of Calne, Wilts, was sent before the Privy Council by Sir Henry Long, as he was suspected as a papist owing to Thomas Becket's name being found intact in one of his service-books. The Privy Council having satisfied themselves that the vicar had " left the same unput out of negligence rather than malice," ordered him to pay forty pounds to the King. He was then dismissed " with a letter to Sir Henry Long to see the same fulfilled accordingly."

The Letter Books of Christ Church, Canterbury,

The Shrine of Becket

record many miracles at the shrine of Becket in 1394 and 1445, and Richard II. wrote to the Archbishop, expressing his thankfulness to "the High Sovereign Worker of miracles."

Miss Rotha M. Clay writes : "The kings continued to pay pilgrimage visits, and even Henry VIII. sent the accustomed offerings to Canterbury. His subsequent animosity towards St. Thomas was a political move, as is shown by the report of Robert Ward in 1535 ; having spied at the hospital of St. Thomas of Acon a window depicting the flagellation of Henry II. by monks at the shrine, he pointed out to Thomas Cromwell that Becket was slain 'in that he did resist the King.' " Bale afterwards alludes thus to this burning question :—

"A trayterouse knave ye can set upp for a saynte,
And a ryghteouse kynge lyke an odyouse tyrant paynte.
  * * * * *
In your glasse wyndowes ye whyppe your naturall kynges?"

CHAPTER X

PILGRIM INNS

THERE is every reason to believe that in early days pilgrims, like all other travellers and wayfarers, were lodged and entertained in monastic and similar houses.

Aubrey, the gossiping topographer (1678), tells us that " before the Reformation public inns were rare ; travellers were entertained at religious houses for three days together if occasion served."

The transformation from the monastic *hospitium* to the public inn was probably of slow growth, for there is no reason to doubt that those who put up at the religious houses would, if they could afford it, be expected to pay for their accommodation. At the same time, there appear to have been inns that correspond more or less to our public-houses in very early days, although we must bear in mind that the Saxon word *inne*, meaning literally a dwelling or abiding-place, was used comprehensively.

The *hospitium* was the place where travellers and strangers were entertained within the monastery itself. No one was refused admission, all were to be made welcome, especially monks, clergy, poor, and foreigners. No one was to be questioned except by the direct order of the abbot. Passing wayfarers were pressed to partake of a meal before continuing

Pilgrim Inns

their journey, and should they not have time to wait
for the common meal, food was specially prepared
for them. They were to be met by the prior or
his delegate, and after a few words of prayer by
way of salutation the kiss of peace was given and
received. Some such form of hospitality was im-
perative in the days when travelling was attended
by so much difficulty and danger. The monastery
was a religious house, a guest-house, and an infirmary
under one roof ; and when almshouses and hospitals
began to be founded the monastic infirmary plan
was retained, as may be seen with existing examples
at Chichester, Higham Ferrers, Stamford, Wells, and
Glastonbury. Many hospitals exhibited holy relics
to attract pilgrims, and indulgences were granted
to those who would contribute money to the funds
of the institutions.

The custodians of the more famous shrines and
relics had no great love for the poorer class of
pilgrims ; the monastic houses in the neighbourhood of the shrines were filled with wealthy or noble
devotees, with the result that special almshouses and
hospitals were founded and set aside mainly, if not
exclusively, for the poorer classes of wayfarers. A
good example of this type of charitable institution,
a mediæval pilgrims' inn, is the Hospital of Newark
(new work), founded in 1260 by Archbishop Boniface, for the reception of poor travellers, and in
particular for such pilgrims as passed through Maidstone on their way to the shrine of Becket at
Canterbury. The hospital chapel, after being used
for many years as a storeroom, has been restored
and again fitted for worship as St. Peter's Church.
In 1395 the ancient hospital was, by Archbishop
Courtenay, incorporated with a college of secular

priests, and of this foundation there are considerable architectural remains. The college was dissolved about 1538, the existing buildings being in private occupation. These comprise a fine gateway (see illustration), a long range of rooms between it and the river, and a tower guarding the river approach. On the right of the gateway is the master's house, on the left a wing where the bakehouse and other domestic offices once stood. No traces of the cloisters remain. The fine apartment above the crown of the gateway arch is now used by the local lodge of Freemasons.

Before reaching Maidstone to partake of the hospitality of Archbishop Boniface, the pilgrims journeying from London found food and lodging at the ancient guesten-house of Malling Abbey, just without the gates of the quadrangle. The guest-house still remains, with some good windows and a traceried frieze. The building has a large fireplace marking that portion of it which was once the kitchen and later the refectory of the pilgrims. The oaken roof is supported at one end by two grotesque corbels of Kentish ragstone. Over the outer side of the door are a series of shields, on which are carved the symbols of the Passion—the Crown of Thorns, the Hammer, Nails, and the rest. The attached chapel, built for the use of the pilgrims, was restored about the middle of the last century, prior to which it had been used for a variety of secular purposes. At the opposite end of the gatehouse is the pilgrims' bath, with steps leading down to the water, which was supplied from the fishpond. One of the numerous legends attaching to the gatehouse is to the effect that after the murder of Becket the guilty knights on their flight from Canterbury halted

THE BONIFACE HOSPITAL, MAIDSTONE.

Pilgrim Inns

beneath the gateway and asked the nuns for food, which was set out in the refectory ; but before the fugitives could be seated unseen hands scattered the food on the floor. The knights fled from the spot in terror, leaving the sisters amazed at so strange an occurrence, until the mystery was solved when the news of the Archbishop's death reached the abbey.

It is probable that between the *hospitium* of the monastery and the special pilgrim-house there was an intermediate stage, for the *hospitia* at St. Mary's, York, and the " Strangers' Hall " at Winchester were within the monastic precincts. A little later we find the isolation complete, as at Battle (*circa* 1076), where, situated outside the walls, was " the house of the pilgrims which is called the hospital."

During the twelfth century St. Bartholomew's Hospital, Smithfield, was much resorted to by sick pilgrims. Miss Rotha M. Clay writes : " The year 1170 marks an epoch, ushering in the great pilgrimage within and towards England. When the shrine of St. Thomas of Canterbury became the goal of pious wayfarers it was necessary to find accommodation for them. The hospitals of Canterbury and Southwark bearing the martyr's name were among the earliest. Within a few years such houses (often called *Domus Dei*) were founded in most southern ports and along the pilgrims' way, as at Dover, Ospringe, and Maidstone. . . . Norfolk, like Kent, was studded with houses of charity, especially near the highway to Walsingham. Thirteen pilgrims were lodged at Bec, near Billingford. At Thetford there was a hospital near the passage of the river."

In the reign of Edward I. the fine old building still known as the " Strangers' Hall " at Winchester

Pilgrim Life in the Middle Ages

was built at their convent gate by the monks of St. Swithin's Priory for the reception of poor pilgrims visiting the shrine of St. Swithin, the great healing bishop. The great hall where the pilgrims slept, ate their meals, and drank their ale is subdivided and now forms part of the Deanery, and the present entrance, beneath three beautiful pointed arches, was the Prior's door, where the same pilgrims would receive alms and food to sustain them on their way to the next celebrated shrine.

St. John's House, or the Hospital of St. John, in the same fair city, was re-founded by John Devenish for " the sole relief of sick and lame soldiers, poor pilgrims, and necessitated wayfaring men, to have their lodging and diet gratis there, for one night or longer, as their inability to travel might require." Most of the seaports that would be used by pilgrims travelling towards Canterbury made similar provision for poor wayfarers ; and portions of these old foundations still remain, although in some instances much modernised. At Southampton and Dover there was a Domus Dei, the authorities of which permitted an annual expenditure of £28 for hospitality to be given " to wayfarers and strangers from beyond the sea."

At Sandwich the Hospital of St. John was founded in 1280. The brothers were a very poor community, who were allowed to beg down by the ships. At the back of the almshouses was a building called the " Harbinge," where poor pilgrims were lodged.

The chapel of the Domus Dei at Southampton, dedicated to St. Julian (the Hospitaller, not the Bishop), is now used as the French Protestant Church, and although restored has retained much of its Norman character. Within it were buried Lord

Pilgrim Inns

Scrope, the Earl of Cambridge, and Sir Thomas Grey, who were hanged outside the Bar Gate for their share in the conspiracy against Henry V. Of the old Domus Dei at Portsmouth, founded by Peter de Rupibus in the reign of Henry III., only the beautiful early English chapel remains. This was restored by Street in 1866 and is now the garrison chapel of Portsmouth.

Canterbury naturally had many of these charitable institutions for those who could not afford the fashionable quarters of " the Chequers," and to whom the hospitality of the wealthy priory of Christ Church or of the Abbey of St. Augustine would not be extended. The Hospital of St. Thomas the Martyr, now generally known as King's Bridge Hospital, was founded and endowed by Archbishop Hubert Walter (1193-1205) for the reception of pilgrims to the shrine of St. Thomas, when the food supplied was limited to a cost of fourpence a day for each pilgrim, who was also given a night's lodging. Stephen Langton (1207-29) was a great benefactor to the foundation, which is still one of the most important charities in the city. At the visitation of Cardinal Archbishop Pole (1556-8) it was recorded that : " They are bound to receive wayfaring and hurt men, and to have eight beds for men and four for women to remain for a night, and more if they be not able to depart ; and the Master of the Hospital is charged with the burial ; and they have twenty loads of wood yearly allowed, and twenty-six shillings a year for drink." In the reign of Elizabeth, Archbishop Parker enlarged the foundation and added a school, but the latter has fallen into abeyance. It appears that, apart from their charitable and scholastic duties, the authori-

Pilgrim Life in the Middle Ages

ties of this hospital were required to keep the East or King's Bridge in good repair.

The foundation had the right of burying such pilgrims as died there in that portion of the cathedral churchyard which was set apart for the interment of pilgrims. The registers, which date from the early years of the sixteenth century, record that sixpence a week was spent on beer for the poor guests, twenty shillings a year for the poor woman who waited upon them, and £10 6s. 8d. for a chantry priest. Part of the revenues were paid in kind, such as the " cocks and hens " paid for the rent of hospital lands in the Forest of Blean. The sum total was a rather inconvenient quantity : " Sum total of the cocks and hens, a hundred and nineteen, *and a third part of a hen, and a half of a hen.*" Eventually this " poultry " payment was compounded for in money, a cock being estimated as equivalent to 2½d. and a hen valued at 3d.

Chaucer does not mention the name of the Canterbury hostel at which the pilgrims alighted at their journey's end ; and it is from the author of the " Epilogue " that we first hear of the " Chequer of the Hope," [1] which is said to have been the most frequented of all the inns of the city. The building, portions of which still stand at the corner of High Street and Mercery Lane, has been much altered and pulled about, although as recently as 1845 the greater part of the old hostelry was intact. The old Merceria was rebuilt by Prior Chillenden about 1400, and here were the rows of stalls and booths for the sale of pilgrims' tokens and other trifles of a like nature.

[1] The chessboard on the *hoop*-(barrel), an intimation that games and drink were provided.

Pilgrim Inns

The position of the inn, near the entrance to the cathedral, would make it a convenient centre. The spacious cellars with vaulted roofs may still be seen ; but the inner courtyard and the great dormitory

THE CHEQUER OF THE HOPE, CANTERBURY.
(From an old print.)

of a hundred beds were burned down some thirty years ago. The old street front, however, with its broad overhanging eaves, makes a mute appeal, and so renders Mercery Lane one of the most attractive corners of Canterbury. That it was a galleried inn is certain, for Gostling, in his " Walk Round Canter-

Pilgrim Life in the Middle Ages

bury," mentions a wooden staircase that led originally to the gallery round three sides of the inner court.

The description of the arrival of Chaucer's party, written apparently not long after Chaucer's death, and printed by Urry, tells us how the pilgrims arrived in Canterbury at " myd-morowe " (in the middle of the forenoon), and took up their lodgings at the " Chequer ". :—

> "They toke their in and loggit them at mydmorowe I trowe
> Atte cheker of the hope, that many a man doth knowe."

After Harry Bailey, the host of Southwark, had ordered dinner for his merry troop, they all proceeded to pay their devotions at the shrine of St. Thomas. At the cathedral door they were sprinkled with holy water :—

> "Then at chirch dore the curtesy gan to ryse,
> Tyl the knyght, of gentilness that knewe right wele the guyse,
> Put forth the prelatis, the parson and his fere.
> A monk, that took the spryngill with a manly chere,
> And did as the manere is, moilid al their patis,
> Everich aftir othir, righte as they were of statis."

The knight and some companions went direct to pay their devotions at the various " stations," but others began to wander about the nave, while the miller entered into a warm discussion concerning the armorial bearings displayed on some of the painted windows.

At length the host of Southwark asserted his authority, called the party together, and reprimanded them for their negligence ; whereupon they hastened to make their offerings : —

Pilgrim Inns

"Then passid they forth boystly gogling with their hedis
Knelid adown to-fore the shrine, and hertlich their bedis
They preyd to Seint Thomas, in such wyse as they couth ;
And sith the holy relikes ech man with his mowith
Kissid, as a goodly monk the names told and taught.
And sith to othir places of holynes they raught,
And were in their devocioune tyl service were al doon."

As noon approached they bought *signs of Canter-*

ROOM IN THE CHEQUER OF THE HOPE, CANTERBURY.
(From an old print.)

bury brooches, and returned to the " Chequer " for
dinner.

After the meal they changed their garments and
went forth to " sport and pley " them, " eche man
as hym list," until supper-time.

Pilgrim Life in the Middle Ages

The knight, with an eye to his profession of arms, and accompanied by his son, went to examine the fortifications :—

"The knyght with his meyné went to se the walle
And the wardes of the town, as to a knyght befalle ;
Devising ententflich the strengthis al about,
And apointid to his sone the perell and the dout
For shot of arblast and of bowe, and eke for shot of gonne,
Unto the wardis of the town, and how it might be wonne
And al defence ther-ageyn, aftir his intent
He declarid compendiously, and al that evir he ment."

The monk, accompanied by the parson and the friar, went to visit a mutual friend, and to sample his wines ; while the ladies remained at home, and visited the garden of their hostess of the " Chequer " :—

"The wyfe of Bath was so wery she had no wyl to walk,
She toke the priores by the honde, 'Madame, wol ye stalk
Pryvely into the garden to se the herbis growe,
And aftir with our hostis wife in hir parlour rowe ?
I wol gyve yewe the wyne, and ye shul me also,
For tyl we go to soper we have naught ellis to do.'
The priores, as woman taught of gentil blood and hend,
Assentid to hir counsel, and forth gon they wend,
Passyng forth softtly into the herbery."

The other pilgrims amused and entertained themselves in a variety of ways. The supper ended in mirth and jollity, which lasted " tyl the tyme that it was well within eve." The more sober of the company retired early to rest ; but the noisy ones continued to drink and " jangle," until those in their beds became annoyed at the disturbance and persuaded them to go to rest :—

"Save the pardoner, that drew apart, and weytid by a cheste,
For to hide hymself till the candill wer out."

Pilgrim Inns

With the "candill" out the pardoner stole away to pursue a low amour.

In the morning the knight and all the fellowship set forth homeward as the sun began to draw upward. The host of Southwark suggested that they should not cast lots to decide who should tell the next story, as some of the revellers might still be feeling the effects of the previous evening's libations, or, in the words of the host, from their having been "semi-boozy over-eve."

Another favourite gathering-place of the Canterbury pilgrims was the great priory of Christ Church, while royal visitors were lodged in St. Augustine's Abbey. For ordinary strangers at Christ Church there was the Guesten Chamber, repaired and enlarged early in the fifteenth century by Prior Chillenden, since when it has borne the name of "Chillenden's Guest Chamber," which now forms part of the Bishop of Dover's house. Here the statutes of Archbishop Winchelsea provided that poor pilgrims should be fed daily with fragments of bread and meat, while another privilege granted by the Prior to pilgrims of all ranks and nationality, who might die at Canterbury, was that of burial at Christ Church, under the shadow of the cathedral walls.

Many pilgrims to Canterbury would doubtless call at the famous Leper Hospital of St. Nicholas, situated on the London Road, one mile from the city. Halting at the hospital, which was founded by Lanfranc in 1084, they would be offered certain relics to kiss, and would probably drink a cup of water from the holy well. The existing building, although partly rebuilt with brick in the reign of James II., contains a considerable portion of the original Norman structure, while the interior walls are covered with a number of

Pilgrim Life in the Middle Ages

old fresco paintings. A curious feature of the church is the downward slope of the floor from the altar to the west doorway. The same thing is observable at Shaftesbury, and in many of those churches built to accommodate large bodies of pilgrims. In many of the churches the pilgrims, with clothing, feet, and bodies covered with the dust and filth of the journey, would spend the whole night before the hallowed shrine or saintly relic, with the consequence that the necessity arose of devising some simple method for flushing the floor with water. At Harbledown the slope of the floor would allow the water to drain off after the lepers had attended Mass in the church.

Guernes du Pont St. Mayence, an Anglo-Norman poet who wrote a metrical Life of Becket immediately after the primate's death, relates an interesting anecdote to the effect that when, in 1174, Henry II. made his memorable pilgrimage to Canterbury, he stopped at Harbledown, and " for the love of St. Thomas he gave in grant twenty marks of rent to the poor house." From the hospital he walked barefoot to do penance at the shrine of Becket. The following extract is from the contemporary MS. in the British Museum :—

> " Juste Cantorbire unt lepros un hospital,
> U mult ad malades de gent plein de mal ;
> Près une liwe i ad del mustier principal,
> Là ù li cors saint gist del mire espirital
> Ki manit dolent ad mis en joie e en estal.
>
> Dunc descendi iluec li reis à Herebaldun,
> E entra el mustier, e a fet sa oreison,
> De trestuz ses mesferz ad requis Deu pardun ;
> Pur amur Saint Thomas a otrie en dun
> Vint marchies de rentes à la povre maison."

Some interesting relics are preserved in the

Pilgrim Inns

hospital, including the famous " Erasmus " money, or
alms-box, of which tradition gives the following
account. When Erasmus visited the hospital in the
company of Dean Colet, one of the brethren presented
a holy relic, a portion of Becket's shoe, for the
travellers to kiss before being sprinkled with holy
water. The dean declined the proffered favour with
such an outburst of wrathful rhetoric that the
courteous Erasmus must needs made amends by
dropping a goodly donation into the box, at that time
fastened by a chain, of which a few links remain,
to a tree near the hospital gate, or at the end of a
long pole, so that the passer-by might give his donation at a safe distance from the infected lepers.

The well at Harbledown is commonly called the
Black Prince's Well, according to the popular tradition that water from it was sent to the hero of
Poictiers when on his deathbed at Canterbury. This
tradition is unsupported by evidence, while the fact
that the Black Prince did not die at Canterbury is
entirely against the supposition. It may, however,
be connected with the prince in another way, for after
the battle above referred to the Prince and his
prisoner, King John of France, passed through
Harbledown (April 19, 1357) on their way to Canterbury and London, when they may have been refreshed with a cup of water at the well. Be this as it
may, the keystone of the semicircular arch above it
bears, in somewhat deep carving, the well-known
cognisance of the Prince—the three feathers and the
motto, *Ich Dien*, but there is no evidence to show
when the stone was inserted or the motto cut upon
it. A woodcut of the well made in 1845 shows
neither feathers nor motto.

The " Tabard," or, as it was called in later times,

Pilgrim Life in the Middle Ages

the " Talbot," at Southwark, was the great London
starting-point for the Canterbury pilgrims in the
days when every other building in Southwark appears
to have been either a brewery or an inn.   The vast

THE TABARD INN, SOUTHWARK.
(*By permission of Mr. Philip Norman, F.S.A.*)

number of Southwark inns has been attributed
to the large amount of accommodation required
for those travellers who arrived after the gates of the
bridge had been closed, and had perforce to wait
until the morning before they could enter the city.

Pilgrim Inns

Canterbury is more fortunate than Southwark, as portions at any rate of the "Chequer" may reasonably be supposed to remain, whereas all traces of the original "Tabard" had disappeared for centuries before the modern public-house that occupied the site was sold in 1865, and finally pulled down about 1886.

It must be confessed that the early history of the "Tabard" is not of a very engrossing kind, and had it not been for Chaucer, to whom it owed all its fame, it is doubtful if its history would have ever been written. As the authors (William Rendle, F.R.C.S., and Philip Norman, F.S.A.) of "The Inns of Old Southwark" say : "The 'Tabard' owes all its fame to the fact that it was depicted by Chaucer as the place of assemblage for his Canterbury pilgrims."

> "In Southwerk at the Tabard as I lay
> Redy to wenden on my pilgrimáge
> To Caunterbury with ful devout coráge,
> At night was come into that hostelrie
> Wel nyne and twenty in a companye,
> Of sondry folk, by aventûre i-falle
> In felawschipe, and pilgryms were thei alle,
> That toward Caunterbury wolden ryde."

A good view of the inn, with the pilgrims setting out on their journey, is given in Urry's "Chaucer," published in 1721 ; and if absolute reliance could be placed on this woodcut we should have much to compensate us for the loss of the actual building. The print shows a range of low buildings with a swinging sign across the roadway, and what appears to be stone steps leading to the galleries, which, in hostels of this character, were placed on three sides of the yard. It is possible that the woodcut was based on or copied from an older drawing ; but the fact remains that the original " Tabard " of Chaucer's day was burned to the ground half a century before the publication of Urry's book. This fire of 1676 left nothing but the foundations, on which, in 1681, a new Tabard Inn sprang up.

In 1865, what remained of the Carolean inn, which

THE TABARD INN, SOUTHWARK.
(From Urry's Chaucer.)

had in its turn been patched and altered over and over again, was advertised for sale as the " Tabard Inn, the scene of the opening of Chaucer's Canterbury Pilgrimage." The question of its being retained on national grounds was raised in the *Times*, when the conclusion reached was that nothing remained sufficiently authentic to justify its retention as a genuine relic of old London.

" The Rood of Barmsey " (Bermondsey Abbey)

Pilgrim Inns

would doubtless be visited by many pilgrims before setting out on their long journey to the shrine of Becket. John Paston, in 1465, prays " his mother to visit the North Door and St. Saviour at Bermondsey, and take his sister Margery to pray for a good husband ere she come home again."

The route taken by the London pilgrims would be along what is now the Old Kent Road, through Kent Street, and by the Bars and the Lock, the streamlet of St. Thomas a Watering. This " waterynge of Seint Thomas " was just beyond the second milestone on the road to Kent. It was a recognised place of execution, and the first halting-place of Chaucer's pilgrims.

If the " Tabard " of Southwark has vanished utterly, and the " Chequer of the Hope " is in almost equally bad case, we have fortunately at Glastonbury a late but good example of a pilgrims' inn which remains much as when it was first erected. At Winchcombe, in Gloucestershire, considerable portions of the pilgrims' inn remain. The New Inn at Gloucester is a galleried inn that is said to have been built to accommodate the pilgrims who visited the tomb of Edward II. ; and the " Bell " at Tewkesbury makes a similar claim. All along the roads that led to the great shrines a certain amount of accommodation for travellers must have been provided ; and if they could be definitely located through the veil of modernity that has descended over them, old pilgrims' inns would be found to have existed along the roads that led to Hayles, Walsingham, Gloucester, Glastonbury, and Canterbury.

The old George Inn at Salisbury still stands in High Street, although no longer used as a hostelry. A doorway in the yard and a few other portions of the structure have been said to date back to the time of Edward II. The gateway, of ornamental woodwork, has been assigned to the fifteenth century, and two large projecting bay windows should be noticed. The inn is thought to have been built to accommodate the pilgrims who came to visit the shrine of St. Osmund in the neighbouring cathedral. That it was a flourishing hostelry in the coaching days there is abundant evidence, and Pepys records having paid an exorbitant sum for the luxury of " a silken bed and a very good diet."

The " George " or the Pilgrims' Inn at Glastonbury is unquestionably the best example we have of a building erected for the housing of pilgrims, and one which recent research has provided with a touch of romance. The inn was built originally as a hostel for pilgrims resorting to the abbey and its famous shrines, and in 1490 was, together with two plots of land on the north side, given by Abbot Selwood to the chamberlain of the abbey. The interior has naturally been somewhat modernised for the benefit of the modern pilgrims to Glastonbury ; but the front is a very decorative piece of building, richly ornamented with shields of arms, carvings, and the other architectural conceits of the fifteenth century. The majority of the windows are later insertions. The clock bracket that now supports a heavy stone sign was copied by the builder of " Napper's Mite," Dorchester, a charming little almshouse erected in 1615. For many years there existed at Glastonbury traditions and legends relating to the secret passages without and within the abbey precincts. One of the most persistent of these rather scandalous rumours alleged that an underground passage led from the Pilgrims' Inn to either the Abbey gates or

The Pilgrims'
Inn, Glastonbury

Sidney Heath.

Pilgrim Life in the Middle Ages

the Abbot's dwelling. From time to time many archæologists, attracted by so romantic a legend, have inspected the cellars and other portions of the inn without result, and have denied the truth of the tradition. Warner, who wrote a history of the town and abbey in the nineteenth century, mentions the passage, which furnishes him with an excuse to suggest that it was used by the abbots for the purpose of visiting ladies staying at the Pilgrims' Inn. During the past few months Mr. Bligh Bond, who is in charge of the excavations at the abbey, came across an old journal containing the following reference to the inn :—

"Under the house is a vault which leads into the abbey, so low that a man must crawl on his knees to pass it ; but there are benches, or little narrow places, to rest the elbows on, in order to ease the knees. It comes out into a large vaulted place, used for a cellar, and after about five or six paces turns aside to the right into another passage, high enough for a man to walk upright ; this passage is about five or six paces long, and leads to a flight of steps which conducted privately to the abbot's chamber."

Having discovered something definite, a precise description by some one who had evidently traversed the passage in question, Mr. Bligh Bond lost no time in asking the permission of the proprietors of the building to make a thorough examination of the premises. After a close scrutiny of the cellar walls some traces of what appeared to be a low filled-in archway were discovered. At this point the masonry was attacked with a crowbar, with the result that before many stones had been removed the opening of a small tunnel was fully revealed.

Pilgrim Inns

Further examination showed that the passage corresponded exactly with the description given in the old journal ; the stone elbow rests were there, and a drainage channel for water was found in the centre of the floor. The passage has been proved to take a downward course, and then continues on an upward slope beneath the High Street, south-west towards the abbey gates and monastic buildings. The air was very foul, but the explorers were able to penetrate some distance along the passage until a solid obstruction barred their further progress. At the time of writing (June, 1911) it has been decided to try and locate the passage from the abbey end.

The contributor of a short account of the discovery to the *Western Morning News* of June 14, 1911, writes as follows : —

" Although not generally known, what may have been a portion of the passage was revealed some years ago. At the north-east corner of the Abbey enclosure is a house built on the site of some of the ancient monastic buildings, and known as ' St. Dunstan's.' Some years ago the then owner of St. Dunstan's was having alterations made in the basement of the house, when the workmen broke into a large, dark place, which had all the appearance of an underground passage. This was examined for a short distance, and was found to be empty, save for a few small objects which were found upon the floor, amongst them being an ancient lamp. On a report of the discovery being made to the occupier of the house, she gave orders that it must be sealed up, and this was accordingly done before any one possessing antiquarian knowledge had any chance of investigating it."

The hospitals, commanderies, and preceptories

founded by the military orders—*i.e.*, by the Knights Hospitallers and the Knights Templars—have been purposely omitted from this chapter, although both orders were the recognised guardians of travellers and pilgrims, and the charitable work of their foundations had many points of similarity to the humbler kind of wayfarers' hospitals.

It is curious to notice that just as many churches were re-dedicated at the Reformation, so the names of many old hostels and taverns were altered; and it is very interesting to note how such comparative trifles as inn signs were affected by the spirit of the Reformed religion. At the same time, we have many examples of the tavern nomenclature of pre-Reformation days. Have we not all at some time or other in our wanderings through rural England, found entertainment and refreshment at a " Salutation " village inn? The only salutation to justify such a title to-day is that which is exchanged between the thirsty traveller and the landlord; but in its original form this was the " Hail, Mary! " or Salutation of the Blessed Virgin. The signboards of these inns usually depicted the Annunciation, and one of the best known hotels in the Lake Country displays such a sign to this day. At the Reformation the figure of the Virgin was erased, or painted over, but that of the angel Gabriel was left on the board, so that the old tavern, which had for centuries rejoiced in the name " Salutation," was by a simple and easy step to come down to us as the " Angel," a name common all over the country. We have many other survivals of a similar nature, such as the " Cross Keys," the symbolical keys of heaven, and the attributes of St. Peter. The " Cardinal's Hat " was very popular with the John Barleycorns of ancient days, when the great Cardinal Wolsey was at the height of his power, and although now generally extinct it was the sign of a well-known tavern that stood in Lombard Street in 1459. We have also doubtless refreshed the inner man at some " Pope's Head," or " Pope's Arms " taverns, of both of which several remain, in name. In 1636, nearly a century after the Reformation, there were four " Pope's Head " taverns in London, the most famous being that in Cornhill, dating possibly from the reign of Edward III., and certainly from that of Edward IV. This remained until 1856, when it was pulled down.

This " Pope's Head " on Cornhill was situated in Pope's Head Alley, a thoroughfare still existing opposite the Royal Exchange ; and, as Stow tells us, there was a " Cardinal's Hat " tavern in the same alley, the Papacy was well represented in the topographical and tavern nomenclature of Cornhill. The " Pope's Head " in Cornhill is mentioned in the fourth year of Edward IV. (1464) in the account of a wager between an Alicant goldsmith and an English rival; the foreigner contending that " Englishmen were not so cunning in workmanship of goldsmithry as Alicant strangers." Stow, however, puts the date of the actual house much earlier than this. He says: " This Pope's Head tavern and other houses adjoining, strongly built of stone, hath of old time been all in one pertaining to some great estate or rather the King of this Realm." Stow's evidence for this statement is that the Arms of England, as they were borne previous to the reign of Edward III., were " fair and largely engraven on a stone towards the High Street." Pepys refers to a fine panelled room in the tavern in 1668-9, and here on April 14,

Pilgrim Life in the Middle Ages

1718, Quin, the actor, killed, in self-defence, his fellow-comedian, Bowen.

In the old ballad " London Lyckpenny " it is stated that in the reign of Richard II. wine was sold at the " Pope's Head " at one penny a pint, with bread included. It is related how a traveller coming to Cornhill, the wine-drawer of the tavern takes the man by the hand and says, " Will you drink a pint of wine? " whereunto the country-man replies : " A penny spend I may," and so drank the wine. This is Stow's version. In the ballad the taverner, not the drawer, solicits the man's custom, and the latter, instead of getting the bread for nothing, complains of having to go away hungry.

> " The taverner took me by the sleeve,
>   ' Sir,' saith he, ' will you our wine assay ? '
> I answered, ' That cannot me much grieve,
>   A penny can do no more than it may ' ;
>   I drank a pint, and for it did pay ;
> Yet sore a hungered from thence I yede,
> And wanting money I could not speid."

There is still at Lytchett Minster, Dorset, an old inn called " Peter's Finger," on the signboard of which is a representation of the saint holding up one hand from which the blood is dripping. The title " Peter's Finger," however, does not refer to a saintly relic or mutilation, being merely a corruption of *St. Peter-ad-Vincula* (St. Peter in Chains), a term applied to certain lands or manors, some-times called Lammas Lands, the occupants of which had to perform on St. Peter's Day (which corres-ponds with our Lammas Day, August 1st) prædial service as a condition of their holdings. The chapel

Pilgrim Inns

within the precinct or liberty of the Tower of London is dedicated to St. Peter-ad-Vincula, a title that is also given to a small tract of land lying between Salisbury and Alderbury.

One of the signs under which some famous old taverns did a thriving business was the "Mitre," of which the *doyen* was that in Mitre Court, Fleet Street, one of Dr. Johnson's favourite haunts, where Goldsmith and his contemporaries used to meet for literary and other, less dry, .refreshment. There are possibly more "Mitre" taverns of historical interest than those of any other name. In the "Quack Vintners," 1712, the reason given for the partiality shown by innkeepers for this sign is explained as follows:—

> "May Smith, whose prosperous Mitre is his sign,
> To show the Church no enemy to wine,
> Still draw such Christian liquor none may think,
> Tho' e'er so pious, 'tis a sin to drink."

Of "Saints" inn-signs we have several, in addition to those whereon are depicted the national saints —St. George, St. Andrew, St. Patrick, and St. David. The "Cat and Wheel" is a curious corruption of the Catherine Wheel, intended originally as an emblem of the instrument by which St. Catherine was martyred. St. Martin, the vintners' patron saint, has fallen from the high place he once held among tavern signs, and with him have gone St. Dunstan, St. Luke, and the celestial hierarchy whose individual forms and emblems were once almost as prominent on inn-signs as they were in churches. In conclusion, we should remember that old hostels and inns bearing the above signs over the city pavements or

Pilgrim Life in the Middle Ages

amid the trees of the village may, many of them, have refreshed the weary pilgrim of other days, as they refresh the equally weary pilgrim of to-day. They are not hotels or restaurants. They are taverns, and they are English.

CHAPTER XI

THE BOXLEY ROOD OF GRACE

FOR the mechanical working image we have no need to go abroad, for one of the most ingenious of these working *automata*, the Boxley Rood of Grace, adorned an English Cistercian Church, founded at Boxley, near Maidstone, in 1144, by William de Ipres, Earl of Kent. This rood or crucifix is said by tradition to have been brought to Boxley by a horse which had strayed from its owner. The monks told themselves that this was a miracle and laid claim to the object, which is thus described in the " Perambulation of Kent," written in 1570, by William Lambarde :—

" But now if I shoulde leave Boxley, the favourers of false and feyned Religion would laugh in their sleeves, and the followers of God's trueth might justly cry out and blame me.

" For it is yet freshe in mind to bothe sides, and shall (I doubt not) to the profite of the one, be continued in perpetuall memorie to all posterite, by what notable imposture, fraud, juggling, and Legierdemain, the sillie lambs of God's flocke were (not long since) seduced by the false Romish foxes of the Abbay.

" The manner wherof, I will set downe, in such sorte onely, as the same was sometime by themselves published in print for their estimation and credite,

227

and yet remaineth deepely ᴸ⸱printed in the minds
and memories of many on live, and to their ever-
lasting reproche, shame, and confusion.

" It chaunced (as the tale is) that upon a time
a cunning Carpenter of our country was taken
prisoner in the warres betweene us and Fraunce,
who (wanting otherwise to satisfie for his raunsome),
and having good leysure to devise for his deliver-
ance, thought it best to attempt some curious enter-
prise, within the compasse of his own Art and skill,
to make himselfe some money withall: And therefore, getting togither fit matter for his purpose, he
compacted of wood, wyer, paste, and paper, a
Roode of such exquisite Art and excellencie, that it
not onely matched in comelynesse and due proportion of the partes the best of the common sorte;
but in straunge motion, variety of gesture, and
nimbleness of joints, passed al other that before
had been seene; the same being able to bow downe
and lifte up it selfe, to shake and stirre the handes
and feete, to nod the head, to rolle the eies, to wag the
chaps, to bende the browes, and finally to represent
to the eie, both the proper motion of each member
of the body, and also a lively, expresse, and significant shew of a well contented or displeased minde;
byting the lippe, and gathering a frowning, forward,
and disdainful face, when it would pretend offence:
and shewing a moste milde, amyable, and smyling
cheere and countenaunce, when it woulde seeme to
be well pleased.

" So that now it needed not Prometheus fire to
make it a lively man, but onely the helpe of the
covetous Priests of Bell, or the aide of some craftie
College of Monkes, to deifie and make it passe for
a verie God.

The Boxley Rood of Grace

" This done, he made shifte for his libertie, came over into this Realme, of purpose to utter his merchandize, and laide the Image upon the backe of a Jade that he drave before him.

" Now when hee was come so farre as to Rochester on his way, hee waxed drie by reason of travaile, and called at an alehouse for drinke to refreshe him, suffering his horse neverthelesse to go forwarde alone along the Citie:

" This Jade was no sooner out of sight, but hee missed the streight westerne way that his Maister intended to have gone, and turning Southe, made a great pace toward Boxley, and being driven (as it were) by some divine furie, never ceased jogging tell he came at the Abbay church doore, where he so beat and bounced with his heeles, that divers of the Monkes heard the noise, came to the place to knowe the cause, and (marvelling at the straungenesse of the thing) called the Abbatt and his Convent to beholde it.

" These good men seeing the horse so earnest, and discerning what he had on his backe, for doubt of deadly impietie opened the doore: which they had no sooner done, but the horse rushed in, and ran in great haste to a pillar (which was the verie place where this Image was afterwarde advaunced) and there stopped himselfe, and stoode still.

" Now while the Monkes were busie to take off the lode, in commeth the Carpenter (that by great inquisition had followed) and he challenged his owne: the Monkes loth to lose so benificiall a stray, at first made some deniall, but afterward, being assured by all signes that he was the verie Proprietarie, they graunt him to take it with him.

" The Carpenter then taketh the horse by the

head, and first assayeth to leade him out of the
Church, but he would not stirre for him: Then
beatheth hee and striketh him, but the Jade was so
restie and fast nailed that he woulde not once remoove
his foote from the pillar: at the last he taketh off the
Image, thinking to have carried it out by selfe, and
then to have led the horse after: but that also
cleaved so fast to the place, that notwithstanding
all that ever he (and the Monkes also, which at
length were contented for pities sake to helpe him)
coulde doe, it woulde not be mooved one inch from
it: So that in the ende partly from wearinesse in
wrestling, and partly by persuasion of the Monkes,
which were in love with the Picture, and made him
beleeve that it was by God himselfe destinate to their
house, the Carpenter was contented for a piece of
money to go his way, and leave the Roode behinde
him.

"Thus you see the generation of this the great
God of Boxley, comparable (I warrant you) to the
creation of that beastly Idoll Priapus, of which the
poet saith:—

> "'A figtree blocke sometime I was,
>   A log unmeete for use:
> Till Carver doubting with himselfe,
>   Wert best make Priapus,
> Or else a benche? resolv'd at last
>   To make a God of mee:
> Thenceforth a God I am of birdes,
>   And theeves most drad, you see.'

"But what? I shall not neede to reporte, howe
lewdly these Monkes, to their owne enriching and
the spoile of God's people, abused this wooden God
after they had thus gotten him, bicause a good sort

The Boxley Rood of Grace

be yet on live that sawe the fraude openly detected at Paules Crosse, and others may reade it disclosed in bookes yet extant, and commonly abroad."

The figure was worked by hidden mechanism and its movements were regarded as miraculous.

From the account given in Foxe's "Book of Martyrs," it appears that the image was capable of assuming every kind of facial expression, according to the value of the offering tendered. A piece of silver, we are told, was received with frowning lip, but a piece of gold caused the "jaws to wag merrily." Many other picturesque details grew up around this wonderful figure, as that it could foam at the mouth, weep from the eyes, and raise its hands in blessing. However, when the monastery was dissolved by Henry VIII., certain curious folk discovered that the figure was full of cleverly concealed wires, of which Foxe tells us there were a hundred, but Foxe, honest man though he was, may have exaggerated.

Be this as it may, the miraculous rood which had bowed its head, and stirred its eyes, was paraded through the roads from market town to market town, exhibited as a piece of jugglery before the Court, exposed to ridicule at Maidstone and St. Paul's Cross, and eventually was publicly burned, together with many images of the Virgin and saints.

Latimer, when sending the image of the Virgin to London from his own Cathedral of Worcester to be burned, is recorded as having exclaimed : " She with her old sister of Walsingham, her younger sister of Ipswich, and their two other sisters of Doncaster and Penrice, would make a jolly muster at Smithfield." Burnet, in his " History of the Reformation," tells us that when one of the effigies of the

Virgin in Worcester Cathedral came to be unfrocked, it was found to be a figure of one of the bishops of the diocese.

At Boxley also was a famous image of St. Rumald, Rumbold, or Grumbald, the son of a Northumbrian king and of a daughter of Penda, King of Mercia. He died when three days old, but not before he had repeated the Lord's Prayer and the Apostles' Creed in Latin, a feat for which he gained canonisation.

His image at Boxley is said to have been small, and of a weight so light that a child could lift it, but that it could at times become so heavy that it could not be moved by persons of great strength.

Thomas Fuller, the quaint old divine, tells us that " the moving hereof was made the conditions of women's chastity. Such who paid the priest well might easily remove it, whilst others might tug at it to no purpose. For this was the contrivance of the cheat—that it was fastened with a pin of wood by an invisible stander behind. Now, when such offered to take it who had been bountiful to the priest before, they bare it away with ease, which was impossible for their hands to remove who had been close-fisted in their confessions. Thus it moved more laughter than devotion, and many chaste virgins and wives went away with blushing faces, leaving (without cause), the suspicion of their wantonness in the eyes of the beholders; whilst others came off with more credit (because with more coin), though with less chastity."

The relics of this very youthful saint were carried to Buckingham and deposited in a shrine in an aisle of the church dedicated in his honour. In 1477, Richard Fowler, Chancellor of Edward IV.,

The Boxley Rood of Grace

left a bequest for rebuilding this aisle and the making
of a new and costly shrine for the relics, which
continued to attract pilgrims up to the Reformation.
Foxe, in his "Book of Martyrs," relates how several
Lollards, having renounced the "new doctrine," were,
nevertheless, forced to walk to Buckingham and
deposit an offering at the shrine of St. Rumald.

Churches dedicated in honour of this infant saint
are very rare, but there was one at Shaftesbury, in
Dorset, outside the borough boundary. To-day this
church is more commonly spoken of as Cann Church.

Boxley is situated a little over two miles to the
north of Maidstone, the roads from the latter place
being numerous. Standing some way off the village
are a few ruins, including part of the refectory, which
mark the site of the old abbey, where the nave of
the church has been turned into a garden containing
a lily-pond. A small portion of the original entrance
remains, while the size of the tithe-barns speaks more
eloquently than words of the former wealth of the
foundation.

When the abbey was dissolved, Jeffrey Chamber,
the Commissioner chosen by the Vicar-General, reported that "upon the defacing of the late monastery
of Boxley and plucking down of the images of the
same, I found in the Image of the Roode of Grace,
the which heretofore hathe ben hadde in great venera-
cion of people, certen ingynes and old wyer with olde
roton stykes in the back of the same that dyd cause
the eyes of the same to move and stere in the hede
thereof lyke unto a lyvelye thyng. And also the
nether lippe in lykewise to move as thoughe it shulde
speke. Which so founde was not a litle strange
to me and other that was present at the plucking
downe of the same."

Pilgrim Life in the Middle Ages

There have been many apologists for the Boxley Rood of Grace, and similar working *automata*, and although Cromwell's commissioners may not have been too scrupulous in their descriptions of these figures, the fact remains that throughout the whole of the Tudor period the strong Catholic party let judgment go by default, and made no attempt to refute the evidence, unreliable and biassed as much of it was, of Cromwell's agents. The truth is we do not know, we probably never shall know, the real history of these things, especially as those most competent to tell us all about them, the learned ecclesiologists of the Roman Catholic Church, are silent. This being so the Holy Rood of Boxley remains one of the unsolved problems of religious history.

As Mr. F. C. Elliston-Erwood, in his charming little volume on "The Pilgrims' Road," reminds us: "Boxley village and Park House are intimately connected with Tennyson. 'The broad ambrosial aisles of lofty limes,' that are the scene of the village festival in the opening of 'The Princess' are part of Boxley Park. . . . Tennyson stayed here in 1842, and the old road was often the scene of his rambles. We can picture him treading the path and beating out those musical lines that come so frequently in his nature poems." From the fact that in 1261 Archbishop Boniface built a hospital on the banks of the Medway at Maidstone, for the reception of pilgrims on their way to Canterbury, it is probable that large numbers of devotees used this route at that time, although Maidstone lay out of the direct course for the majority of the pilgrims who would cross the river at either Cuxton, Snodland, or Aylesford. The London pilgrims to Canterbury would have to make a detour to reach Boxley, as they

The Boxley Rood of Grace

generally proceeded by way of the direct road from Chatham. Miss Julia Cartwright (Mrs. Ady) writes : " The Abbey of Boxley owned vast lands, and the Abbots were frequently summoned to Parliament, and lived in great state." Be this as it may at the Dissolution no more serious personal charge was brought against the monks than that there were too many flowers in the convent garden, and that therefore they had turned "the rents of the monastery into gilly flowers and roses." If nothing more serious than an excess of horticultural zeal had been preferred against all the monastic brethren, what pleasanter reading the history of the Reformation would have made !

CHAPTER XII

OUR LADY OF WALSINGHAM, AND OTHER NORFOLK SHRINES

"Gentle heardsman, tell to me,
  Of curtesy I thee pray,
Unto the towne of Walsingham
  Which is the right and ready way.

Unto the towne of Walsingham
  The way is hard for to be gon ;
And verry crooked are those pathes
  For you to find out all alone."

THE scene of this charming old ballad, of which the first two verses are quoted above, is laid near Walsingham, in Norfolk, where the famous image of the Virgin and the even more famous relic of her milk, gave the little town a European reputation from the numerous pilgrimages made to it and the immense riches it possessed. The Walsingham pilgrimage formed the basis for many a popular ballad such as the following :—

"As ye came from the holy land
  Of blessed Walsingham,
O met you not with my true love
  As by the way ye came ?
        *   *   *   *
How should I know your true love,
  That have met many a one,
As I came from the holy land,
  That have both come and gone ?"

236

Norfolk Shrines

Second only to the shrine of Becket at Canterbury in popular esteem, in the numbers of pilgrims it attracted, and in its great riches, was the great shrine of Our Lady of Walsingham, situated in a remote corner of North Norfolk, a few miles from the sea. The history of this shrine is, to a very large extent, a history of one side of English religious life from before the Conquest down to the Reformation.

Erasmus informs us that Walsingham was supported almost entirely by the vast numbers of persons who came to make their offerings to the Virgin, and he adds that there was scarce a person of any note in England who had not at some time or other paid it a visit or sent a present thither. King and peasant, foreigner and native-born, cleric and layman, all wended their way to Walsingham.

In May, 1469, Edward IV. and his queen made a pilgrimage to Walsingham, as is recorded in a letter from James Hawte to Sir John Paston :—

" As for the king, as I understand, he departs to Walsingham upon Friday, com sev' night, and the queen also, if God send her health."

In 1470 John Paston wrote to his mother to tell her that the Duchess of Norfolk would visit Norwich on her way to Walsingham, and, accompanied by her husband, the duchess paid another visit to the shrine on foot, in September 1471.

In 1478 Henry Stafford, Duke of Buckingham, was one of the pilgrims to Walsingham.

There is no reason to doubt that this Norfolk shrine rivalled the earlier one of Our Lady of Loretto, in Italy, and a large number of inns and hostels were built for the accommodation of the pilgrims, not only in Walsingham and the immediate vicinity

Pilgrim Life in the Middle Ages

of the shrine, but along all the Norfolk highways that led to it.

The original chapel was founded five years before the Conquest by Ricoldie de Faverches, or Taverches, and was reputed to be an exact copy of the Santa Casa, or Home of the Virgin, which was conveyed in so miraculous a manner from Nazareth to Loretto.

With the return of the Crusaders from Palestine a portion of the Virgin's milk found its way to Walsingham, and the popular belief of the day was that the Virgin herself had come to establish herself in Norfolk in consequence of the infidels having invaded the Holy Land. The result was that a splendid priory soon stood beside the primitive and original chapel. This priory was founded in 1420 by Godfrey de Faverches, and given to the Order of St. Augustine.

It appears that the pilgrims who arrived here entered the sacred precincts by a low narrow gate, purposely made difficult to pass as a precaution against relic-snatchers. On the gate was nailed a copper figure of a knight on horseback, whose miraculous preservation on that spot by the Virgin formed the subject of one of the numerous legends with which the shrine abounded. Passing through the gate, the pilgrim found himself in a small chapel, where, on giving a suitable offering, he was allowed to kiss a gigantic bone, said to have been the finger-bone of St. Peter. He was then conducted to a building thatched with reeds and straw, enclosing two wells of water which had attained great fame for their medicinal properties, but more so, perhaps, on account of the rare virtue they were reputed to have possessed of granting whatever the pilgrim might wish for.

Norfolk Shrines

Passing through the outer gateway, an unfinished building in the time of Erasmus, the devotee found himself before the Chapel of the Virgin, a small wooden building with a door in each opposite side, through which the pilgrims made their entrance and exit. Within this chapel stood the celebrated image of the Virgin, on the right of the altar. Incense was kept burning perpetually before it, and by the light of the many tapers Erasmus beheld the gold and jewels with which the effigy was adorned. After kneeling awhile in prayer the pilgrim arose and deposited his offering, which was immediately taken up by a priest to prevent the next comer from stealing it when depositing his own coin. At another altar, probably in the outer chapel, was exhibited the far-famed relic of the heavenly milk, enclosed in crystal and set up in a crucifix.

Erasmus saw the sacred relic, which he tells us looked excessively like chalk, mixed with white of egg, and quite solid.

Of Walsingham in general the same writer says : "This house depends chiefly on the Virgin for support, for the greater offerings only are laid up, but if money or things of small value are offered, they are applied to the maintenance of the convent, and their superior, whom they call their prior. The church is neat and elegant, but the Virgin dwells not in it. This place, as out of respect, she has resigned to her Son. She has her temple so placed as to be at her Son's right hand, nor does she dwell even there. The building is not finished, and the wind comes in at the doors and windows, for the ocean, father of winds, is just by. In the unfinished church is a narrow wooden chapel, into which the worshippers are admitted by a narrow door on each

side. It has but little light, and that only from
wax tapers, which give a very agreeable smell. If
you looked in, you would say it was the mansion of
the gods, it glitters so with jewels, gold, and silver."
The following extracts from the " Household Book
of the Earl of Northumberland " will show what
constant tribute was paid to Our Lady of Walsingham :—

" Item : " My lord useth yearly to send afore
Michaelmas for his lordship's offering to our Lady
of Walsingham—4d. Item : My lord useth and
accustometh to send yearly for the upholding of the
light of wax which his lordship findeth burning yearly
before our Lady of Walsingham, containing eleven
pounds of wax in it after—7d. Ob. For the finding
of every pound ready wrought by a covenant made
with the channon by great, for the whole year, for
the finding of the said light burning—6s. 8d. Item :
My lord useth and accustometh to send yearly to
the channon that keepeth the light before our Lady
of Walsingham, for his reward for the whole year,
for keeping of the said light, lighting it at all service
times daily throughout the year—12d. Item : My
lord useth and accustometh yearly to send to the
priest that keepeth the light, lighting of it at all
service times daily throughout the year—3s. 4d."
The gifts, offerings, and benefactions made to
the shrine were many and various. In 1369 Lord
Burghersh bequeathed to it a silver statue of himself on horseback, and Henry VII. gave a silver
image of himself, kneeling on a table, with " a brode
border, and in the same graven and written with
large letters, blake enameled, theis words : ' Sancte
Thoma, intercede pro me.' "
Among the many royal visitors were Henry III.,

Norfolk Shrines

Edwards I. and II., and Charles V. Henry VIII.
walked barefoot from Barsham to present a necklace, and this monarch, when dying, is said by
Spelman, but by no other historian, to have left
his soul in charge of Our Lady of Walsingham,
but this is quite unsupported by evidence. Catherine
of Arragon, however, did so bequeath her soul, and
a sum of 200 nobles, to be given to a pilgrim to
spend in charity on his way to the shrine.

About the middle of the fifteenth century Sir W.

Walsingham Sign

Yelverton, in a letter to his cousin, John Paston,
wrote : "Right worshipful cousin, I recommend
one to you, thanking you as heartily as I can for
myself, and especially that ye do so much for our
lady's house of Walsingham, which I trust verily
ye do the rather for the great love that ye deem
I have thereto, for truly if I be drawn to any worship
or welfare, and discharges of mine enemies' danger,
I ascribe it unto our lady."

We also find Margaret Paston writing to her
husband to inform him that " my mother behested

241

Pilgrim Life in the Middle Ages

[vowed] another image of wax of the weight of you to our Lady of Walsingham, and she sent four nobles [£1 6s. 8d.] to the four orders of friars at Norwich, to pray for you, and I have behested to go on pilgrimage to Walsingham and St. Leonard's for you."

The offering of an image of wax of the weight of the person for the good of whose soul it was provided was a somewhat rare, and, considering the price of wax in the fifteenth century, a very costly gift.

The church of the Priory of St. Leonard, at Norwich, referred to by Margaret Paston, was in great repute with pilgrims for its images of the Virgin, the Holy Cross, and St. Anthony, but was afterwards rendered more famous by the pilgrimages made to the effigy of Henry VI., by whose miraculous intervention great cures are supposed to have been performed.

Mr. W. A. Dutt, in his book on " The Norfolk and Suffolk Coast " (Fisher Unwin), tells us that " Endowments and offerings of pilgrims made the priory [Walsingham] exceptionally rich—in one year the offerings alone amounted to £3,000 of our money —and it may be that it was in consequence of its being so wealthy that it became, early in the sixteenth century, the most disorderly and demoralised religious house in the county. When it was dissolved its yearly revenue amounted to about £5,000 present money. The site was then sold to Thomas Sidney, the governor of a hospital at Walsingham, ' for the use of the people,' but he kept it, we are told, for himself."

Although the modern pilgrim will find but a few fragments remaining of the old Priory of Walsing-

ham, he can, if he be so minded, find his way there
from London along the first road set down in
Holinshed's " English Itinerary," by way of Waltham
and Ware, or along the road that leads to Brandon,

The Gateway, Walsingham
Priory.

Swaffham, and Fakenham, although all of these
deviate very much from the Walsingham Green
Way, of which practically no traces remain, although
local enthusiasts will tell you otherwise. The
original shrine of Our Lady was destroyed at the
Reformation, but an interesting and possibly accurate

copy of it may be seen in the Roman Catholic Church at King's Lynn, not very far away.

A portion of the entrance gateway, a tall fragment of the great eastern window of the abbey church, and the pilgrims' bath and wishing wells are the most important features that remain of this ancient building, of which, long after its destruction, Philip, Earl of Arundel, who died in the Tower in 1595, penned the lines :—

> "Bitter, bitter, oh to behould
> The grasse to growe
> Where the walls of Walsingham
> So stately did shewe
>
> Levell, levell with the ground
> The towers do lye
> Which with their golden glittering tops
> Pearsed once the skye.
>
> Owls do shriek where the sweetest hymns
> Lately were sung ;
> Toads and serpents hold their dens
> Where the palmers did throng.
>
> Weep, weep, O Walsingham,
> Whose days are nights,
> Blessings turned to blasphemies,
> Holy deeds to despites !
>
> Sin is where our Lady sat.
> Heaven turned is to hell,
> Satan sits where our Lord did sway,
> Walsingham, oh, farewell !"

The pilgrims' wells, two in number, have been described by Erasmus in his "De Peregrinatione." They were no doubt enclosed in a building and had an attached chapel. When Erasmus visited them he found that between the two wells was a stone on which the votary of Our Lady knelt with his right knee bared ; he then plunged one hand in each well, so that the water reached to the wrist, and silently wished his wish, after which he drank as much of the water as he could hold in the hollows of his hands. It was also customary for the pilgrims to carry the water away in leaden *ampullæ* for their own future use, or for the benefit of their friends and relations.

In an old " Guide to Norfolk," published early in the nineteenth century, we read, with regard to Lynn Regis, as the town of King's Lynn was then called : " About halfway between the south and east gates stand the remains of an ancient oratory, a singular kind of building, with several vaults and cavities under the ground, over which are some dark cells, where the priests were used to take confessions in, and above them is a small chapel, in the figure of a cross, arched above, and enriched with carvings. It was dedicated to the Blessed Virgin, and commonly called Our Lady's Mount, whither the Romish peni-tents, in their pilgrimage through this town to the holy wells and the monastery of Our Lady at Walsing-ham used to resort and perform their devotions." This building, which remains much as when first erected, is the only complete example we have left of a pilgrim chapel, although traces of several others have been found in various parts of the country. Having seen what an early nineteenth-century topographer said of this chapel, the account given one hundred years later by Mr. W. A. Dutt may be quoted, not only as being the latest description of the build-ing, but as a confirmation of a fact which has often struck the present author, namely, that the guide-book and topographical writers of a century ago were, considering the limited amount of material they had to draw upon, singularly accurate in their general statements. With regard to this particular chapel, Mr. Dutt writes : " The most remarkable building in Lynn is the Chapel of St. Mary-on-the-Hill, better known as the ' Red Mount Chapel.' It was built about 1485 by Robert Curraunce, and consists of a red-brick octagonal tower containing an exquisite little cruciform chapel of stone, measuring eighteen feet from east to west, fourteen feet from north to south, and thirteen feet in height. The roof almost exactly resembles that of King's College Chapel, Cambridge, and its workmanship is of a very high order. This perfect church in miniature has beneath it a vestry with a small chapel attached, while in the basement of the small tower, below the level of the top of the mound, is another chapel or vault in a state of decay." The building has served a variety of uses, and has been successively a conduit, stable, powder-magazine, and pest-house, but was carefully restored in 1828, and placed under the care of the Corporation authorities. The date of its erection, 1485, is borne out by entries in the municipal records of the town, relating to a dispute between the Prior of Lynn and the Commons.

Mr. Ralph Surridge, an architect who has drawn out plans and made a minute study of the fabric, considers it to be one of the most interesting architectural studies in the district. Writing to *The Builder* (February 1, 1908), he says : " This chapel, dedicated to St. Mary, was built for the use of pilgrims on the way to the shrine at Walsingham. Outside the building is a platform of earth, which is retained by a surrounding wall supported by buttresses. . . . The lower chapel is entered from the

CHAPEL OF THE RED MOUNT KING'S LYNN.

WEST ELEVATION

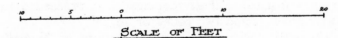

SCALE OF FEET

By permission of "The Builder."   Drawn by Ralph Surridge.

Pilgrim Life in the Middle Ages

north-east door in the outer wall, although at one time this was the priests' entrance only, and the people's entrance was by a passage under the west door, which is now blocked up—it is vaulted in brick and at present in a very uninviting state, all the decorations and pavement having gone. Just inside the west door is a window from which the service in the lower chapel could be seen. To the right of this entrance are the main stairs to the west door of the upper chapel. In passing the east end of the chapel a passage is formed under the altar, the walls being supported by two arches. The interior of the upper chapel is a most beautiful piece of fifteenth-century work. It has a nave, transepts, and choir, vaulted in stone, and is lighted by four quatrefoil windows. Near the south door are the steps to the priests' chapel and vestry and to the doorway in the north-east outer wall."

The Roman Catholics of Lynn and the surrounding district make an annual pilgrimage on May 25th to this chapel, attended by priests and acolytes, and with a carved effigy of Our Lady borne high before them.

At Hillborough, between Brandon and Swaffham, the pilgrims' chapel is little more than a mass of ruins, but the beautiful little building at Houghton-in-the-Dale, which had been converted into cottages, is once more in the hands of the Roman Catholics, for whom it has been re-dedicated. This was known as the " Shoe House," or " Chapel of the Slipper," as it was here, according to tradition, that the pilgrims discarded their footwear, and proceeded to Walsingham, some two miles or so away.

The only serious rival in the county of Norfolk to the shrine of Our Lady at Walsingham was that

Chapel of the Red Mount
King's Lynn

Scale of Feet

10   5   0   10   20

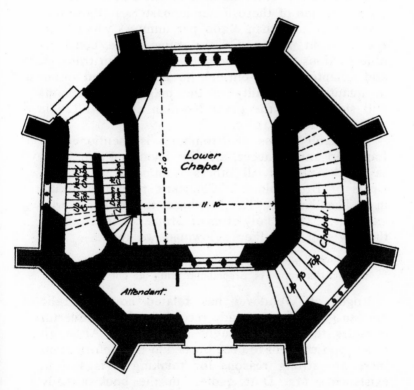

Lower
Chapel

15.0

11.10

Up to North Chapel

Lower Chapel

Up to Top Chapel

Attendant

Ground Floor Plan

By permission of "The Builder."   *Drawn by Ralph Surridge*

of the Holy Cross at Bacton Abbey, or, more correctly, Bromholm Priory, a monastery of the Cluniac Order founded in 908. Until 1295 this was merely a " cell " or dependency of the larger monastery of Castle Acre, belonging to the same order, but its possession of so famous a relic brought it fame and made it independent of the parent abbey, where they had nothing more attractive to show pilgrims than a spurious arm of St. Philip. Bromholm was one of those lesser monasteries (those with incomes of less than £200 per annum) which were dissolved in 1536. Of the ruins some considerable portions remain—the gate-house, north transept, and Chapter-house—but not to be compared either in quantity or quality to the magnificent remains still standing of the great Norman abbey of Castle Acre, founded in 1085.

The Holy Cross of Bromholm is mentioned by Langland and Chaucer, also by Thomas Fuller, who says : " Amongst all others, commend me to the Cross of Bromholme." Chaucer's reference occurs in " The Reeve's Tale," where the miller's wife exclaims, " Help, holy crois of Bromeholme ! " and in the " Vision " of Piers Plowman we read :—

> " But wenden to Walsingham, and my wife Alis,
> And byd the roode of Broomholm bring me out of dette."

Roger. of Wendover has related how the relic got to Bromholm, and recorded the wonderful miracles that were wrought by its aid. Although it is supposed to have been burned at the Reformation there are strong reasons for thinking it is still in existence. Mr. Dutt quotes, in the book already referred to, a note that appeared in " Eastern Counties Collectanea " (1872-3), as follows : " A

convent of nuns in Yorkshire, who have a large piece
of the Cross of our Lord, set in silver in the shape of
a Jerusalem cross, desire to trace its history. A
member of the family of Paston was at one time
Superioress of this convent. Now the Pastons were
intimately connected with the Priory of Bromholm,
and lived in the next parish, and it does not seem
improbable that at the Dissolution the celebrated
relic of the true Cross, for which Bromholm was
famous, may have come into the possession of the
Paston family."

It would be interesting to learn which of the convents of Yorkshire desired this information, and if
the relic is still in their possession.

The Pastons were the great patrons of Bromholm, and when John Paston was buried, in 1466,
his " wake " was held in the monastery, and attended
apparently by a great concourse of people. For
three days one man was employed in flaying beasts,
and provision was made of " 13 barrels of beer,
27 barrels of ale, a barrel of beer of the great
assize, and a runlet of red wine of 15 gallons." A
barber found employment for five days in smartening
up the brethren and their guests, who, on this aus-
picious occasion, consumed no less than 1,300 eggs,
20 gallons of milk, 8 gallons of cream, 41 pigs,
49 calves, and 10 'neat stock.' "

Matthew Paris has also recorded the story of this
wonderful cross, to the effect that Baldwin, Count of
Flanders, being harassed by infidel kings, and
neglecting in his march against them to take the
Cross of Christ and other relics with him on his
campaign, was in consequence defeated and slain.
A chaplain of English extraction had been left in
charge of the relics, and he, on learning of the

Count's death, hurried from Constantinople with the sacred treasures. He came to England with his spoil and commenced business at St. Albans Abbey by selling to the monks some jewelled crosses and images of St. Margaret, but he failed to induce them to purchase the piece of the true Cross. After offering the relic to several wealthy monasteries without disposing of it, the chaplain came at length to the poor chapel of Bromholm. " There he sent for the Prior and some of his brethren, and showed them the above-mentioned Cross, which was constructed of two pieces of wood, placed one across the other, and almost as wide as the hand of a man ; he then humbly implored them to receive him into their order with the cross and the other relics which he had with him, as well as his two children." The chaplain was admitted into the monastery, and before long miracles began to work by the aid of the holy wood, when the dead were restored to life, the blind received sight, the lame walked, the lepers were made clean, and devils were exorcised.

The arm of St. Philip at Castle Acre was by no means the only spurious relic to be seen in Norfolk, for at Winfarthing, near the Suffolk border, the monks exhibited the " good sword of Winfarthing," a relic invaluable for the recovery of lost property, stolen or strayed horses, while perhaps its great popularity was due to the power it was said to have possessed of shortening the lives of refractory husbands. To invoke its aid for this purpose the impatient helpmate was required to enter the church on every Sunday throughout the year and set up a lighted candle before the relic, which is supposed to have been originally the sword of a robber who took sanctuary in the churchyard. It was laid up in the church for years, when the clergy, being hard-pressed for a relic, bethought them of the old sword, which they proclaimed a relic, and made a handsome revenue out of it.

A writer of the Georgian era, referring to this relic, said, somewhat unkindly : " What pilgrimages would be made in the days of modern gallantry, was the sword of Winfarthing now in existence."

CHAPTER XIII

THE LEGEND OF WINCHCOMBE AND THE BLOOD OF HAYLES

SITUATED on the picturesque Clent Hills, not far from the busy city of Birmingham, is a very small but highly interesting church dedicated to God in honour of St. Kenelm (A.D. 820), one of some half-dozen churches in Britain so dedicated.

According to legendary lore, St. Kenelm was a king, *sub-regulus*, or chieftain of Mercia, when Winchcombe in Gloucestershire was the head town of that kingdom. Kenelm being but a boy when he came into his inheritance, an elder sister, Quendrede, became his guardian. The princess being ambitious and in love, was desirous of possessing her brother's kingdom, and the little Kenelm was removed from Winchcombe to a royal hunting lodge on the Clent Hills, where he was slain while hunting with his sister's betrothed, who buried the body at a lonely spot and placed a large stone over it.

The extraordinary part of the legend is to the effect that on a certain day in Rome, when the Pope was celebrating Mass before the High Altar of St. Peter's, a dove flew into the great basilica, bearing in its beak a scroll of parchment on which was inscribed :—

> "In Clent, in Cowbage, Kenelme Kyngborn,
> Lyeth under a thorn, his hede of shorn."[1]

Puzzled by this strange message, delivered in so unusual a way, the Pope, making inquiries, and finding that Kenelm was a member of one of the regal houses of Britain, dispatched messengers with instructions to solve the problem. The scene now shifts again to Clent and an old woman whose herd of cows fed on the hills there. It appears that one of the herd, a white cow, always went to a certain spot near a large stone and there remained, eating nothing but daily growing fatter and sleeker than the rest of the cattle. This unusual circumstance being reported to the papal emissaries, they followed the animal to the stone, which, on being removed, disclosed the remains of the murdered Kenelm and the sword with which he had been slain. From beneath the stone a spring of water gushed forth, and both spring and stone may be seen on the Clent Hills to-day.

It was highly improbable that such valuable relics authenticated by the papal messengers would remain long without claimants, and two parties of monks, one from Winchcombe the other from Gloucester, set out in haste from their respective convents to claim the body. Unfortunately, both parties arrived on the scene at the same moment, with the result that a violent dispute arose as to which monastery the relics should adorn. The wrangling continued until the

---

[1] There are several versions. Mr. J. C. Wall, in "Shrines of the British Saints," gives : "In Clento cou bathe Kenelm, Kynebearn lith under thorne havedes bereaved."

evening, when one of the monks proposed that they
should all lie down for the night, and those who
awoke first in the morning should have the body.
The suggestion was agreed to, when it doubtless
became a trial as to who could remain awake until
daylight appeared, and we may be sure that not one
of the company closed his eyes until overcome by
fatigue. Be this as it may, when morning came
the Winchcombe men had disappeared with the booty.
Thereupon the Gloucester contingent started off in
pursuit, to be perceived by the victors of the night's
vigil as, exhausted by the heat of the day, they
toiled up a hill with their burden. At last, when
their strength was nearly spent and their pursuers
close at hand, the Abbot thrust his staff into the earth,
when water immediately gushed forth for the refreshment of his weary monks, who, having quenched
their thirst, renewed their journey, and reached their
destination in safety.

Kenelm's wicked sister, Quendrede, learning that
the bells were pealing because the remains of her
brother were being brought by a party of monks
into Winchcombe, took up a service book and began
to read the prayers backwards, but as the procession passed her dwelling both her eyes fell from
their sockets on to the pages of her book.

The remains of Kenelm were buried beside those
of his father, King Kenulf, in Winchcombe Church,
and his tomb was visited by an immense number
of pilgrims until the Reformation, as also were the
church dedicated to him at Clent and the well
beside it.

The story is, to a certain extent, supported by
the evidence of the tombs, which, when opened in
1815, revealed two stone coffins, within the smaller

of which was the skeleton of a boy and the rusted remains of an iron sword, the instrument of martyrdom.

Mr. J. C. Wall writes : " The relics of the saint and the dust of the king were thrown to the ground ; the shrine and the coffin were afterwards sold and placed in the grounds of Warmington Grange." Be this as it may, two stone coffins may be seen to-day in Winchcombe Church, with an inscription placed over them setting forth the main incidents of the legend. If the original coffin of St. Kenelm was removed to Warmington Grange in 1815, it would be interesting to know when and by whom it was replaced in the church. The once famous abbey of Winchcombe was entirely destroyed at the Dissolution, although a few memories of its old-time activities still cling to the place. The " George " is one of those ancient pilgrims' inns which abounded in the vicinity of shrines. The initials R.K., still to be seen on the building, are those of Richard Kyderminster, abbot in the days of the seventh Henry. It is an interesting old building with a galleried yard, the view from the far end of which is one of great charm. Within the church vestry is a memorial in the shape of a door, once abbey property and marked with the same initials as those on the inn. This has been recently rescued from a neighbouring farmhouse. There are many other treasures in the vestry —old chalices and flagons—to describe which would take us far beyond the limits set for this volume. The church has an aisled nave of eight bays, with octagonal shafts and depressed arches. East of the choir is a presbytery, with triple sedilia on the south side, and farther east is a lady chapel, or reliquary, having no connection with the church except by a narrow doorway. Until 1872, when the church was " restored " by that terrible vandal Wyatt, the altar stood centrally, with seats for the communicants on the south, east, and north sides respectively. The same arrangement existed at Deerhurst, and still exists in Jersey, and at Lyddington, Rutlandshire, among a few other places.

While at Winchcombe the devotional pilgrim of the Middle Ages would not fail to make his way to the Cistercian Abbey of Hayles, some two or three miles off, famed for its relic of the Holy Blood.

Mr. St. Clair Baddeley, in his very interesting paper on " The Holy Blood of Hayles," tells us that " relics known by the title of *Sanguis Christi*, other-wise ' drops of the Holy Blood,' belonged to several categories. They sometimes derived from the blood shed at Calvary—from hands, feet, or side of the Christ ; sometimes from the blood issuing from His forehead, wounded by the crown of thorns ; others still (as was the case with the Lateran relic) derived from the occasion of the circumcision ; still others (and these were not uncommon in the thirteenth and fourteenth centuries) derived from crucifixes which had been struck, or had accidentally fallen ; or from ' Hosts ' which had either been called in question or had been profaned by impious hands, and had bled." With the latter type of relics we are not much con-cerned ; but the former class, those purporting to be genuine drops of our Lord's blood, have a common history, in that they all claimed to be drops of the blood contained in a vase, enclosed in a leaden chest inscribed *Jesu Christi Sanguis*, which was dis-covered at Mantua, in 804. The tradition concerning the Holy Blood of Hayles is, as told by the authority above quoted, to the effect that : " It came to Europe,

Gallery of the
Pilgrims' Inn
Winchcombe

Pilgrim Life in the Middle Ages

into the possession of William II., Count of Holland,
Zealand, and Friesland, authenticated by the seal and
guarantee of Jacques Pantaleon, Patriarch of Jerusalem 1255-61, afterwards Pope, as Urban IV. As
this pontiff was both a Cistercian and the Institutor
of the great festival of Corpus Domini, the monastery
of Hayles at a later day no doubt considered its relic
to be above all question. He died in 1264. Three
years later we find Edmund, son of Richard, Earl
of Cornwall, the Founder of Hayles, purchasing the
relic from Florenz V., Count of Holland, and taking
it back to England with him."

Only one-third of the Holy Blood was given to
Hayles, the remainder was kept until 1297, when it
was presented to the Augustinian House of Bonshommes at Ashridge, Bucks, which had been founded
in 1283. The Blood of Hayles was deposited in its
shrine with great ceremony, and placed in charge of
a custodian, or *Altararius*, whose duty it was to
display it to the pilgrims and to collect their fees.

Richard, Earl of Cornwall, and the founder of
Hayles Abbey, was a brother of Henry III., and he
held the title of King of the Romans from the year
1257, and married Sanchia of Provence, a sister of
Eleanor, the queen of Henry III. Edmund, the
purchaser of the Holy Blood, was their second son,
born at Berkhampstead on December 26, 1250.
When he died, at Ashridge, in 1300, his body was
taken to Hayles for burial.

The abbey was founded in 1246, and dedicated on
November 5, 1251, in the presence of Henry III.,
Eleanor, and a vast company of nobles and ecclesiastics. The church, consumed by fire in 1271, was
rebuilt by Richard, the original founder. By the
middle of the fifteenth century the buildings were

in a bad state of repair, until the popes came to the rescue by granting indulgences (see Chap. XV.), the sales of which must have been enormous, as with this "pardon" money the monks repaired their church, rebuilt the cloisters, and paved the Chapter House with tiles. On December 24, 1539, the abbey and the whole of its possessions were surrendered by Stephen Sagar, its last abbot, who, together with his twenty-one monks, were pensioned out of the revenue, which was returned at £330 2s. 2d.

The Commissioners, headed by Bishop Hugh Latimer, issued their certificate, in which they stated, among other things, that the supposed relic was enclosed within a round beryl, garnished and bound on every side with silver. They also stated that the contents of the phial proved to be an unctuous gum coloured a glistening red resembling somewhat the colour of blood, "and after we did take our part of the said substance and matter out of the glass then it was apparent glistening yellow colour, like amber, or base gold, as doth cleave to as gum, or bird-lime."

On November 24, 1539, one month before the abbey was formally surrendered, the Holy Blood of Hayles, that had brought such fame and wealth to this secluded corner of Gloucestershire, was publicly destroyed at Paul's Cross by John Hilsey, Bishop of Rochester, who declared it "to be no blood, but honey clarified and coloured with saffron."

As Mr. St. Clair Baddeley says : "This statement seems to give the lie to the calumnious affirmations which had been sown broadcast, describing it as the blood of a duck . . . which were repeated by Fuller, Burnet, Herbert, and others who followed Holinshed, Fox, and other writers, all of whom derived from

the testimony of William Thomas, Clerk of the
Council to Edward VI." Whatever it may have
been composed of it is generally agreed that the relic
was not that which it professed to be, so that whether

Ruins of Chapter
House Hayles Abbey

it was a concoction of duck's blood or clarified honey
is a question of little moment.

In 1899 investigations were commenced on the
site of the Abbey of St. Mary, at Hayles, under
the auspices of the Bristol and Gloucestershire
Archæological Society, and in the summer of the
following year the cloister walks and their adjacent

Winchcombe and the Blood of Hayles

walls were cleared of rubbish, and the falling arches supported with dry masonry. The Chapter House and Sacristy were excavated, and the church located. In the Chapter House six beautiful bosses of thirteenth-century date were found, and six others bearing the arms of Huddleston, Compton, Percy, and Evesham Abbey were discovered in the cloister walk. Other things brought to light were some sixteenth-century tiles, and fragments of stained glass, pottery, and ironwork, all of which have been deposited in a small museum within the grounds. The excavation of the presbytery revealed some fragments of a stone effigy in chain mail, which have been conjectured to be portions of the effigy that surmounted the tomb commemorating Edmund, Earl of Cornwall. Miss Ida M. Roper, F.L.S., the author of some valuable monographs on "Monumental Effigies," writes : " The pieces consist of a portion of an arm in mail showing the relieving strap at the wrist, a hand grasping the hilt of a sword, and a portion of the thigh, also in mail, the rings carved in the stone."

The uncovering of the foundations proved the church to have been about 320 feet in length, or, as figures convey little meaning except to the professional architect, as long as Gloucester Cathedral without its Lady Chapel. The exposure of the eastern limb of the church, always the most important part of such buildings, proved the plan to have been what architects call *periapsidal;* that is, the apsidal termination had polygonal chapels (at Hayles five in number) and semicircular ambulatories, an arrangement very popular with those greater churches where provision had to be made for a processional path or ambulatory round a high altar,

Pilgrim Life in the Middle Ages

presbytery, or shrine. At Hayles the eastern limb of the church would have the shrine of the Holy Blood as its base centre. Mr. Francis Bond, writing without particular reference to Hayles, tells us that " the one great advantage of the plan, which led our builders to prefer it to the plan in vogue in the mother-churches in Normandy, probably was that it fulfilled the requirements of processional ritual. It enabled a procession to pass right round the high altar without entering the sacred enclosure of the presbytery." For pilgrimage churches the plan was equally convenient, and there is little doubt that the plan originated in the pilgrim churches of the Continent about the end of the ninth century. The plan would not only provide ready access to the eastern chapels, but it allowed the pilgrims to circulate round the whole of the eastern end of the church, without retracing their steps to the inconvenience of their companions. The Holy Blood of Hayles naturally calls to mind a similar relic to be seen at the present day (among other places on the Continent) in the beautiful chapel of Saint Sang, or Holy Blood, at Bruges, that most interesting of Belgium's ancient towns. The building is two-storied, the lower one forming the church founded by Thierry d'Alsace and Sibylle d'Anjou, in 1148, and consecrated to the honour and glory of God and of His servant St. Basil, in 1150. The upper church was rebuilt in the fifteenth century. The Holy Blood had been given to Thierry d'Alsace by the Patriarch of Jerusalem, in consideration of the valour he had shown in the second Crusade. It was taken to Bruges in a glass bottle by its recipient and his friend Leonius, Abbot of St. Bertin, and placed in a rich reliquary in the chapel, to which four chaplains were appointed.

Winchcombe and the Blood of Hayles

Every Friday up to 1325 the blood liquefied in a similar manner to that of St. Januarius at Naples ; but after this date the miracle ceased for a time, until the phial was placed in a new reliquary by the Bishop of Ancona in 1388, when the miracle began to work again. The original *châsse* was stolen by Gueux in 1570, and the one now to be seen was made at the commencement of the seventeenth century by a noted goldsmith of Bruges, who bore the English name of John Crabbe. It is a beautiful piece of silver-gilt work, loaded with precious stones and medallions. At Bruges, also, in the Hospital of St. John, is a singularly beautiful reliquary, the panels of which, painted by Memling, illustrate the legend of St. Ursula.

CHAPTER XIV

NOTES ON SHRINES OF BRITISH SAINTS

WITH the lives of the early British saints and the traditions which have gathered about them we are not much concerned, although there is a fascination about saintly legends and traditions, even if they are unsupported by evidence. At the same time, to dismiss many of the legends as myths presents more difficulties than to accept the idea that the majority of them contain a certain amount of truth. The shrines and tombs, the churches and chapels connected with the saints of old are very numerous in the British Isles, so numerous that it is not possible in this chapter to attempt more than a brief reference to a few of the more prominent saintly shrines or royal tombs to which pilgrimages were made.

Historically considered, any account of English shrines should commence with that of St. Alban, the proto-martyr of Britain; but our present purpose will be served best if the subject is treated in the nature of a cathedral tour, beginning in the far west at the lonely little city of St. David's.

Here, on a promontory of Wales, jutting far out into St. George's Channel, stands the venerable cathedral of the great Welsh saint. On the summit of a cliff overlooking the sea are the ruins of a

Shrines of British Saints

little chapel that marks the reputed birthplace of
St. David, and where " St. Non's Well," a spring
that bubbled up in answer to her prayer, may still
be seen. St. David studied at Llanwit Major, and
after his ordination lived with Paulinus, Abbot-bishop
of Ty Gwyn, for about ten years, after which time
he built a hermitage for himself in the Vale of Ewias,
where the ruins of Llanthony Priory now stand.
After the lapse of several years he returned to his
native place, and founded a monastery on the site
of the present cathedral. He was formally
canonised by Pope Callixtus in the twelfth century,
although for many years previously his shrine had
been an object of veneration. In course of time
St. David was accounted the patron saint of Wales.
Part of the shrine remains in the cathedral, where
it occupies the space between two piers in the presbytery. A low seat for the pilgrims is supported on
three pointed arches, in the spandrils of which are
deeply-cut quatrefoils, the two middle ones being
pierced through the stonework into the aumbries at
the back of the shrine for the reception of offerings. Three blind arches above the seat are surmounted by crocketed moulding, terminating in head
corbels, now much mutilated. At the back of the
shrine, which is very plain, are two square and three
round-headed aumbries. The relics of the saint were
placed in a portable reliquary, and a niche behind
the altar is considered to be the place where the
reliquary was kept after its periodical exhibition to
the pilgrims. The Rev. Hermitage Day says :
" When the niche was opened a few years ago there
were found in it some human bones, which had
been embedded in a mass of mortar, perhaps to
prevent a worse desecration. St. David's relics may

267

yet rest in the cathedral, in a spot unmarked and known only to a few."

So great was the fame of St. David's shrine that the saying arose, *Roma semel quantum, dat bis Menevia tantum,* expressing the popular belief that two pilgrimages to St. David's were equivalent to one made to Rome.

Another Welsh cathedral with saintly relics was that of Llandaff, where the objects of pilgrimage were the shrines or tombs of Saint Dubricius, the founder of the see, and Saint Teilo, his successor. The tomb of the latter saint was held in such veneration that solemn oaths were taken upon it, even as late as the seventeenth century. The tomb is now in an arched recess, with the effigy of a bishop (in vestments and with a mitre) of the early Decorated period lying upon it.

From Llandaff to Hereford is not a far cry ; and in this latter cathedral were two shrines of such importance that pilgrims were attracted from all parts of the country to see the relics.

The first event to bring the cathedral into prominence as a place of pilgrimage was the murder of Ethelbert, King of the East Angles, by Offa, King of Mercia. Ethelbert had been invited to Offa's palace, near Hereford, as the suitor of the latter's daughter Alfrida, but was foully murdered, at the instigation, it is said, of Offa's wife. Various reasons have been assigned for the deed, among them that Queen Quenrida wished to become possessed of East Anglia in addition to Mercia. The legend is to the effect that on the night of the burial a column of light rose towards the sky, brighter than the sun ; and three nights afterwards the murdered king appeared to his friend Brithfrid and asked him to

Shrine of St David.

Niche at back of High
Altar where the relics
were kept.

Sketches in St David's
Cathedral

Sidney Heath

remove his body to the monastery near Hereford. Other miraculous events happening, Offa sent two bishops to ascertain the facts, and then, possibly repenting of his deed, caused an elaborate monument to be erected over Ethelbert's tomb, and presented gifts to the church, which became known as the Church of Saints Mary and Ethelbert. Ethelstan II., Bishop of Hereford from 1012 to 1056, had a magnificent shrine made for the relics, but in 1055, during an invasion of the Welsh, the church was so completely destroyed by fire that only a tooth of St. Ethelbert is said to have been preserved. With the rebuilding of the cathedral another shrine was erected, to which pilgrims continued to flock until the Reformation. The destruction of the original shrine was a source of great trouble to the monks, who feared that pilgrims would pay their devotions elsewhere ; but the situation was saved by the timely advent of another saint, Thomas de Cantilupe, Bishop of Hereford from 1275 to 1282. During his episcopate he went to Rome to appeal against a decree issued by the Archbishop of Canterbury which he considered unjust. On the way to Rome he died of fever, and Richard Swinfield, his chaplain, being deputed to bring home his bones, boiled the deceased bishop, and returned with his heart and his bones, the former being given to the College of Bonshommes at Ashridge, the latter deposited in the Lady Chapel at Hereford.

With the bones enshrined, miracles soon began to work by their aid, and over three hundred afflicted persons are said to have been healed at the tomb, with the result that the shrine of St. Thomas became one of the most popular in the West of England. In cases of sickness it was customary for an offer-

The Cantilupe Shrine Hereford

Sidney Heath

To face p. 270.

ing of wax to take the form either of a taper corre-
sponding to the length of the donor, or a quantity
equal to his weight, and this form of offering appears
to have been used whether the saintly benefits
were asked for human or bestial beings. We are
told that Edward I., hearing of the great healing
virtue of the shrine, caused a model in wax to be
made of his favourite falcon, which was ailing, and
sent it, with a valuable offering, to the shrine. The
relics were translated several times, and part of the
shrine remains in the north transept of the cathedral.
It consists of the base which supported the reliquary.
It is an elaborate piece of work in Purbeck marble,
and is in two parts, the lower in the form of an
oblong tomb, with fourteen figures of Knights
Templars, of which Order St. Thomas was Pro-
vincial Grand Master. On its surface is the matrix
of a brass. The upper portion consists of an oblong
slab, supported on an open arcade.

From Hereford we pass to Gloucestershire, famed
for the Holy Blood of Hayles, the tomb of St.
Kenelm, at Winchcombe, and in the Cathedral of
St. Peter at Gloucester that of Edward II. Before
the murder of this monarch Gloucester was in the
same position as Canterbury previous to the martyrdom of Becket. There were no popular shrines
and consequently no funds for the beautifying of
the cathedral. In 1327 the deed that deprived
England of a king was to bring to Gloucester wealth
undreamed of by the monks and abbot. After
Edward's escape into Wales he was recaptured by
the Queen's party and imprisoned. In the spring
of 1327 he was removed by night to Berkeley Castle,
where he was at first well treated by his custodian,
Lord Berkeley, who, on that account, was ordered

to give up the keys of the castle, which he did with a heavy heart, fearing that violence was intended towards the King. After Berkeley's removal Edward was subjected to horrible tortures, and his shrieks of despair are said to have been heard by the villagers. He is said to have " ended his life with a lamentable loud cry heard by many both of the towne and the castle." The news of his death soon spread abroad, but the neighbouring religious houses of Malmesbury, and Kingswood, in Gloucestershire, and of St. Augustine, in Bristol, refused to receive the body for burial, fearing the vengeance of Isabella, his widow, the " she-wolf of France." Abbot Thokey of Gloucester saw his opportunity, and begged the body of Edward for interment, and, his request having been granted, the royal remains were conveyed to the monastery and buried with all the rites of the Church.

With the fall of Queen Isabella and the accession of Edward III. one of the first acts of the new King was to raise a stately tomb over the resting-place of his predecessor. Then a reaction set in, and all England wended its way to Gloucester to pay their devotions at the tomb of the murdered Edward and to honour the brave old abbot who had given him burial. Dean Spence writes : " It was a strange cult this of the murdered sovereign, and one hard to explain. It seems as though men in England felt that a curse lay on them, and on their homes and hearths, owing to their having suffered the Lord's anointed to be cruelly done to death in their midst. So thousands came and prayed at the dead King's shrine. Their offerings enriched the abbey coffers. Soon there was wealth enough to have rebuilt the whole church from its very foundations. At all events, the desire of the monks to adorn their ancient house with new work could now be gratified." Pilgrims came in such numbers that the " New Inn " is said to have been erected specially for their accommodation.

The monument, with its effigy and beautiful canopy, may still be seen in the cathedral choir. The figure is of alabaster, and it has been frequently stated that the face was modelled from a death mask of the monarch. This was not the opinion of the late Mr. Albert Hartshorne, a very great authority on monumental sculpture, who wrote : " It appears to be a conventional bearded statue, with regal attributes, but bearing a certain general resemblance to the original. . . . It is highly improbable that a cast, for the use of a sculptor, was taken of the royal face . . . and the circumstances of the revolting crime were specially unfavourable to such a departure from the usual conventional practice of sculptors of that period."

The canopy of the tomb is of Decorated work that terminates aloft in delicate pinnacles. By the time sufficient offerings had been made to complete the building Abbot Thokey was a very old man, and on his resignation, in 1329, John Wygmore was appointed abbot. He it was who began the great architectural changes that gave Gloucester the honour of forming the cradle of the Perpendicular style, which was a little later to be carried to such perfection by Bishop Edington and William of Wykeham, his successor in the see of Winchester.

The not far distant cathedral of Worcester was fortunate enough to possess four bishops who were thought worthy of canonisation—St. Egwin, St. Oswald, St. Dunstan, and St. Wulstan, the shrines of two of whom were erected in the cathedral. St. Oswald, who succeeded St. Dunstan in the bishopric, built the first cathedral, in the Saxon style, of which no portion remains, with the exception, perhaps, of part of the wall of the prior's passage leading into the eastern cloister. In 1084 Bishop Wulstan began to build his Norman cathedral, of which the greater part was destroyed by fire.

During Bishop Sylvester's episcopate another cathedral was erected, and at the time of its consecration, in 1218, the relics of St. Wulstan were enclosed in a new shrine, the ceremony being attended by Henry III. and William Trumpington, Abbot of St. Albans. On the return of the latter to his abbey he took with him a rib of St. Wulstan, which he enclosed in a shrine and placed it over an altar dedicated in honour of the saint. Many pilgrimages were made to the relics of St. Wulstan, who died in 1095, and was canonised eight years later. William II. enriched the shrine with fine gold and silver work, and King John was a frequent visitor to it. So highly did the latter King esteem this shrine and that of St. Oswald that on his deathbed he expressed the wish that he should be buried between their respective shrines, and that they, together with the cowl which was to be placed upon his head, would ensure for him an easier passage through purgatory. After his conquest of Wales, Edward I. made a special pilgrimage to St. Wulstan's shrine, where he gave thanks for his victory. Prince Louis of France levied a tribute of three hundred marks on the monastery, to meet which the monks, in 1216, were compelled to melt down the gold and silver trappings of the shrine.

Near the Chapter House at Worcester are the

beautiful remains of the Guesten Hall, built in 1320 by the prior for the reception of the noble and wealthy pilgrims.

Another famous Worcestershire pilgrimage-place was Evesham, with its shrine of St. Egwin, and later that of Simon de Montfort. St. Egwin is said to have made a pilgrimage to Rome with his feet fettered, and in the Tiber he found the key which he had thrown into the Avon before starting on his journey, and was thus able to free himself from the fetters. He was the founder of Evesham Abbey, the site of which was determined by the vision of the swineherd Eoves, to whom the Virgin appeared while he was tending his swine, and pointed out the spot where the intended abbey should be erected, all of which is depicted on the old monastic seal of Evesham Abbey, of which St. Egwin became first Abbot, and who bore for his conventual arms *a chain and horse block* in chevron between *three mitres*, in allusion to his pilgrimage.

In 1265 the great Battle of Evesham was fought, and resulted in the defeat and death of Simon de Montfort. An old writer has called this battle " the Murther of Evesham," and after de Montfort's death one of the Royalist leaders ordered the earl's body to be dismembered and his limbs dispersed, his hands being cut off and sent, still in their bloody bandages, to his wife, who had followed the fortunes of the fight from the abbey walls. The monks of Evesham took up de Montfort's cause, proclaimed him saint and martyr, and took portions of his body into the abbey and laid them before the high altar, when miracles began to work, both here and at the little spring of water on the hillside that spouted out on the spot where de Montfort is said to have fallen.

Pilgrim Life in the Middle Ages

Again to quote Dean Spence : " The enormous popularity of de Montfort among the people is abundantly testified by the remains which we still possess of the folklore of that period. . . . He was especially the people's loved hero, and their love endured beyond the death of their champion. He was even invoked and received a kind of worship from his countrymen, who came in numbers to the tomb in the abbey, and kneeling, there prayed their passionate prayers to their dead patron saint."

A well-known saint was Frideswide, the first builder of Christ Church, Oxford [1] (729), where she was laid to rest. The church was partly burned down during the massacre of St. Brice's Day in 1002 ; but the tomb of the saint appears to have been unharmed, for on Ethelred rebuilding the church about two years later, he placed the shrine in the centre instead of on the south side as previously.

In 1180 the relics were translated to another place with great pomp and ceremony, and many miracles are recorded. On two other occasions the relics were translated, each time to a richer and more splendid shrine, to which Henry III. and Edward I. made pilgrimages ; and shortly before its destruction it was visited by Catherine of Arragon. Although the reliquary has vanished, portions of the marble shrine were discovered recently among the stones forming the lining of a well near the western end of the cathedral. A length of plinth, containing two quatrefoils and two queens' heads, was found doing duty as a step, and another portion of the shrine was discovered in a wall of an adjoining cemetery. The workmanship is of the early Decorated period, the

[1] The present cathedral.

276

spandrils being filled with delicately-carved foliage. As far as possible the shrine has been rebuilt, the missing portions filled for the present with blue stone, pending the discovery of further fragments.

The actual relics were said to have been preserved up to the Reformation, and are now thought to lie with other bones beneath the pavement of the lady chapel.

To St. Alban belongs the honour of being the protomartyr of Britain, and one of the most remarkable facts connected with him is that he had only just become a convert to Christianity when his martyrdom took place. His home was in the Roman city of Verulam, which was proud in later days to become known as St. Albans in honour of the saint. During the Diocletian persecution a priest named Amphibalus, of Caerleon, fled to St. Alban for shelter. At this time St. Alban was not a Christian, but he protected the fugitive, and noticing the hours the priest spent in prayer and devotion, made inquiries of him which led to his being instructed in the new faith, and in a short time St. Alban embraced Christianity. He was soon denounced as a protector of Christians, and soldiers were sent to search his house, but this having become known to St. Alban, he gave Amphibalus his clothes, and sent him out in safety through a secret door. Then, robing himself in the other's vestments, he awaited the soldiers, who took him before the judge. His disguise was soon penetrated, and the enraged official ordered him to do sacrifice at once to prove himself a true worshipper of the gods. On his refusal to sacrifice or to disclose the whereabouts of Amphibalus he was ordered to be scourged, a punishment endured so patiently that he was then condemned

Pilgrim Life in the Middle Ages

to death. He was taken to the top of a hill over-looking the city, when, owing to a miracle, the soldier who had been appointed executioner refused to do the deed, and he was also put to death with St. Alban, in 303. Many legends grew up around the name of the saint, one to the effect that the night after his burial a clear stream of light came down from heaven and rested upon his sepulchre. Angels hovered round the light, sing-ing, among other songs, " Alban, the glorious man, is a noble martyr of Jesus Christ." Many people beholding this heavenly vision were turned from their heathen gods and became Christians. Tradition says that Amphibalus was found in Wales, whence he was brought to Redbourne, near Verulam, and sub-jected to horrible tortures. On the spot where St. Alban was martyred a chapel was built, to be destroyed during an invasion of the Danes in the sixth century.

Towards the end of the eighth century King Offa of Mercia founded a monastery on the site, urged thereto, it is said, by a vision, and St. Alban's relics, which had been concealed for safety, were suitably enshrined. The fourteenth abbot, Paul of Caen, built a fine Norman church, using Roman bricks from Verulam for the edifice. The monastery of St. Albans soon became the most important Bene-dictine house in England. Throngs of pilgrims visited the shrine of the saint, which had several royal benefactors.

To this shrine Henry III. made a pilgrimage, and presented a valuable bracelet, rings, and embroidered palls. Edward I. gave an image of silver-gilt, Edward III. valuable jewels, and Richard III. a necklace of precious stones for the

278

image of the Virgin, that stood on the west end of the shrine, which was several times despoiled of its treasure, twice to relieve the poor after famines, and a third time for the purchase of the manor of Brentfield. Yet after each succeeding dismantling the shrine arose in more magnificence than before. In 1302-8 Abbot John rebuilt the whole structure on which the reliquary rested, and this remained until it was so thoroughly pulled down at the Dissolution that all traces of it were thought to have vanished. During a slight alteration of the church, however, in 1847, some beautifully worked fragments of Purbeck marble were found built into the walls, and when, several years later, still more fragments were discovered, over two thousand in all, they were pieced together and the shrine was re-erected in its old position eastward of the High Altar and westward of the retro-choir. The lower part of the pedestal consists of quatrefoil panels, and above these are twelve canopied niches, the backs filled in with thin plates of clunch, on which are still visible the three lions of England and the *fleurs-de-lis* of France, emblazoned in vermilion, blue, and gold. Scenes from the martyrdom of St. Alban are sculptured around the pediment, which is further ornamented with statues of kings, prelates, and angels censing. The whole is capped with a richly sculptured cornice. Originally the shrine was surrounded by fourteen slender square shafts, and three cable-pattern shafts on each side for holding tapers. Fragments of these shafts have been found, and when more of them have been unearthed it is possible that the restoration of one of the most beautiful pieces of fourteenth-century work in the country will be completed.

Dean Farrar wrote : " The numerous pilgrims to

the abbey probably approached the shrine by the wax-house gate (now an archway leading from the town), where tapers could be obtained for offering at the shrine. Then they must have entered by the north transept door, and would see in front of them the back of the great stalls. These, as we may judge by the places cut to receive them, must have been about twenty feet high, and have effectually prevented the public in either transept from intruding into the presbytery or monks' choir."

To the north of the shrine is the watching-gallery, occupying the space between two piers. It is of two stories, where the monks kept watch and ward lest any thief should attempt to rob them of their treasures. Some carved figures on the gallery represent a variety of subjects, including a woman milking a cow, a man mowing barley, a cat with a rat in her mouth, and many others.

John Lydgate, the "Monk of Bury," wrote for Whetamstede, Abbot of St. Albans, the Latin legend of St. Alban about the year 1430, and was paid for translating, writing, and illuminating it a hundred shillings (in present value about £70). The book, when finished, was placed upon the altar of the saint.

Just to the north of the watching-gallery of St. Alban is the shrine of St. Amphibalus, this also restored from fragments found in the walls. Around the base are some curiously carved stones, on one of which appears part of the name of Amphibalus. Surmounting the base is an open arcade and above the whole a deep cornice.

The only real survival we have of an old English shrine is that of Edward the Confessor at Westminster. This, although much mutilated when it was robbed of its valuables by Henry VIII.'s commissioners, was restored during Mary's reign. The

Shrine of St Amphibalus S.H.

Confessor died on January 5, 1065-6, and was buried before the High Altar of the church which he had himself erected. Long before his canonisation by the Pope, in 1161, he had been hailed as a saint by the people, not only on account of his peculiar sanctity but also in consequence of the wonderful miracles that took place before his tomb. William I. paid his devotions, and gave rich offerings to the shrine. He also rebuilt the tomb in a sumptuous manner, owing, it is said, to the miracle of St. Wulstan's staff. This prelate, having been commanded to resign his bishopric by William, laid his pastoral staff on the tomb of St. Edward, who had appointed him to the see ; but no one was able to take it up again but St. Wulstan himself.

The remains of the Confessor were afterwards translated by Archbishop Becket to a magnificent shrine prepared by Henry II. Mr. J. C. Wall [1] writes :—

"In a manuscript Life of St. Edward in the University Library, Cambridge, is a representation of the translation. Archbishop Thomas and King Henry themselves lifted the body from the old to the new tomb, assisted by the Abbot of Westminster and other prelates, the monks of St. Peter's holding aloft the lid of the feretory. This picture shows the decoration of the sides and roof, the shape of the ends and finials, and the top-cresting of the feretory, which stands on a stone base draped with embroidered hangings.

"Another illustration gives the elevation of one of the ends of the feretory. Here a number of pilgrims are venerating the relics, while one of them creeps through an aperture in the base . . . hoping thereby to receive relief from some infirmity."

[1] "Shrines of British Saints."

Shrines of British Saints

The translation of St. Edward's body took place in 1163, two years after his canonisation ; yet, according to monkish historians, his body was still entire and uncorrupted and his vestments undecayed, a fact which still further enhanced the sanctity of the saint, and his tomb became more venerated by pilgrims.

When the choir and eastern part of the abbey church had been completed sufficiently by Henry III. for Divine service, this King gave orders for the re-translation of the body of St. Edward into the new shrine which he had prepared for it in a special chapel behind the High Altar. The anniversary of the translation, October 13, 1269, was celebrated for nearly three centuries afterwards. On St. Edward's Day the citizens of London, in their corporate capacity, used to visit the shrine, and grand processions, with lighted tapers, were made to it by all the religious communities of the city. Frequently the presence of the reigning sovereign and his Court gave an additional splendour to the festival. In 1390 Richard II., who had adopted St. Edward the Confessor as his patron saint, and his Queen sat crowned in the abbey, while Mass was celebrated at the anniversary. At the three great festivals of Christmas, Easter, and Whitsuntide the shrine of St. Edward was visited by immense crowds of pilgrims of all ranks and of all ages ; the prince, the noble and the peasant flocked thither with their offerings.

Here on March 20, 1413, on the eve of his departure for the Holy Land, Henry IV., while performing his devotion to this saint, was seized with the sudden illness from which he never recovered.

The shrine of St. Edward the Confessor became

283

Pilgrim Life in the Middle Ages

one of the wealthiest in the kingdom.   At Henry III.'s
marriage with Eleanor, in 1236, he caused an image
of his Queen to be made for the adornment of the
shrine, and he also presented a golden vessel containing the heart of his nephew Henry.   At this
shrine Edward I. offered the Scottish crown and
sceptre, and the Stone of Destiny from Scone.   The
same monarch also gave a piece of the True Cross,
set in gold and precious stones.   At his coronation
Edward II. gave sufficient gold for the making of
two figures to decorate the shrine, one of St. John,
the other of St. Edward.   The choice of the figures
to be fashioned rested on the allusion to the old
legend which stated that one day Edward the Confessor was asked for alms by an aged beggar.   Having
nothing with him in the way of coin, and unwilling
to send the old man away unsatisfied, he took the
rings from his finger and gave them to the beggar,
who was really St. John in disguise, and who
eventually returned the rings by two pilgrims and
revealed his identity.

Henry VII. had an image of himself made in
a kneeling attitude, covered with gold plates and
enamelled, placed upon the top of the shrine.

The shrine stands to-day in the Chapel of the
Confessor, where it was placed by Henry III., and
although the lapse of centuries has deprived it of
its brilliant colouring and gilding, yet it remains still
a splendid example of the work of Peter of Rome,
whom Henry employed, together with one Oderic,
of the same city, to erect a fitting shrine for the
relics of the great St. Edward.

An inscription around the cornice was plastered
over by Abbot Feckenham at the Marian restoration, but this has fallen away in places, leaving a

284

few words exposed. The inscription has been translated thus by Rapius :—

"In the year of our Lord 1270, this work was finished by Peter a Roman citizen. Reader, if thou wilt know how it was done ; it was because Henry was the present saint's friend."

The lower part of the shrine has arcaded recesses, with trefoil heads, into which pilgrims thrust themselves when afflicted with diseases they wished to cure by a personal contact with the saintly relics. The step is deeply worn by the knees of innumerable pilgrims, although these hollows are now on the inner instead of the outer edge, owing to the stone having been reversed in a relaying.

The original wooden canopy which covered the feretory was totally destroyed. The present cover is attributed to Abbot Feckenham, but was probably never finished. In the reign of James II. the chest containing the body of St. Edward the Confessor having been broken open by the fall of some scaffolding, the contents were exposed to view, and " under the shoulder-bone of the monarch was found a crucifix of pure gold, richly enamelled, and suspended to a golden chain twenty-four inches in length, which, passing round the neck, was fastened by a locket of massive gold, adorned with four large red stones. The skull, which was entire, had on it a band or diadem of gold, one inch in breadth, surrounding the temples, and in the dust lay several pieces of gold, coloured silk, and linen." [1]

A choirman of that time who examined the relics took out the valuable crucifix and chain, which, after passing through various hands, were sold by auction

[1] "British Costume," J. R. Planché.

285

Pilgrim Life in the Middle Ages

as late as 1830, but their present whereabouts are unknown.

It was to prevent such sacrilege that James II. commanded the chest to be enclosed in one bound round with strong ironwork.

At Canterbury were the remains of St. Anselm, St. Elphege, St. Dunstan, St. Odo, and St. Wilfrid; and with this goodly array of saintly relics it is possible that, notwithstanding the immense popularity of the shrine of St. Swithin at Winchester, these tombs would have attained greater notoriety had it not been for the overwhelming devotion paid to the relics of Becket.

Very little is known of the resting-places of St. Anselm and St. Elphege. The relics of St. Odo and St. Wilfrid were translated to the " corona " of St. Thomas. It was St. Elphege who carried the skull of St. Swithin to Canterbury in the eleventh century.

The bones of St. Dunstan were the cause of much bitterness between the monks of Glastonbury and those of Canterbury, both foundations claiming to possess the true relics. Although St. Dunstan became Archbishop of Canterbury after a short period as Bishop of Worcester, it was at Glastonbury that he spent the greater part of his life. He died on May 19, 988, after a celebration of the Eucharist. He was at first buried in the crypt at Canterbury, but on the rebuilding of the choir his relics, and those of St. Elphege, were translated to new shrines on the south and north sides of the High Altar respectively. The monks of Glastonbury claimed to have possession of the true relics of St. Dunstan, but no shrine was erected there until 1184. With the raising of a shrine the monks fabricated a tale concerning the relics to the effect that after the burning of Christ Church certain monks were sent to Canterbury for the remains. Arrived at the city, they found the cathedral still smouldering, and discovered the bones of St. Dunstan, with which they returned to Somerset. As they neared Glastonbury the bells rang of their own accord to welcome the relics of the saint, which were at first buried near the door leading from the cloisters to the nave, in a spot known only to two monks. Here the relics remained for 170 years. After the destruction of the abbey by fire the bones were found and enshrined in a reliquary, to which many pilgrimages were made. So famous and wealthy did this shrine become that it roused the jealousy of the Canterbury monks, who sent a protest to the abbot, stating that the real bones of St. Dunstan were in their own monastery of Christ Church. Notwithstanding the spurious nature of the Glastonbury relics, pilgrimages continued to be made to them until 1508, when Archbishop Warham examined the tomb of the saint at Canterbury and found in the wooden chest a leaden case containing the skull and bones, together with a plate of lead, bearing the inscription, *Hic requiescit Sanctus Dunstanus, Archiepiscopus*. Thereupon he sent word to Abbot Beere that, as the true bones of St. Dunstan rested at Canterbury, the claim of Glastonbury must be abandoned under pain of excommunication.

At Chichester a famous shrine was that of Richard de la Wych, Bishop of the see, and an erstwhile Chancellor of Oxford University. He was canonised in 1260, seven years after his death, by Pope Urban IV. In 1276 his relics were translated with great ceremony, in the presence of Edward I., his Queen and

Pilgrim Life in the Middle Ages

Court. The shrine was placed to the east of the High Altar, and a watching loft was built to guard its treasures, which was not removed until 1820. Pilgrims came in such crowds to the tomb that the body of the saint was dismembered, and three separate stations were made: one at the original tomb, another at the shrine, and a third at a head-shrine, or reliquary containing his skull.

Mr. J. C. Wall writes: " On April 3rd—St. Richard's Day—the concourse of pilgrims was of such magnitude that in 1478 Bishop Storey made stringent rules whereby the crowds might approach the shrine in seemly order. The pilgrims were accustomed to carry staves, and the struggles for precedence led to the free use of these on each other's heads, often leading to serious injury, and in one case even death. The Bishop directed that, instead of staves, they should carry crosses and banners, and the members of the several parishes should approach reverently from the west door in prescribed order, of which notice was to be given by the parish priests in their churches on the Sunday preceding the festival."

In the fifteenth century the cathedral was sadly in need of repair, and to meet the expenses of the restoration, indulgences were granted to all making pilgrimage to the shrine of St. Richard on Whit Sunday and on Trinity Sunday. By way of penance for poaching on the preserves of the Bishop in Hoghton Chace, the Earl of Arundel was granted absolution only on condition that he made a pilgrimage to the shrine.

The shrine was destroyed on the " XXth day of November, the XXXth yere of the reyne of Henry the VIII ; by Wyllm. Gorgny, Knygth, and Willm

Shrines of British Saints

Erneley, esquyer," who have left an inventory of the valuables and money taken for the King.

In the neighbouring county of Hampshire was the great and popular shrine of St. Swithin, known to most people as the " weather saint," from the tradition that when the monks of Winchester attempted to remove his relics from the lowly grave he had chosen " where the feet of passengers and droppings from the eaves " should beat upon his grave, a heavy rain began to fall and continued so severely for the following forty days, that it was regarded as a warning that he resented the proposed disturbance of his bones.

St. Swithin was the friend and tutor of King Alfred, whom he accompanied on a visit to Rome. He died about 862, and his body lay in its humble burial-place, on the north side of the cathedral, for more than a century, when King Edgar had a splendid shrine prepared within the church into which his relics were translated in 963, by St. Ethelwold, Bishop of Winchester. The translation was the occasion of many miracles. In the library of Gloucester Cathedral are three MS. leaves, written about 985, recording some of these miracles. The accounts have been published under the title of " Gloucester Fragments," and relate the remarkable appearance to a poor smith of the saint who asked him to go to Eadsige, a priest who had been ejected from the abbey, and desired him to go to Bishop Ethelwold and command him to open the grave and remove his bones to the interior of the church.

Many miracles were performed at the tomb of St. Swithin, where the sick were said to be healed at the rate of from three to eighteen a day. The saintly remains were divided in the eleventh century his skull going to Canterbury and an arm to Peter-borough. In 1150 Bishop Walkelyn translated the residue of the relics to a new shrine, when he re-built the cathedral. On September 21, 1538, the shrine was destroyed.

St. Swithin was essentially a " home-made " saint, as he was never formally canonised.

Although Salisbury never attained the popularity extended to many other pilgrimage centres, it was in this cathedral that on his canonisation, in 1456, the shrine of St. Osmund was erected. His supposed tomb, removed by Wyatt to the nave when he destroyed the Beauchamp Chantry in which it for-merly rested, is now placed between the Lady Chapel and the south aisle. No trace remains of the shrine, but legends of the miracles wrought by its aid and the indulgences granted to pilgrims prove its former existence. The reputed tomb bears the date MXCIX in Roman numerals, but their authenticity has been questioned, so that of satisfactory evidence connecting St. Osmund with this incised slab we have none. When Wyatt opened the tomb it was empty, a fact which proves nothing one way or the other, as the relics may have been removed to a secret hiding-place if not destroyed at the Reformation.

At Malmesbury, in the same county, stood the shrine of St. Aldhelm, Abbot of Malmesbury and first Bishop of Sherborne. He died in 709 at Doulting, and in 837 King Ethelwulf erected a costly shrine for the relics. This shrine appears to have been a wonderful piece of work, with the back enriched with silver panels, gilt. In embossed work were representations of the four miracles wrought by the saint—the Book, the Beam, the Boy, and the Chasuble. In the front were figures in solid silver,

the pediment of crystal, and the inscription in letters
of gold.

The shrine was looted by the Danes, but the bones
of the saint had been safely hidden and were eventually taken up again by the secular canons who
displaced the regular monks at Malmesbury, they
having been installed there by King Edwy in order
to vent his wrath on St. Dunstan. The relics were
again enshrined and attracted great crowds of
pilgrims—so many, indeed, that on special occasions
a troop of mounted soldiers was required to maintain order.

The Abbey of St. Mary the Virgin at Shaftesbury
was one of the best endowed in England, and when
the body of King Edward the Martyr was brought
hither in June, 980, the importance of the foundation was greatly increased by its becoming a place
of pilgrimage to the shrine of the sainted King.
Tradition associates Corfe Castle with the murder
of Edward, but this is doubtful, although the
" Saxon Chronicle " recording the event says the foul
deed took place at " Corfes Geat," where stood the
domus Elfridæ. The body is said to have been first
buried in a lowly grave, possibly at Wareham; until
Ethelred, who had come to the throne on his brother's
death, became stricken with remorse, and commanded that the relics should be duly honoured.
This resulted in the bones being placed in a reliquary
and deposited in the " Holy of Holies " at Shaftesbury. The shrine attracted many pilgrims, who
brought offerings and purchased indulgences. No
trace of the shrine remains, although a tomb was
uncovered a few years ago which is thought may
have been the resting-place of St. Edward. In the
little village of Whitchurch Canonicorum, in the same

county of Dorset, and not a very great distance from Shaftesbury, an interesting discovery has lately been made of the ancient leaden reliquary containing the relics of St. Candida. The recessed tomb, known locally as the " saint's shrine," stands in the north transept of the church, and consists of two portions, the lower part pierced by three openings through which pilgrims placed their hands to obtain contact with the healing virtues of the relics.

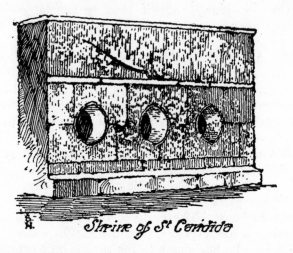

Shrine of St Candida

The upper slab is of older date. In March, 1900, a crack appeared in the north wall, and an old fracture in the shrine became widened. On examination the leaden reliquary was found inside with an inscription recording that the casket contained the relics of St. Wita, or Candida. The remains were replaced and the shrine cemented to prevent further damage.

Every one is familiar with the legend of the Holy Thorn at Glastonbury, and of the landing of St.

Shrines of British Saints

Joseph of Arimathea near by, where an oak-tree was planted in commemoration called the Oak of Avalon. St. Joseph and his companions, being weary after their journey, sat down to rest on the slopes of a hill near the town, which hill still bears the name of Weary-all-Hill. Here St. Joseph struck his staff, a dry hawthorn stick, into the ground, when it commenced to grow, and became a large tree which constantly flowered on Christmas Day.

From very early days Glastonbury was considered

CT·RELIQE·SCE·W

✠hICREQESCT·RELIQE·SCE·WITE

Inscriptions on Reliquary of St Candida.

a sacred spot, for here King Arthur was buried. The first church is said to have been a little wattled building erected by St. Joseph, but the early ecclesiastical history of the place is very obscure, although two early charters mention the little wooden church, the forerunner of the famous monastery.

In the sixth century St. David is reputed to have built a new church near the old one, and still later King Ina built and endowed a monastery. After the Danish invasions the foundation declined, but was brought into prominence again by St. Dunstan, who caused Glastonbury to become famous throughout Europe for its culture and learning, and whose spurious shrine in later days attracted thousands of

293

pilgrims, some of whom found accommodation in the old Pilgrims' Inn described in a former chapter.

The beautiful ruins of the Lady or St. Mary's Chapel, frequently called St. Joseph's Chapel, are the remains of the church built in the twelfth century on the site of an older building, which was practically destroyed by fire in 1184. The ruins show some beautiful Transitional work, and the fine north and south doorways, although mutilated, are lavishly enriched with carving. Beneath the chapel is a crypt containing a well. In the sixteenth century Abbot Beere built a chapel, of which portions remain, in memory of King Edgar, a great benefactor to the abbey, whose bones were enshrined with much ceremony in his chapel. In the Glastonbury Museum are preserved many interesting mementoes of the days when the town was thronged with pilgrims, such as staffs, "counters" made by the monks for use as coins, leather bottles, and a reliquary containing a small piece of bone said to be that of St. Paulinus, and given to the monastery by St. Augustine.

Apart from Our Lady of Walsingham and the Cross of Bromholme, a popular pilgrimage in the eastern counties was that made to the shrine of St. Edmund, at Betrichesworth, now called Bury St. Edmunds. The saint was born at Northemberg, in old Saxony, of which his father Alkmund was prince, and to his father's Court came Offa, King of the East Angles, when Edmund was about twelve years old, on a pilgrimage to Rome and the Holy Land. Having no heir to the throne, as his only son Fremund was a hermit, Offa adopted Edmund as his successor. Offa died at Constantinople on his homeward journey, and Edmund proceeded to

The Lady Chapel
Glastonbury

Pilgrim Life in the Middle Ages

England and landed near Hunstanton, where it is said springs of water gushed forth when Edmund prayed for his new kingdom on landing. During his reign the Danes harried the country, and in 870 they again invaded the fenland, sacking monasteries, whose riches they seized. Then Hinguar, the Danish leader, sent a message to Edmund demanding his submission, but he, knowing that this would mean the downfall of Christianity, refused. He then ordered his men to retreat, and he himself, with the faithful Bishop Humbert, awaited the Danes before the altar of the church. He was eventually seized and bound, then suffered the indignity of a mock trial, and he was led in the evening outside the village, bound to an oak-tree, and left as a target for the archers. Many arrows buried themselves in his body, but to prolong the torture, no fatal wound was inflicted. Then Hinguar promised him his life if he would renounce his faith, but the King made no reply and was beheaded, together with Bishop Humbert. When the Danes had left the district the friends of the martyrs began to search for their relics, and the legend runs that the head of the King could not be found, when in the wood they heard a voice say, " Here, here! " and going to the spot, they saw the head guarded by a wolf. The arms of Bury St. Edmunds are : Azure, three royal crowns, or, each crossed by two arrows; the crest being a wolf guarding the head of Saint Edmund.

The relics were first buried at the scene of the martyrdom, now Hoxne, but in 903 they were translated to Betrichesworth, and here, in course of time, a stately abbey arose over the saintly remains. Cnut made a pilgrimage to the place, and Edward the Confessor was a frequent visitor. Before setting

Sidne Heath.
Doorway of Lady Chapel
Glastonbury

out on the crusade, Richard I. came to the shrine, to which he gave sufficient land to maintain a perpetual light before the relics. The two wax torches thus provided were the cause of a great catastrophe, for one night, while the guardians of the relics slept, one of the tapers fell over and set fire to the table and burned the shrine. The relics were unharmed and a new shrine was quickly prepared, into which the remains were placed. Other royal visitors to the shrine were Queen Eleanor, who gave valuable jewels, King John, Henry III., who prepared a still more costly shrine for the relics, Edward I., and Henry VI.

In Westgate Street, Bury St. Edmunds, stands the Roman Catholic Church dedicated in honour of St. Edmund, and in it may be seen an altar-statue of the saint and a painting representing his martyrdom. A silver reliquary, inscribed " From the bones of St. Edmund, the Martyr King of England," contains a relic of the saint presented to the church by Cardinal Duprez, in 1867, and an alms-box at the west end is said to have been made from a portion of the oak-tree at Hoxne to which St. Edmund was bound.

John Lydgate wrote a volume of poems in honour of Edmund, the patron saint of his own monastery of Bury, the " precious charbuncle of martirs alle," which MS., in addition to illuminated letters, is adorned with over a hundred illustrative and contemporary pictures, one of which depicts Lydgate himself kneeling at the shrine of St. Edmund.

Lydgate was about thirty years old when Chaucer died. He was born at the village of Lydgate, some seven miles from Newmarket. He was ordained subdeacon in the Benedictine Monastery of Bury St.

Shrines of British Saints

Edmunds in 1389, deacon in 1393, and priest in 1397. He is generally spoken of as "the monk of Bury," and was the chief poet of the generation after Chaucer.

According to tradition, St. Augustine himself founded a church in the Isle of Ely, or Eel Island, among the fens, "and therefore," says Beda, "it has its name from the great plenty of eels taken in those marshes." Nothing is really known about the church in the fens until the stately building arose in the honour of Etheldreda, Queen and Abbess, whose sanctity was such that she is said to have retained her virginity although twice married. Her first husband was Toulbert, a prince of East Anglia, and her second Ecgfrid, the son of Oswy, of Northumbria, who had wrested Mercia from Penda. Etheldreda soon returned to the Abbey of Coldingham, where she had retired after her first marriage. It was not long before Ecgfrid regretted having given her permission to resume a religious life, and he set out for Coldingham with an armed band to take her away by force if necessary. Ebba, the abbess, became advised of the project, and counselled her niece Etheldreda to fly southwards and take refuge in her own land of Ely. On the way miracles were worked in her favour, for being almost overtaken by her husband near St. Abb's Head, the sea surrounded the hill on which she and her attendants had taken refuge, and remained there for seven days, until Ecgfrid grew weary and left her in peace. At Ely in 673 she founded the great abbey of which she was consecrated abbess. She died in 679, and was buried at her own desire in the cemetery among the nuns. During her last illness she suffered great pain in her throat, which she said "is a fitting punishment to me for the pleasure I once took in wearing neck-laces there." From Etheldreda, or Awdry, is said to be derived the word "tawdry," from St. Awdry's Fair, where cheap necklaces and other ornaments were offered for sale.

Etheldreda's sister Sexburga succeeded her as abbess, and sixteen years later she resolved to trans-late the bones of her sister to a fitting shrine. Some monks were given the task of obtaining a slab of stone large enough for the purpose, and as there was none to be found near by, they went by boat to Grantchester, an abandoned Roman city near Cam-bridge, and there they saw beside the walls " a white marble coffin, most beautifully wrought, and neatly covered with a lid of the same sort of stone." Believing it to have been placed there by Divine agency, they gave thanks to God, and returned with their treasure to Ely, and the remains of Etheldreda were translated to the shrine with great ceremony on October 17, 695. On two other occasions the relics of St. Etheldreda were translated. In 1106 the relics of her sainted relatives were translated with hers ; St. Sexburga being enshrined eastward of her, St. Ermenilda, her niece, on the south side, and St. Werburga, St. Ermenilda's daughter, on the north.

In 1541 the shrine was despoiled and nothing now remains of the silver reliquary, the jewels, or the white marble tomb at which pilgrims used to kneel. The watching loft is still there, although removed from its original position. The Rev. Father Lockhart is said to have been able to recover some relics of the saint, which are now enshrined in the chapel connected originally with the town house of the Bishops of Ely, at Ely Place, London, now a Roman Catholic church. A remarkable series of sculptures representing scenes in the life of St. Etheldreda somehow escaped destruction at the Reformation, and may yet be seen on brackets supporting richly canopied niches at each angle of the great octagon of Ely Cathedral. The subjects comprise : (1) The marriage of St. Etheldreda with Ecgfrid of Northumbria. (2) Her taking the veil at the monastery of Coldingham. (3) Her staff taking root and bearing leaves and shoots while she slept during her flight from the monastery. (4) Her miraculous preservation on the hilltop by the rising of the waters. (5) Her consecration as Abbess of Ely. (6) Her death and burial. (7) The legend of St. Brithstan, who is said to have been released from his bonds by the saintly merit of Etheldreda. (8) The translation of her relics. In the northern counties popular shrines were those of St. Cuthbert and St. Beda. The Life of the former contains much that is legendary. He is said to have worked many miracles, and on one occasion stilled a tempest. In early youth he was a shepherd, and it was while tending his sheep by night that he had the vision which resulted in his adopting the religious life. He became Prior of Lindisfarne, and in 685 was Bishop of the island. Two years later he died. In accordance with his wish his body was wrapped in a linen cloth given him by the Abbess Yeoca, and buried in a stone coffin, the gift of the Abbot Cudda. After the lapse of eleven years the monks wished to remove his relics to a reliquary above ground, and obtained the consent of Bishop Eadbert to their plan. On opening the stone coffin, however, the body was found in such a wonderful state of preservation that the monks hastened to inform the bishop, who directed

Pilgrim Life in the Middle Ages

that a fresh garment should be placed on the saint's body, which should then be put into a wooden coffin and placed on the sanctuary pavement.

About one hundred and fifty years later the ravages of the Danes so alarmed the monks of Lindisfarne for the safety of their relics, that they fled and took with them the body of St. Cuthbert and their sacred vessels and books. Then commenced the historical wanderings of the monks for over one hundred years, with their precious burden, which ended in the founding of the cathedral church of Durham, where the relics of St. Cuthbert had a new resting-place. Many legends grew up around the journeyings of the monks, many of which state that the saint himself often came to their assistance. For years the monks remained at Chester-le-Street, to which place the see was removed for a time, and while here, Athelstan, son of Edward the Elder, visited the shrine, on his way to the Court of the Scottish King, Constantine. In the British Museum is a manuscript recording his gifts to the shrine, among which were a stole with a maniple, and fabrics of gold and tapestry, now preserved in the cathedral library at Durham. Of the latter part of their journey, the story is told how that, coming to a place called Wardenlawe, to the east of Durham, the saint's body became fastened to the ground and could not be moved. Being in great trouble, the monks fasted and prayed for three days, when it was revealed that the body should be taken to Dunholme. Not knowing where this place was, the travellers remained unenlightened until they heard a woman call to her companion to know if she had seen her cow. The other replied that the cow was in Dunholme. "This was a happy and heavenly Sound to the distressed monks, who thereby had Intelligence that their Journey's End was at Hand, and the Saint's Body near its Resting-place ; thereupon

The Don Cow. Durham. Sidney Heath.

with great Joy they arrived with his Body at *Dunholme* in the year 997."

To commemorate the event Bishop Flambard erected a monument of a milkmaid and her cow, the original panel being replaced in the eighteenth century by the one still to be seen on the north-west turret of the Nine Altars Chapel of Durham Cathedral.

On their arrival at Dunholme the monks erected a temporary shelter for the relics, until such time as they could build a more fitting resting-place. Several times the relics were removed, until at last, in 1104, they were translated into the present cathedral by Bishop Carileph. Thousands of pilgrims visited the shrine, among them William I., Henry III., Edward II., and Henry VI., each of whom brought valuable offerings. The shrine appears to have been of a similar type to those of St. Edward at Westminster and St. Edmund at St. Edmundsbury, and near it was a box known as the " pix of St. Cuthbert," into which the offerings of the poorer pilgrims were placed, these not being of sufficient value to be hung on the actual shrine, which was dismantled at the Dissolution, when the relics were buried beneath the spot where the shrine had stood. Some doubt has been expressed as to whether these were the authentic relics, or bogus ones placed in the shrine so that the real ones could escape desecration at the hands of the Commissioners. A tradition is extant to the effect that the actual hiding-place of St. Cuthbert's body was known only to three Benedictines, who have handed down the secret on the death of one of their number to a member of the same order. The tomb in the Nine Altars Chapel was opened in 1827, and the contents corresponded so well with ancient accounts of the saint's body as to leave no doubt whatever that the remains still treasured in Durham Cathedral are those of St. Cuthbert. Two maniples, a stole, a girdle, and two bracelets of gold, and a large golden cross of ancient workmanship were removed from the tomb and may be seen in the library of the Dean and Chapter.

The annual Feast of St. Cuthbert, which lasted for a week, attracted pilgrims from all over the country. From the rolls of the cellarer, preserved at Durham, we find that in 1347 the consumption of provisions included the following: Six hundred salt herrings, four hundred white herrings, thirty salted salmon, twelve fresh salmon, fourteen ling, fifty-five " kelengs," four turbot, two horse-loads of white fish, nine carcasses of oxen, seven carcasses and a half of swine, fourteen calves, three kids, twenty-six sucking porkers, seventy-one geese, fourteen capons, fifty-nine chickens, five dozen pigeons, five stone of hog's lard, four stones of cheese and butter, a pottle of vinegar, a pottle of honey, fourteen pounds of figs and raisins, and one thousand three hundred eggs.

St. Cuthbert appears to have had a strong aversion to women, and at Lindisfarne he had a separate chapel set apart for them, and the Galilee Porch or Chapel at Durham is said to have been built originally for their use. Be this as it may, no woman was allowed to enter the chapel containing St. Cuthbert's shrine, or, according to some writers, even a church dedicated in his honour. A dark-coloured line in the nave of Durham Cathedral marks the limit beyond which no woman was allowed to pass eastwards. Reginald of Durham relates that an embroideress, " nobly skilled," determined to pass the limits assigned to women, but was at once detected and ignominiously expelled from the church.

In the Galilee of Durham is the grave marking

the site of the once magnificent shrine of the venerable Beda, to whose great work on " The Ecclesiastical History of England " we owe our knowledge of the early history of the English Church in these islands. The greater part of his life was passed at Monkswearmouth and Jarrow. He died in the latter place and was buried in the monastery chapel, where pilgrimages were made to his tomb. It was not until a century later that the title " Venerable " became attached to his name; the legend concerning it is that the monk who was composing the inscription for his tomb had got as far as

> *Hac Sunt in `fossa,*
> *Bedæ   ossa,*

but could not find a suitable word with which to complete the rhythm of the line, and at last retired to rest disheartened. The next morning on returning to his task he found to his surprise that the line had been completed by angelic hands :—

> *Hac Sunt in fossa,*
> *Bedæ Venerabilis ossa.*

In 1020 the relics of Beda were stolen from Jarrow by a pilgrim and taken to Durham, where they were placed in a small linen sack in St. Cuthbert's coffin. In 1155 Bishop Hugh Pudsey translated the remains to a magnificent shrine of gold and silver, which was removed in 1370 to the Galilee by Richard de Castro Barnardi. Here they remained until the Reformation, when, in 1542, the relics were re-interred on the site of the shrine, which was destroyed with the exception of the plain

Shrines of British Saints

slab of stone which still indicates the spot where the relics were buried.

The only shrine of any importance in York Minster was that of Archbishop William Fitzherbert, canonised as " St. William of York " in order to provide in the northern counties a counter-attraction to the shrine of the great Becket at Canterbury. On March 18, 1226, Pope Honorius issued a letter " tied with thread of silk, and a Bull " saying that William (Fitzherbert) having been nominated by the Dean and Chapter of York, for the honour of canonisation, was henceforth to be included in the catalogue of the " Saints of the Church Militant." No efforts appear to have been made to enshrine the relics until William de Wickwaine was raised to the episcopate, when one of his first acts was to translate them to a lofty shrine, prepared behind the High Altar on a platform raised upon arches from the crypt, removed thence for the purpose. The expenses of the translation were defrayed by Anthony Bek, then Bishop of Durham, who afterwards became Patriarch of Jerusalem. The shrine was dismantled by Dr. Layton, one of Cromwell's Commissioners, who had become Dean of York, and the desecrated relics were buried in the nave beneath a marble slab.

At Lincoln were four shrines, St. Hugh the Bishop, and " Little St. Hugh " having been canonised by the Pope, while the other two, Robert Grosseteste and John of Dalderby, both of them Bishops of the diocese, were hailed as saints by the people.

Bishop Hugh was buried at his own desire in the chapel dedicated to St. John the Baptist, near the cloister door. " Bury me there," he said, " where I have so often loved to minister; but lay me by

the side of the wall, where people will not be in
danger of tripping over my tomb." The Bishop was
not allowed to stay for long in so lowly a place.
Miracles began to work at his tomb, and on his
canonisation, in 1220, such throngs of pilgrims
flocked to the place that it was found necessary to
enlarge the church. The apse built by St. Hugh
was pulled down and the cathedral lengthened by
five bays. When completed the relics were translated to a shrine at the back of the High Altar,
and in the midst of the beautiful "Angel Choir."
The ceremony was carried out with impressive
grandeur, Edward I. and his Queen, Edmund his
brother, and the Queen of Navarre being present
at the time. The head of St. Hugh was placed in a
separate head-shrine or reliquary of gold and
precious stones. "Little Saint Hugh" was said to
have been crucified by the Jews in 1255, and in
consequence was canonised, but recent investigation
has proved that his death was the result of an
accident. Robert Grosseteste, the successor of St.
Hugh in the see of Lincoln, was regarded as a saint
by the people owing to the miracles wrought at his
tomb, which was visited by thousands of pilgrims,
although his relics were never formally enshrined.
The remains of John of Dalderby were translated
to a costly silver shrine enriched with precious stones.
The shrines of SS. Hugh and John were destroyed
at the Reformation, but that of "Little Saint Hugh,"
which does not seem to have attracted so much
wealth, was left untouched, and remained *in situ*
until the time of the Great Rebellion.

To Derby the relics of St. Alkmund, the son
of a King of Northumbria said to have been
treacherously slain by the Danes, were hastily trans-

lated for fear of the invaders. In the midland town he was hailed as their patron saint, and the festival of his translation, March 19th, was kept with due honour. His shrine became famous for miracles and was much visited owing to its being situated on one of the most frequented highways connecting the north and south portions of the country. A special church dedicated in his honour was built for the reception of his relics. A short distance to the north of St. Alkmund's Church at Derby is a well which bears the saint's name, and was credited with healing properties, while the old custom of decorating the well on the festival of St. Alkmund has been revived in recent years.

The churchyard of St. Mary's, Lichfield, was the first resting-place of the remains of St. Chad, the great Celtic saint, who became first Bishop of Lichfield. The " Book of St. Chad," a beautiful manuscript now preserved at Lichfield, was probably the work of the saint. Originally a plain little wooden shrine was erected over his remains, and Beda said it was " made like a little house covered, having a hole in the wall, through which those that go thither for devotion usually put in their hand and take out some of the dust, which they put into water and give to sick cattle or men to taste, upon which they are presently eased of their infirmity and restored to health." When the church of St. Peter was built on the site of the present cathedral, his relics were translated into it. On the rebuilding of the cathedral in 1148 an elaborate shrine was prepared, and in 1296 the relics were translated again to a yet more magnificent shrine. About a century later the saint's relics were once more translated, the base of this shrine being of marble, and the feretory of gold enriched with precious stones. On the occasion of one of these translations the head of St. Chad was removed from the body and separately enshrined in the Chapel of the Head of St. Chad. This chapel has been restored recently, and it still contains an aumbry and a fifteenth-century stone gallery, whence the pilgrims viewed the relics. At the Reformation Bishop Lee begged the King to spare the shrine of their first Bishop, a request which was granted, owing, it is said, to Lee having secretly married the King to Anne Boleyn. Soon afterwards, however, the shrine was despoiled, but the relics were taken and preserved by Prebendary Dudley, and the story of their preservation and continuous transmission is told at length in the " Records of the English Province of the Society of Jesus," edited by Henry Foley, S.J. In 1841, on the consecration of the Roman Catholic Cathedral at Birmingham, the relics of St. Chad were conveyed into the sanctuary, and placed in a reliquary of oak, adorned with jewels, gilding, and painting, above the High Altar.

In the cathedral at Chester may be seen a portion of the shrine of St. Werburgh, which, although destroyed at the Dissolution and its stone used for other purposes, and particularly in the making of the Bishop's throne, has been restored recently as far as possible, the missing portions being replaced by plain stone to distinguish them from the original. Doubts have been expressed as to whether the St. Werburgh at Ely and she of Chester are one and the same person, or whether there were two saints bearing the same name. It is now generally accepted that the same saint had shrines in both places. St. Werburgh is said to have been buried at Dereham, and when the grave was opened after many years,

LICHFIELD CATHEDRAL.

being found untouched by decay, was translated into the church, where the usual miracles began to work. In the ninth century, during a Danish invasion, the relics were conveyed to Chester for safety, and afterwards the stately church was built as a home for the shrine. So great was the reputation of this saint in Chester that her relics were carried in procession in the streets in 1180, when their aid was invoked to arrest a terrible conflagration. A portion of her relics appear to have been left at Dereham, for we find that the monks of Ely obtained possession of them by a stratagem, and carried them to their church, where they were enshrined with great rejoicing.

Although the list is by no means exhausted, we need not continue any further these " devotional items " that are left to us with much of their fragrance of past times, all the pathos of old memories, and the distinct characteristics of successive phases of religious and political life. Each example of the shrines that stirred the devotional instincts of our ancestors, and stimulated the architectural genius of the monkish craftsmen, is highly suggestive to the beholder. Who can doubt that saintly relics provided the inspiration for much that is noblest in our national ecclesiastical architecture?

Around the sacred relic, rapturously enshrined, grew the chapel, monastery, or cathedral. The architectural genius of the Middle Ages caught at the idea bred of devotion, and developed it magnificently in buildings which we can copy only in a soulless way, mainly, perhaps, because science, in killing the belief in holy relics, scotched the germ of faith, which was the great driving force behind the marvellous architectural achievements of the Mediæval

Shrines of British Saints

Period, buildings whereof every stone was a Paternoster and each piece of delicate carving an Ave Maria.

> "Firm was their faith, the ancient bands,
>   The wise of heart in wood and stone,
> Who reared with stern and trusting hands
>   Those dark grey towers of days unknown;
> They filled the aisles with many a thought,
>   They bade each nook some truth recall,
> The pillared arch its legend brought,
>   A doctrine came with roof and wall."
>   (Hawker of Morwenstow).

CHAPTER XV

INDULGENCES AND PENANCES

THE history of indulgences and penances is a very,
interesting one, particularly, perhaps, as the granting
of the former is by no means an obsolete custom
in the Church of Rome, and the ecclesiastical law
relating to the latter has never been abrogated by
the Church of England. By the Church of Rome
the indulgence is regarded as " a releasing, by the
power of the keys committed to the Church, the debt
of temporal punishment which may remain due upon
account of our sins, after the sins themselves, as to
the guilt and eternal punishment, have been already
remitted by repentance and confession " (*vide*
" Grounds of Catholic Doctrine," Chapter X.,
Question 1).

There are two main classes of indulgences—plenary
and non-plenary—which are subdivided under such
headings as partial, temporary, indefinite, local,
perpetual, real, and personal.

A *plenary* indulgence is that by which a remission
is obtained of *all* the temporal punishment due on
sin, either in this world or the next. A *non-plenary*
or *partial* indulgence is that which remits a part only
of the punishment due to sin, and usually operates
in the remission of so many days, weeks, or years
of penance, which would otherwise have to be

Indulgences and Penances

observed before the penitent was cleansed from his sin.

Temporary indulgences are those which, as the name implies, are granted for a certain specified time, as distinct from the *indefinite* indulgences, the duration of which is unlimited.

Perpetual indulgences are granted in perpetuity, while *local* ones operate only in connection with particular chapels, churches, shrines, holy springs, and sacred places. A *personal* indulgence is granted to certain individuals, corporate bodies, fraternities, general assemblies, and religious brotherhoods of various kinds.

Other indulgences are termed " enjoined penances " (*pœnitentiœ injunctœ*), and by them is conferred the remission of so much of the punishment due to sins as the delinquent would have to pay by the more regular canonical penances, or by those pronounced by the priest. Lastly, there is what is called a *real* indulgence, which is attached to material and movable things, such as rosaries, medals, and crosses, and is granted to those who wear these and similar articles with devotion and contrition. After the bishops had enjoyed the privilege of granting indulgences for many centuries, the popes at length discovered what a powerful instrument it might become in their own hands ; therefore, in the eleventh century, when the papal dominion was approaching its zenith, the heads of the Roman see assumed to themselves the exclusive prerogative of granting indulgences and dispensing pardons. The result was that the net of repentance was spread far and wide, and indulgences were no longer confined to their original institution as a form of ecclesiastical discipline, but were extended to remit the punishment of the wicked in the future world. The sale of indulgences received an immense stimulus when it was decreed that by them relief could be granted to the dead, and the people were reproached if they showed unwillingness to contribute the sums of money necessary to deliver their deceased relatives and friends from the horrors of purgatory.

To vindicate in an authoritative manner some of the really extraordinary pontifical measures relating to indulgences, a document was produced, which was modified and embellished in the thirteenth century by St. Thomas Aquinas, and which affirmed, among other declarations, that there existed an immense measure of merit composed of the pious deeds of the saints—an excess above such virtue and holiness as was required for their own salvation, and was available for the benefit of those who purchased indulgences. The guardian and wholesale dispenser of this surplus piety was the Pope, who was empowered to assign such quantities of the precious material to sinners as would suffice to free them from the punishment due for their crimes. Moreover, it was asserted that this overflow of saintly virtue was inexhaustible, and one wonders somewhat if it were stored in a liquid or a tabloid form. That it was well paid for we may be sure.

This singular traffic was carried on for many years both in this country and on the Continent, and the revenues of many ecclesiastical, monastic, and charitable institutions must have been swelled enormously by those wishing to secure the privilege of sinning for a cash payment.

In buying an indulgence the purchaser was not *in theory* excused or exempted from the duty of

Indulgences and Penances

repentance, but was released only from the penances imposed by ecclesiastical authority, the endurance of which was intended originally to be a sign of the penitents' sincerity in the renunciation of evil. Authorised indulgences were intended originally for the benefit of penitents who had confessed their sins and received absolution. The monks, however, and the other retailers of indulgences, did not trouble their heads much about repentance, and multitudes of buyers went away with the comfortable assurance that no troublesome consequences would attend the commission of the offences specified on their " pardon-tickets." Be this as it may, the sale of indulgences brought a golden harvest to the coffers of the Vatican ; in the fifteenth century, in particular, the disposal of them was a well-organised business, and a public sale of them was generally preceded by some specious pretext—for example, to provide funds to wage war against heretics, or for the prosecution of a crusade against the Neapolitans.

All students of the Reformation will remember that Martin Luther's first great controversy with the Church of Rome related to the sale of indulgences, which Pope Leo X. had instituted for the purpose of obtaining funds for the completion of St. Peter's, which had been begun by his predecessor, Pope Julius II. On the 31st of October, 1517, there appeared on the door of the castle church at Wittenberg a document, written in Latin and signed by Luther, which was destined to occupy a great place in history. This was his discussion on the sale of indulgences, in a series of ninety-five theses, which, although moderate in form, were a scathing condemnation of the mechanical system of the Church in the sixteenth century.

317

Pilgrim Life in the Middle Ages

The right of promulgating Leo X.'s indulgences, with a plenary remission to all such as should contribute towards the completion of the magnificent fabric of St. Peter's, together with a share in the profits arising from the sale of them, was granted to Albert, Elector of Mentz and Archbishop of Magdeburg, who selected as his chief agent in Saxony a certain Dominican monk, John Tetzel, whose licentious character was reputed to be on an equality with his enterprising spirit and his popular eloquence. Assisted by the monks of his order, he was soon heard to boast that he had saved more souls from hell by his indulgences than St. Peter had converted by his preaching. In the usual form of absolution, written by his own hand, he said :—

" May our Lord Jesus Christ have mercy upon thee, and absolve thee by the merits of His most holy passion. And I, by His authority, that of His apostles Peter and Paul, and of the most holy Pope, granted and committed to me in these parts, do absolve thee, first, from all ecclesiastical censures, in whatever manner they have been incurred ; and then, from *all thy sins, transgressions, and excesses, how enormous soever they may be*, even from such as are reserved for the cognizance of the holy see ; and, as far as the keys of the Holy Church extend, I remit to thee all punishment which thou deservest in purgatory on their account ; and I restore thee to the Holy Sacraments of the Church, to the unity of the faithful, and to that innocence and purity which thou didst possess at baptism ; so that, when thou diest, the gates of punishment shall be shut and the gates of the paradise of delights shall be opened ; and if thou shalt not die at present, this grace shall remain in full force when thou art at

Indulgences and Penances

the point of death. In the name of the Father, and of the Son, and of the Holy Ghost. Amen."

This indulgence is so comprehensive in character that we are not surprised to learn that when Tetzel was eventually expelled from Saxony, he established himself in a village on the border, where he continued to do a big business with those persons anxious to secure the privilege of sinning on easy terms.

The sale of unauthorised indulgences was very common in England and many spurious " pardons " were disposed of by unscrupulous persons. Bishop Grandisson of Exeter (1327-69) forbade the sale of fictitious and unauthorised pardons within the diocese.

So recently as the year 1800 a Spanish vessel was captured near the coast of South America, freighted, among other things, with numerous bales of indulgences for various sins, the price of which, varying from half a dollar to seven dollars, was marked upon each. They had come from Spain, and were intended for sale among the Roman Catholic communities of South America. At the present day many of the churches of Rome, Italy, and the Roman Catholic countries generally, have inscribed over the altar the words *indulgentia plenaria,* an intimation that a plenary indulgence is attached to the Masses offered there. In some cases the meaning is more than implied, as in the Church St. Maria della Pace, where hangs the famous fresco by Raphael, and where, above one of the altars, the visitor may read :—

"*Ogni Messa celebrata in quest' altare libera un anima dal purgatorio.*"

which may be translated :—

" Every Mass celebrated at this altar frees a soul from purgatory " ;

and a similar notice, posted up near the altar, is in the church of St. Croce di Gerusalemme.

All matters pertaining to indulgences are discussed and settled by the " Congregation of Indulgences," an assembly or committee consisting of cardinals and various prelates, whose duty, it is to examine the reasons put forward by all persons applying for indulgences, and to grant or refuse them, as they may think fit, in the name of the Pope.

The Tax of the Sacred Roman Chancery sets forth the scales of payment for various indulgences, and the fees levied for offences are peculiar, as may be gathered from the following :—

	s.	d.
For murdering a layman	7	6
For lying with a mother or sister	7	6
For procuring abortion	7	6
For taking a false oath in a criminal case ...	9	0
For defiling a virgin	9	0
For keeping a concubine	10	6
For simony	10	6
For sacrilege	10	6
For robbing	12	0
For burning a neighbour's house	12	0

From the " Informacion for Pylgrymes," printed by Wynken de Worde, we learn that in the sixteenth century there was a scale of payment for admission to all the holy places, graduated according to the reputed sanctity of each, and " to every pylgryme at the firste fote that he setteth on londe there is graunted plenary remyssion *de plena et a culpa*." At the majority of the sacred spots a similar remission was given. Thus at Rama, the reputed scene of the martyrdom of St. George, a " groat venetian " was demanded, for which, in addition to a view of the place, the pilgrim was entitled to indulgence for

Indulgences and Penances

" seven years and seven Lents," and it would be difficult to mention any noteworthy shrine or holy place where such advantages were not granted to the traveller in exchange for his fee. It has been fittingly said by Langland that pilgrims came home so loaded with indulgences that they " had leave to lie all their lives after."

A few extracts from this Pilgrim's Guide Book may be given :—

"The fyrste is before the temple of the sepulcre doore. There is a foure square stoon whyte. Where up pon Christe restyd him wyth his crosse whan he went towarde the mount of Caluarie. Where is Indulgence VII yeres & VII lentes."

" Also a lytyll thens is a place & a stoon on whyche our lady rested her upon, visytynge the holy places. VII yeres & VII lentes."

" In the vale of Syloe is a welle where our lady wasshyd the clothes of Ihehu Cryfte. Ther is VII yeres & VII lentes."

" Also a lytyll thens aboue hangynge on the hyll ben places lyke caues where the apostles were hydn in the time of the passyon of Cryste. VII yeres & VII lentes.

" Atte the hyhe awter of mount Syon there is a place there Crist made his maundy with his discyples. VII yeres & VII lentes."

Mediæval indulgences are worthy of attention if only because they help us to mark an important epoch. The famous Mainz indulgences were circulated in 1454, " a date," as Mr. Walter Crane reminds us, " which appears to be the earliest definite date that can be fixed on to mark the earliest use of printing." [1] Indulgences carved or inscribed after the continental manner on some portion of the fabric are extremely rare in English churches at the present day, and possibly the only example that has survived is that inscribed on the west jamb of the south door of the little chapel, or *ecclesiola*, of

[1] "Decorative Illustration," Walter Crane.

321

Pilgrim Life in the Middle Ages

St. Catherine, at Milton Abbey, Dorset. The inscription, of thirteenth-century date, is in Lombardic capitals, and reads :—

INDVLGENCIA : H' : SCI : LOCI : C : E : X : DIES :

The Rev. Herbert Pentin writes : " The indulgence was offered, presumably, to those who would contribute to the fabric fund of the chapel." [1]

Although these inscribed indulgences are so rare, we have a very large number of records relating to the granting of indulgences to those who would contribute to the relief of the poor in hospitals and almshouses, and Pope Martin V. granted special indulgences to all pilgrims who should visit St. Winifred's Well.

When any doubt was thrown on the authenticity of a relic, or from some other cause a shrine lost prestige in the eyes of devotees, the popes frequently granted indulgences in the hope of restoring the temporary loss of popularity. Thus when St. Thomas Aquinas expressed his opinion that Holy Blood did not, and could not, exist, for the simple reason that at the moment of our Lord's resurrection the blood that had been shed had perforce been reunited to the resuscitated body, the custodians of the shrines which attracted pilgrims by their claim to possess some phial of Christ's blood were much perturbed by the arguments of the greatest theologian of his century. The relic of the true Blood preserved in Hayles Abbey, Gloucestershire, which had been so rapturously enshrined and adored, fell into disrepute until Popes John XXIII., Eugenius IV., Callixtus III., and Paul II. came to its rescue by granting indulgences to its venerators.

[1] "Memorials of Old Dorset."

Indulgences and Penances

Eugenius IV. (1431) granted absolution for four confessions at Corpus Christi, and seven years and three Lents to all " who give anything to the worship of God and that precious Blood." A little more than a quarter of a century later Callixtus III. granted full remission " at Corpus Christi and at Holy Rood in May and Harvest, gave one hundred days' pardon to those who put their helping hands to the welfare of the Monastery of Hayles." There is no doubt whatever that the Holy Blood of Hayles was saved from oblivion, if not from something worse, by the aid of indulgences. Mr. St. Clair Baddeley writes : " From these documents [indulgences] we gather two important facts—first, that these Pontiffs regarded the relic favourably ; secondly, that Hayles Abbey during the Wars of the Roses, like many another convent, was tumbling about the ears of its inhabitants, and was looking to its relic of the Holy Blood to save it from perdition. As we presently (in A.D. 1470) find the Abbot of Hayles, William Whitchurch, practically rebuilding the church of Didbrook, we may safely conclude that papal favour toward the relic was proving really efficacious and brighter days had dawned on the monastery."

It may be of interest to mention that episcopal indulgences will generally be found to differ from those issued by the Pope, inasmuch as while the former rarely remit penance for more than seven, thirteen, or forty days, the papal indulgences knew no such limits.

In Trinity Hospital, Salisbury, an ancient charity for twelve old men, founded by William Chandler, *obiit* 1411, the visitor may still see a precious parchment in the form of a bull of Pope Boniface, dated 1379. The document, which is a splendid specimen

Pilgrim Life in the Middle Ages

of fourteenth-century caligraphy, promises a fortnight's indulgence to those who obey its behests.

The interesting Hospital of St. Bartholomew, near Oxford, is used as a farm, with the exception of the chapel. In addition to the relics preserved there (see Chapter II.), Burgwash, Bishop of the diocese in 1336, granted forty days' indulgence to all who would come to the chapel within the octave of the saint, and worship, with " Prayers, Oblations, and Gifts, and contribute relief towards the leprous Alms-folk." " Upon which," Mr. J. Oxley [1] tells us, " multitudes of people obeyed this injunction, and set up the image of the saint in the windows and on the wall of the chapel."

On January 9, 1449, Adam Moleyns, Bishop of Chichester, was brutally murdered near the Domus Dei (now the Garrison Chapel), at Portsmouth. Fifty years later a " Process " was held for the absolution of the inhabitants of Portsmouth from the sentence of excommunication, which had been passed upon them at the time of the crime.

For the " Process " the Bishop of Winchester issued a highly interesting document relating to the services and Masses he ordered to be said for the deceased Bishop, and, " at the end of the procession, the said Master John Dowman intimated to the same parishioners and to others present, that the said Reverend Father granted forty days' indulgence to all persons visiting the said place and making stations there, so often as they should say the *De Profundis* and the Lord's Prayer five times, with the Salutation of the Angels five times, and the Apostles' Creed."

The indulgences quoted above were, with the exception of the Salisbury example, granted by bishops,

[1] The *Antiquary*, vol. v., No. 12, New Series.

Indulgences and Penances

and may be compared to the following extract from a deed, dated the sixteenth year of Henry VIII., referring to a papal indulgence given to those who should contribute to the funds of the ancient Hospital of St. Margaret, at Wimborne, Dorset. The deed recites that " Pope Innocent IV., in the year 1245, by an indulgans or bulle did assoyl them of all syns foregotten, and offences done against fader and moder, and all swerynges neglygently made. This indulgans, grantyd of Peter and Powle, and of the said pope, was to hold good for *51 yeres and 260 days*, provided they repeated a certain specified number of Paternosters and Ave Marias daily."

Miss R. M. Clay, in " Mediæval Hospitals of England," gives a very interesting example of a papal brief, dated 1392 :—

" Relaxation of seven years and seven *quadragene* to penitents who, on the principal feasts of the year and those of St. James in the month of July and the dedication, the usual octave and six days, and of a hundred days to those who, during the said octaves and days visit and give alms for the sustentation and recreation of the chapel of St. James's poor hospital, without the walls, London."

Penances are closely allied to indulgences, the latter, indeed, being frequently granted to redeem the former, and the imposition of a penance was often the *raison d'être* of a pilgrimage. As early as the fifth century penance began to be commuted, and in place of the ancient severities prayers, Masses, and alms were substituted, to be superseded in their turn, to a considerable extent, by the granting of indulgences.

The "Codex Pœnitentialis " is the authorative book which contains everything relating to the imposition of penance and the reconciliation of penitents. Very similar are the Roman " Penitential," and those of Beda and Archbishop Theodore, of Canterbury. Equally interesting but far less known is the unpublished " Penitential " of Bishop Bartholomew, of Exeter, of which a copy is among the Cottonian MSS. in the British Museum. The compiler, a native of Brittany, was Bishop of Exeter from 1161 to 1184. The MS. contains 177 folios on vellum, and is beautifully written in the contracted Latin of the twelfth century. After a long exposition on penances in general, he treats in detail the various penances to be done for offences against morality, &c., and those to be enforced against fortune-tellers and soothsayers. If a woman places her son on the roof of her house, or in an oven, to cure him of the fever, she shall do five years' penance. Conjurors, fortunetellers, or sorcerers, being laymen, shall do penance three days, and abstain from wine, beer, and meat ; others shall do penance twelve days for the same offence. Whosoever shall eat unclean flesh, or flesh torn from a beast, shall do penance forty days, but if necessity from hunger has driven him to this, the penance shall be much lighter. Such are a few extracts from a mass of curious matter contained in the " Penitential " of Bishop Bartholomew. The seller or retail vendor of indulgences was called the Pardoner, an important ecclesiastical official, whom Chaucer describes thus :—

> "But of his craft, from Berwick unto Ware,
> Ne was there such another pardonere,
> For in his mail he had a pillowbere,
> Which, as he saidë, was our Lady's veil.
> He said, he had a gobbet of the sail
> That Saint Peter had, when that he went
> Upon the sea, till Jesu Christ him hent.

Indulgences and Penances

He had a cross of laton full of stones,
And in a glass he haddë piggës bones.
But with these relics, whennë that he fond
A poorë parson dwelling upon lond,
Upon a day he gat him more money
Than that the parson gat in moneths tway;
And thus with feigned flattering and japes,
He made the parson, and the people, his apes."

In *Piers Plowman* we may read about the pilgrims and palmers who went to St. James of Compostella and the saints of Rome, also of the " long lubbers " who made their way to our Lady of Walsingham, in the hope of obtaining an indulgence :—

"There preached a Pardoner, as he a Priest were,
And brought forth a bull with bishop's seals,
And said that himself might assoil them all
Of falseness of fastings, of vows to-broke.
Lewéd men lieved [believed] him well and likeden his words,
Comen and kneleden, to kissen his bulls.
He blessed them with his brevet, and bleared their eyne
And raught with his ragéman rings and brooches.
Thus ye giveth your gold gluttons to help."

From the word " ragéman," used by Langland, our word " rigmarole " is thought by some authorities to have been derived.

Long after the Reformation a kind of indulgence survived in the form of church fines, as is shown by many existing records, such as the following from the books of the General Session of Edinburgh.

" 1643
Feb. 10. Given in by Geo. Stuart, advocat,
for not coming to the ile,   20 merks.
Given by Col. Hume's lady for private
marriage with young Craigie,   20 merks.
Given by Mr. Robt. Smyth for private
marriage,   20 merks."

Pilgrim Life in the Middle Ages

"1644
    May 9. Given by M^r. Luis Stuart and Isbell
             Geddes, for fornication,   21 lib. 6s. 8d.
             By Robert Martin, for his private
             marriage,   20 merks."
"1645
    March 13. Given for Wm. Salmond,
             relapse in fornication.   53 lib. 6s. 8d."

Public penance was the customary ecclesiastical
punishment for immorality, and the Church law with
regard to this offence has not been abrogated,
although it is not now enforced. The penitent,
bareheaded and barelegged, and clad in a white
sheet, made an open confession in some public place
of the imputed crime. Several cases occurred during
the last century, as at Liverpool, where, in 1840,
penance was performed by a female at St. Peter's
Church.

The following extracts are from the Churchwardens' Accounts of Woodbury Church, Devon :—

"1701-2. P^d for the charges of a woman
           doeing penance   o o 9
  1702-3. Paid the Charge for a woman
           doing penance   7"

In the Vestry Book of Otterton is the following
entry :—
"June 20th, 1764. It is agreed at a parish
meeting this Day, by us parishioners who were there
present, that the Churchwardens shall take out an
Order of Penance against Pascho Potter, who was
presented at the last visitation for a Base Child,
an'd that the expenses of it be allowed and reimbursed
them either out of the poor or Church Rate."

Indulgences and Penances

At Otterton also we find :—

"1714. Oct. 17. Paid to procure sheet and wand for
Peter Longworth standing penance   oo oi oo
1735. Paid for washing the Parish Sheet for Club's
wife to stand penance in   oo oo o2"

The following example from the Registers of Frithelstock must close the list :—

" Alexander Tuck died at Great Torrington of the small pox aged about 75, August yᵉ 10th 1720, which fellow had the Horrid impudence to tell the minister of Frithelstock that he knew what Anathema Maranatha was as well as Himself only because the aforesaid Gentleman asked his Impudent Daughter whether or no she would do penance or be excommunicated for her Bastard, which she had then in her arms when her Honest uncle Jo : Tuck was buried (who was excommunicated and died so at Crediton in the small pox 1713.) "

It may not be without interest to note that decrees or letters issued by the Pope have from early times been called papal " bulls " because of the attached *bulla*, or seal of lead, without which they were invalid. It is sometimes called the " seal of the fisherman," for the reason that the early papal letters always concluded *Datum Romæ sub annulo piscatoris* (" Given at Rome under the signet of the fisherman "), a reference, of course, to St. Peter.

Papal bulls are dispatched from the Roman Chancery, by order of the Pope, and sealed with lead. They are written on parchment to distinguish them from *briefs*, which are written on paper. Another distinguishing feature between papal briefs and bulls is that whereas the former are dated *a die nativitatis*, the latter *a die incarnationis*. In affairs

329

of the greatest importance *golden* or *silver* bulls were formerly used, and in the Chapter House at Westminster are two golden bulls, one attached to the treaty between Henry VIII. of England and Francis I. of France, the other to the instrument by which Pope Clement VII. conferred on Henry VIII. the title of " Defender of the Faith." Papal bulls are frequently mentioned in early Acts of Parliament, and they were formerly valid in this country. By the statute 28 Henry VIII. c. 16, all bulls obtained from the Bishop of Rome are declared to be null and void ; and the statute 13 Elizabeth, c. 2, pronounces the procuring, publishing, or using of them to be high treason. The historical student will find the most copious collection of papal bulls in the " Bullarium Magnum à Leone Magno ad Benedictum XIV. " (A.D. 461 to 1757), published at Luxembourg, 1747-58, in nineteen tomes, forming eleven large folio volumes.

CHAPTER XVI

THE REFORMATION

IN writing about the Reformation the difficulty is to steer a middle course between the whole-hearted supporters of the monastic system, who describe Thomas Cromwell and his friends as "infamous wretches," and the equally biassed persons to whom the word "monastery" is synonymous with licentiousness and immorality, and who firmly believe that the religious houses were suppressed largely, if not entirely, because they were hotbeds of vice. Notwithstanding the support given them by J. A. Froude, to name but one historian, the greater number of the accusations brought against the abbots and inmates of monastic houses have been proved to be mere fictions, invented for the purpose of aiding the work of spoliation. Although to estimate exactly the precise condition of English monastic life in 1530 is an impossible task at the present day, it is quite true to say that no unimpeachable evidence has yet been produced to show that the cloister fostered vice, or that the occupants of religious houses were not living up to a fairly high standard as compared with that of to-day—a higher standard, at any rate, than was attained by the secular clergy outside monastic jurisdiction and control.

The accounts sent to the Vicar-General by the

four agents of his own choosing—London, Layton, Legh, and Ap Rice—are not supported by evidence, and the methods adopted by the Reformers—the destruction of noble buildings, the burning of valuable manuscripts, the alienation of Church property—have never been excused. At the same time, to condemn the methods employed does not imply that the continued existence of the monastic system would have been for the good of the Church or for the welfare of the realm. All impartial historians are now agreed that the system had reached its utmost limit of usefulness long before it was suppressed, that it had ceased to be a vital factor in religious life, and that its suppression could not have been achieved without at least the passive help of the people, by whom the destruction of the buildings was deplored, as the breaking down of the system was universally welcomed. Indeed, it is quite an open question as to whether such violent and drastic changes could have been carried to a successful issue without the brutal methods of the Vicar-General.

Be this as it may, the monasteries had lost caste and had become lax in many ways, although no student of history can doubt that for many centuries they had played a splendid part in the development of civilisation, and this even after the time when the Papacy had ceased to be a purely spiritual power working for the common good. For more than a century before what we call the Reformation, which was not one event, but a series extending over many years, there had been frequent and loud calls for reform. Religious services had become more and more formal in the observance of an outward routine, and long before the Dissolution the devotional charms of the priest failed to open the fountains of love or dispel the cares of doubt. The outward forms of the faith, the ceremonials and processions, were as picturesque, as gorgeous, and as ascetic as ever ; but they had lost vitality, and even the memory of their original power and significance had become dim and obscure.

It would be difficult to find a fairer statement of the causes that led up to the Reformation than that penned by the Rev. Anthony Deane in the charming notes he used to contribute to the pages of the *Treasury* when he was editing that periodical. " In truth," he wrote, " some change was essential. It was demanded by two facts : the altered condition of the nation and the altered condition of the monasteries themselves. An institution which suited excellently well the needs of the thirteenth century was not necessarily adapted to the needs of the sixteenth. And the tone of the religious houses had deteriorated ; they had been great spiritual centres ; they became powerful administrators of vast estates. Immersed in such business, the religious character of these foundations was greatly vitiated. Of gross sin or immorality there was practically none, but of easy-going worldliness there was more than enough. And a monastic life which is not supremely good becomes at once, from the high claims it makes, more than usually bad ; it degrades its own ideals in the sight of the world. Again, the work of the monasteries to a great extent was finished. For centuries they had been immeasurably in advance of the general standard of learning, but with the progress of the Renaissance they began to fall behind it. And the invention of printing made unnecessary one of their special forms of industry : the laborious copying of manuscripts was needful no longer. But,

above all, the time had come when either the whole
constitution of the monastic system must be reformed
or the episcopal system of the Church reduced to
impotence. From quite early days many of the
regular clergy had declined to recognise the authority
of the English bishops, professing obedience only
to their abbot, and through him to the Pope.
Obviously this meant that there would be incessant
strife between the abbots and the bishops, and the
supremacy of the former was in flat contradiction
to the first principles of Church government. . . .
To imply that no reform at all was needed, that
this dual system of Church government could be continued, that the monasteries were still adapted to
meet the needs of the age, is to let partisanship
obscure historical truth."

Certainly the Reformation quickened the intelligence of the people ; and when the excitement caused
by the momentous changes had subsided, social life
was brought under the dominion of a moral ideal
that struck a happy mean between laxity on the
one hand and severe austerity on the other. To
pilgrimages the Reformation gave the deathblow,
although these had long ceased to be devotional,
and for generations before the destruction of shrines
and relics the blood-exuding crucifix and the weeping images of the Virgin were regarded with a
healthy scepticism ; and even such genuine relics
as the Church possessed had lost a good deal of their
miraculous virtue in the popular mind, with the result
that they were of but little value as alms-drawing
assets. It is interesting to note in this connection that
on the accession of Mary no saint in all England was
replaced in a shrine, with the single exception of
Edward the Confessor at Westminster. Even the

powerful Cardinal Pole at Canterbury left the saints in their obscurity, although he could hardly have believed that the effect of Henry's edicts would be permanent.

A few extracts from the Injunctions of 1559 may be given :—

" 23. Also that they shall take away, utterly extinct, and destroy all shrines, coverings of shrines, all tables (engraved pictures), candlesticks, trindals and rolls of wax, pictures, paintings, and all monuments of feigned miracles, pilgrimages, idolatry, and superstition, so that there remain no memory of the same in walls, glass-windows, or elsewhere within their churches and houses, preserving nevertheless, or repairing the walls and glass-windows, and they shall exhort all their parishioners to do the like within their several houses."

" 32. Item, that no persons shall use charms, sorceries, enchantments, witchcraft, soothsaying, or any such-like devilish device, nor shall resort at any time to the same for counsel or help."

" 35. Item, that no persons keep in their houses any abused images, tables, pictures, paintings, and other monuments of feigned miracles, pilgrimages, idolatry, and superstition."

The Injunctions were followed by the Visitation Articles of the same year, among which we find :—

" 2. Item, whether in their churches and chapels all images, shrines, all tables, candlesticks . . . be removed, abolished, and destroyed."

" 9. Whether they used to declare to their parishioners anything to the extolling or setting forth of vain and superstitious religion, pilgrimages, relics, or images, or lighting of candles, kissing, kneeling, or decking of the same images."

Pilgrim Life in the Middle Ages

" 45. Item, whether you know any that keep in their houses undefaced any images, tables, pictures, paintings, or other monuments of feigned or false miracles, pilgrimages, idolatry, and superstition, and do adore them, and specially such as have been set up in churches, chapels, or oratories."

A glance through the churchwardens' accounts of the period, many of which have been printed, will show how general was the destruction of the shrines and relics to which pilgrimages had been made for centuries. With the passing of the miraculous and saintly *media* the devotional pilgrimage was shattered beyond recovery, and quickly became but a pious memory.

In conclusion, it may be of interest to mention that the general idea that the Reformation disposed once for all of the claims of the Church of Rome to certain abbeys and conventual churches in this country is quite erroneous. With regard to the possessions of the Benedictine Order, at any rate, their claim has been definitely stated in a most lucid manner by Henry Norbert Birt, O.S.B., in a letter to the *Church Times*, dated March 13, 1908, and written particularly with regard to the claim of the Roman Catholics to possess the Abbey of Glastonbury. The letter is so interesting and of so much historical value as an authoritative state-ment from one of the most distinguished members of the Church of Rome in this country that no apology is needed for quoting it at length :—

" After the dissolution of the religious houses by Henry VIII. some of the communities endeavoured to maintain their corporate existence, but in process of time died out. As long as the Orders that formerly existed in England were represented by members lineally descended from them, so long could they maintain a legal claim to their ancient possessions. But as they died out their claims became extinct. Thus the English Carthusians, Dominicans, Franciscans, Augustinians, and the rest came to an end, and their modern representatives have sprung from entirely new beginnings, and can therefore have only a 'sentimental' interest in the ancient possessions of the respective Orders to which they belong. The same may be said of the hierarchy, though of course our contention is that the same authority which sent St. Augustine and his companions to England, and through them founded the Provinces of Canterbury and York and the various dioceses of England, might as legitimately replace them, and actually did so at the restoration of the hierarchy in 1850. The case of the Benedictines is, however, different. When Westminster Abbey was restored by Queen Mary, its abbot, Feckenham, a monk of Evesham, embodied in himself the claim of the corporate body of which he was the head to the former possessions of that body. When his community was dispersed in 1559 by Queen Elizabeth, its members still represented that claim ; and when one solitary member, Sigebert Buckley, finally remained, all the accumulated rights of his spiritual ancestors were centred in him. He, in the providence of God, outlasted Elizabeth's long reign, having spent the whole of those forty-four years in various prisons for conscience' sake. Before his death, which occurred at a very advanced age, in 1610, he had aggregated to himself and the ancient congregation of Black Monks, of which he was the sole survivor, two secular priests who had become monks, and by that act, and their union with Englishmen, professed in the Spanish congregation, that ancient English Benedictine Congregation has grown up again into the numbers it now possesses, and thus, through Sigebert Buckley, the one slender link with the past, the 'Benedictines of the modern Roman communion' are the present-day representatives in unbroken line of the Benedictines who came to England with St. Augustine in 597.

"There has, providentially, never been a snap in the chain of the Benedictine descent, as in that of the other Orders, and therefore the legal claim (by descent) to the old possessions has never ceased, though Anglicans may rest secure in the thought that as Bishop Ellis (himself a Benedictine of the old English Congregation) stated in the reign of James II., the 'Benedictines of the modern Roman communion' will never disturb existing arrangements by urging such a claim to the ousting of present owners. It is merely a 'sentimental' ground which has caused us steadily to uphold our title to Glastonbury, St. Albans, Westminster, and the rest of the pre-Reformation Benedictine houses."

The writer then goes on to say : "It may interest your readers to know that in Charles I.'s reign, when some folk entertained an ill-founded idea that England would shortly return to the obedience of the See of Rome, and that the old houses of religion and the Cathedrals would be restored, the English Benedictines abroad actually allocated their members to the various Cathedral priories they had formerly possessed, as nucleus communities ready to man them whenever they might be handed over ; and from that day to this the said Congregation has maintained the titular Cathedral priorships in its midst, and the succession to Canterbury, Durham, Win-

The Reformation

chester, Worcester, Coventry, Norwich, Ely, Peterborough, Gloucester, Chester, Bath, and Rochester is complete. We have also amongst us the Abbots of Glastonbury, St. Albans, St. Mary's, York, Bury St. Edmund's, Evesham, Reading (the Right Rev. Francis Aidan Gasquet, Abbot-President), and Westminster ; and if the rest, as Colchester or Pershore, are not filled, they are but in abeyance.

" I may further point out that because our claim ' from sentimental grounds only ' to these houses has legally never determined, we form the important link between the old and the restored hierarchy, for it should be remembered that the communities of the above twelve Cathedral priories had the rights of election to their respective sees, as the Canons of the less numerous secular Cathedrals had to theirs ; and whatever a secular Parliament (without the concurrence of its ecclesiastical element, be it borne in mind) may have decreed, those ecclesiastical rights could never cease to be, and endure *in posse*, if not *in esse*."

It is perhaps hardly necessary to point out that the claims set forth above in so crisp and lucid a manner apply only to the Benedictine Order ; and that the Church of Rome as a whole makes no such claim, although the Church of England still recognises the Orders of Rome and admits Roman Catholics to her communion.

If any doubt exists as to the position of Roman Catholics in England at the present day, the following testimony of Father Humphrey, priest of the Society of Jesus, may help to elucidate it : " I do not defend the position, for I do not think it defensible, inasmuch as I do not believe it to be true that we [*i.e.*, Roman Catholics] represent the pre-

Pilgrim Life in the Middle Ages

Reformation Church of England in the sense of our being a continuation of that body. We are a new Mission straight from Rome."

"But with still clearer voice, and sweeter tongue,
Thus speaks the legend, 'Sleep and death are one,
Not diverse, and to death's long sleep there comes
Awakening sure and certain, when the Dawn
Of the Last Day shall come, and shall unseal
The sleepers' eyes, and the swift sun of Spring
Illumes the caves of sleep, and stirs the blood
Which else had slumbered still. Yet since no sign
Comes from the sleepers here, the yearning souls
Which mark the struggling breath come short and faint,
The tired eyes close, and the calm peace which smoothes
The painful brow—and feel 'tis sleep—no more—
Yet find no proof, cherish the legend fair,
Because life longs to be, because to cease
Is terrible, because the listening soul
Waits for some whisper from beyond the grave,
Waits still, as it has waited through all time,
Waits undismayed, whate'er its form of creed,
Nor fails, though all is silence, to believe,
Deep in its sacred depths, too deep for thought,
The Resurrection and the Life to be."

LEWIS MORRIS.

INDEX

341

Index

Index

Index

Index

Index

Index

Legh, 332
Leland, 92, 112
Lenham, 180
Leo, 52
Leo X., Pope, 70, 317, 318
Leonius, Abbot, 264
Lichfield, 103, 147, 309
Lichfield, Bishop of, 93
Lichfield Cathedral, 309
Lidwell, *see* Ladywell
Liège, 156
Lincoln, 111, 307, 308
Lindisfarne, 301, 302, 305
Lipsius, 53
Liskeard, 114
Little St. Hugh, 307, 308
Liverpool, 328
Llandaff, 268
Llanthony Priory, 267
Llanwit Major, 267
Lockhart, Father, 300
Loftie, W. J., 163
Lombardy, 34
London, 42, 56, 57, 63, 66, 71, 84, 104, 126–129, 172, 182, 189, 202, 216, 243, 283, 325, 332
Long, Sir Henry, 198
Looe, 114
Loretto, 29, 67, 68, 122, 237, 238
Lough Derg, 116
Louis VII., 30, 31, 33, 190, 191
Lower Saxony, 99
Lucca, 150
Lucy, Bishop, 171
Luther, Martin, 144, 317
Luxembourg, 330
Lychnoscopes, 87
Lydda, 152
Lyddington, 258
Lydgate, John, 143 280, 298
Lyndsay, 68
Lynn, 131, 244–249
Lyonesse, 115
Lyons, 64
Lytchett Minster, 224

MACAULAY, 17
Magdalen College, Oxford, 174
Magi, The, 61, 63, 68, 69, 141
Magna Charta, 189
Maidstone, 179, 202, 203, 231, 233, 234
Mainz, 321
Malling Abbey, 202
Malmesbury Abbey, 155, 272, 290, 291
Malmesbury, William of, 155
Mantua, 258
Martin V., Pope, 110, 322
Martyrsworthy, 171
Mary, Queen, 197, 281, 334, 337

Masham, Lord Scrope of, 84
Massingham, 84
Mandeville, Sir John, 155, 156
Maundrell, 155
Mawgan, 89
Mediterranean, 18, 20
Medway, The, 179, 234
Mellitus, Bishop, 102
Melrose Abbey, 78
Memling, 265
Memorials of Westminster Abbey, 94
Mentz, Albert of, 318
Merstham, 177
Milan, 37, 53, 64, 68, 189
" Miller," The, 139
Mill, J. S., 144
Milman, 79
Milton, 117, 144, 145,
Milton Abbey, 322
Minto, W., 161, 162
Mohammed, 35
Mole, The, 176
Moleyns, Adam, 324
Monkswearmouth, 306
" Monk," The, 143
Montaigne, 135
Monte Casino, 153, 154
Montfort, Simon de, 275, 276
Monza, 37
More, Sir Thomas, 42, 44, 66
Morice, Master, 46
Morley, Henry, 144
Morris, Rev. John, 195, 196
Morris, William, 133
Mortimer, *family*, 125
Moselle, The, 69
Moses, 60, 100, 101
Moule, Henry, 88
Mull, Isle of, 61
Munich, 156
Musselburg, 68
Muswell Hill, 118, 119
Muswell, Our Lady of, 119

NAPLES, 37, 151, 265
Navarre, Queen of, 308
Nazareth, 152, 163
Nazianzen, Gregory, 53
Newcastle, 85
Newman, Cardinal, 37, 38, 155
Newmarket, 298
New River, The, 104
Nicene Council, 50
" Nonne," The, 138
Nonnus, 53
Norfolk and Suffolk Coast, The, 242
Norfolk, Duchess of, 35, 237
Norfolk, Duke of, 35
Norfolk, History of, 31

Index

Index

Index

Index

Index